STRATEGIC SURRENDER

STRATEGIC SURRENDER
The Politics of Victory and Defeat

PAUL KECSKEMETI

The RAND *Corporation*

STANFORD UNIVERSITY PRESS
STANFORD, CALIFORNIA
1958

STANFORD UNIVERSITY PRESS
STANFORD, CALIFORNIA

LONDON: OXFORD UNIVERSITY PRESS
© 1958 BY THE RAND CORPORATION

LIBRARY OF CONGRESS CATALOG CARD NUMBER: 58-7840
PRINTED IN THE UNITED STATES OF AMERICA

PREFACE

The following study deals with strategic surrender as a problem in political theory. The context in which this theoretical problem arises is that of the transition from war to peace when one side is completely victorious. Such a transition sometimes involves strategic surrender, that is, the orderly capitulation of the loser's remaining forces; sometimes it does not. It is the theorist's task to specify the general conditions that determine whether or not the winding up of hostilities will involve surrender. Since the shape of events depends both on strategic constraints and on the political objective and beliefs of the belligerents, the task is not an easy one.

The theoretical analysis of strategic surrender is presented in a historical context, that of World War II. Four major cases of strategic surrender are examined in order to show the interaction of strategic constraints and of political desires and beliefs in shaping the concluding stage of hostilities. I have made no attempt to present an exhaustive narrative of the four surrenders. My purpose was rather to sketch the broad outlines of the story in each case and to interpret the major decisions made by the protagonists. Interpretation turned out to be inseparable from evaluation; when analyzing the past in political terms, one cannot avoid asking whether the means adopted were suitable to the ends in view, whether the people concerned made errors of judgment which can be traced to a common source, and so on. For this reason the study is frankly critical of the surrender policy of the Western Allies in World War II.

I am aware of the pitfalls involved in attempting to criticize political decisions in retrospect. One of these is the temptation to overestimate the freedom of action possessed by the policymakers; another is the danger of paying insufficient attention to the adverse consequences that might have resulted if some policy other than the one rejected by the critic had been adopted. I can only say that I have tried to avoid the shortcomings which might make this study a gratuitous exercise in hindsight.

I extend my warmest thanks to Bernard Brodie, Herbert S. Dinerstein, Raymond L. Garthoff, Alexander L. George, Joseph M. Goldsen, Leon Gouré, Victor M. Hunt, and Hans Speier for the extremely valuable advice, criticisms, and suggestions I received from them during the preparation of this study.

This study was prepared as part of the research program undertaken for the United States Air Force by The RAND Corporation.

P. K.

CONTENTS

vii

INTRODUCTION

Allied strategy in World War II was dominated by the concept of surrender. In the Western belligerent countries, both the leaders and the populations took it for granted that the enemy's final defeat would take the shape of mass surrender of his forces.

In most earlier wars of the modern era, the image of surrender did not play a similar role in strategic thinking; there were other suggestive images of the victorious termination of wars, such as the "battle of annihilation" or the conquest of the enemy's capital, followed by the dictation of peace terms. Mass capitulations did occur in European wars of the nineteenth century (Ulm in 1805, Sedan in 1870), but those were fortunate windfalls rather than preconceived objectives in terms of which victory was defined in advance, and in fact neither of those capitulations ended the wars then in progress. "Unconditional surrender," the Union's predesigned objective in the American Civil War, was an exceptional war aim in the nineteenth century. It played no role in the international conflicts of that period.

The armistice accord that concluded hostilities in World War I was indeed in the nature of a final mass surrender, but the strategy that led to it emerged only gradually by trial and error, and the terms imposing capitulation came as a surprise. It was only in World War II that surrender, and unconditional surrender at that, was adopted in advance as the final objective of one side.

One of the purposes of the present study is to throw some light on the question of why surrender became such a dominant concept in the last war. From the point of view of the basic strategic constraints under which a war is waged, surrender appears as a strategic (or tactical) concept related to certain distinct types of campaigns or operations. Allied strategists conceived of World War II as one of those types of military activity; that is why they expected it to be terminated by surrender.

It is not sufficient, however, to look at surrender only from the military point of view. Acts of surrender do more than liquidate military operations; they initiate new, nonviolent cycles of mutual dealings between winners and losers. Surrender as a goal concept, therefore, serves to shape ideas of the political relations between states after the termination of hostilities.

A second purpose of the present study is to show how planning for postwar political arrangements was influenced by the Allies' preoccupation with surrender as the epitome of victory.

PART ONE

GENERAL
STRATEGIC AND POLITICAL
CONSIDERATIONS

One

SURRENDER AS
A STRATEGIC CONCEPT

THE STRATEGIES OF ROUT AND ATTRITION

Surrender (capitulation) occurs when a military engagement or a war is terminated by an agreement under which active hostilities cease and control over the loser's remaining military capability is vested in the winner. In such cases one side achieves a monopoly of armed strength and the other is reduced to defenselessness, thus accomplishing the classic objective of total victory, the "annihilation" of the enemy's military power. Annihilation does not mean the physical extermination of the enemy, but merely neutralization of his combat strength.[1] In surrender agreements, immunity of life is expressly guaranteed to members of the surrendering force.

The objective of annihilating the enemy's military power, however, can be achieved in ways other than formal surrender. If a belligerent succeeds in routing the enemy's forces in pitched battle, he also achieves a monopoly of armed strength, but without a formal agreement transferring control over the loser's residual capability to the winner. Rout in battle renders the loser defenseless because the organizational structure of his force is disrupted. In cases of surrender, on the other hand, the loser's forces retain their organized structure. They admit defeat only because they are deprived of the essential means of waging war, either as a result of relentless attrition inflicted upon their sources of strength or because they are surrounded and besieged by an enemy who succeeds in cutting off their supplies.

Total victory, then, can be accomplished by means of either of two basically different strategies: that of disruption, and that of siege or attrition. Which of these strategies will be employed depends on the strategic constraints under which the war is waged. If the enemy's entire strength is concentrated in a field army, disruption is the proper strategy for a belligerent who hopes to achieve total victory. If the enemy is entrenched behind a strong fortification, depriving him of supplies is a far more promising strategy than disrupting the structure of his forces.

A somewhat similar distinction between two basic strategies is familiar from the writings of Delbrück, according to whom "all strategic thinking and action [is] necessarily dominated by the problem of the duality of the strategy of the rout and that of exhaustion."[2]

According to Delbrück and his school, however, only the strategy of disruption is appropriate to the objective of total victory: if a belligerent aims at annihilating the enemy's forces, he must defeat him in pitched battle. The strategy of exhaustion, according to this school, is suited only to wars of maneuver in which no radical decision is sought. In a war of maneuver, the enemy can be bested by the capture of his stores, and it is expected that heavy losses of this kind will make him amenable to concluding a negotiated peace on moderate terms. The strategy of exhaustion, however, cannot reduce the enemy to total defenselessness.

World War I exploded the theory of two basic strategies as these were defined by Delbrück, for it led to the emergence of a third type of strategy based neither on the concept of rout (disruption) nor on that of maneuver. Within the framework of Delbrück's theory, siege operations securing capitulation are only incidents within a war, but a war as such is not visualized as a kind of siege operation directed against the entire war-making strength of the enemy nation; hence total strategic victory is not equated with the enemy's surrender. In World War I, however, decision was sought and attained by gradual attrition of the enemy's entire man-power and matériel reserves, and by choking off his supplies. The war was essentially a gigantic siege operation, in which a radical strategic decision was reached while the enemy's forces still retained their organizational structure. Hostilities, then, had to be liquidated by what was essentially a capitulation agreement, i.e., by the surrender of the loser's residual military capability.

Western strategic thinking in World War II was guided by this experience: the strategic task was defined in terms of reducing Germany by siege. Attrition of the economic base of the enemy, however, was no longer merely a matter of throwing a blockade ring around him to prevent his replacing the matériel used up in static warfare. Strategic bombing added a new dimension to attrition, exposing the enemy's population and industrial centers to destructive blows. This new type of war of attrition turned out to be more destructive, more "total," than were previous wars governed by the strategy of annihilation. The contrast with the Delbrück concept of "exhaustion" as the less extreme form of warfare is obvious.

Technological developments since World War II have introduced further momentous changes into the strategic picture. The "classic" attrition strategy of both world wars and the concept of victory based on it have become obsolete.

SURRENDER AND THE TREND OF ATTRITION

Surrender means that winner and loser agree to dispense with a last round of fighting. Military necessity sometimes requires exposed units (e.g., the garrison of a fortress) to prolong fighting even when it appears certain that they will eventually be overwhelmed; but, apart from such cases, surrender is indicated when an operation or campaign having the characteristics of a siege enters its final stage. The critical point is reached when prolongation of fighting would inevitably break up the structure of the besieged unit. What the loser avoids by offering to surrender is a last, chaotic round of fighting that would have the characteristics of a rout. Surrender is then the only rational decision for the loser, since it means that the losses that would be involved in the last battle are not incurred. By the same token, *accepting* surrender is a rational decision for the winner: he can obtain his objective without paying the costs of a last battle.

Belligerents involved in an attrition situation, of course, will not always act strictly in accordance with military rationality. The information available to military leaders in the course of operations is in general too fragmentary to enable them to make optimal decisions. Nations or military units faced with defeat sometimes assume superfluous losses, either because they refuse to admit that the situation can no longer be reversed or because they wish to avoid the risk of too early surrender, when additional effort could still save the situation.

With perfect foresight, the potential loser would know before the conflict started that he must lose, even if his forces were initially superior. In this case, if he were rational, he would not initiate hostilities. In the absence of perfect foresight, however, the belligerents have to make the best estimates they can about the future shape of the war. Early in the conflict, the data permit of many different estimates. The actual outcome reveals itself only gradually, so that there is no way for the loser to guarantee himself against superfluous losses: he cannot know in advance whether further resistance may not reverse the trend. What the loser can certainly avoid, if he is rational, is that amount of attrition that he would suffer by fighting on when the available evidence definitely excludes everything but defeat. In wars dominated by the strategy of attrition, the supreme strategic question at any given time is whether the curves of the attrition suffered by the two sides have become divergent and, if so, whether the nascent divergence can still be reversed. From a purely military point of view, surrender is definitely indicated when the loser in such a war is forced to conclude that the trend of divergent attrition has become irreversible. But he cannot be sure about this without having already absorbed a certain measure of attrition that was objectively unnecessary.

So far, we have considered surrender as an act by which one side renounces any further use of a residual fighting capability. Seen in this light, surrender is a matter of choice; in fact, it is this choice character of surrender that makes this concept an interesting one in the theoretical analysis of warfare. But it should not be assumed that all actual cases of surrender involve a significant element of choice between two practically feasible courses of action, fighting on and offering surrender. If soldiers survive after fighting until their last round of ammunition is spent, they have no choice between surrendering and fighting on; their only alternatives are running away, deliberately committing suicide by walking into the enemy's fire, and surrendering. If they surrender, the "residual capability" they yield up is zero; the surrender agreement does not cut short a possible last round of fighting, and hence it has no practical military significance.

In cases of this sort, one may speak of "enforced" surrender; since such surrenders lack military significance, they will remain outside the scope of the present investigation. Cases in which prolonged resistance is not literally impossible but would be wholly meaningless also may be called "enforced" in a wider sense; such is, for example, the case of an isolated armed soldier surprised by an enemy party. Such a soldier could achieve nothing by trying to fight except being killed on the spot.

TACTICAL AND STRATEGIC SURRENDER

Surrender of less than the loser's total existing forces can be called tactical surrender, as distinct from strategic surrender, in which the surrender of the loser's entire force brings hostilities to an end.

Tactical surrender is often a matter of individual soldiers or small units cut off from the main fighting body. From the operational, or strategic, point of view, such incidents may be entirely trivial. Tactical surrenders of major scope, however, can have strategic importance. After the tactical surrender of large forces, those remaining in the field may be so inferior that the weakened side must eventually acknowledge defeat.

Indeed the line separating tactical from strategic surrender may be altogether blurred. The strategic surrender of Germany's forces in World War II, for example, was a gradual process, assuming the form of a series of tactical surrenders preceding a final strategic surrender. The mass capitulations which occurred in several theaters prior to V-E Day were strategic in essence though tactical in form: taken together, they added up to strategic surrender, consummated in piecemeal fashion.

Other ambiguities concerning the tactical or strategic nature of surrender arise in coalition warfare. If there are only two belligerents, the strategic surrender of one ends the war, but in coalition warfare individual coalition members may surrender separately. From the point of view of the coalition as a whole, or from that of its leading member, the strategic surrender of a partner still has only tactical scope. And even the total capitulation of the partner need not mean the end of the war for him, since belligerency may be maintained by a government-in-exile.

In other words, what we call strategic surrender, as distinct from tactical surrender, is an act that concerns not merely the belligerent role of military units but the maintenance of belligerency itself. In tactical surrender, troops lay down their arms but the state of belligerency remains. In strategic surrender, the disarming of troops is merely one phase of a more comprehensive act by which a sovereign abandons or loses belligerent status. Thus strategic surrender is a political act as well as a military act. In the present study we examine only the conditions and constraints governing *strategic* surrender.

Strategic surrender is both the terminal act of a war and the initiating act of the new postwar relationship between the belligerents. The military act of surrender strips the losing sovereign of his war-making capability. It is followed by a political act that provides for the belligerents' postwar status and relationship on the basis of this one-sided military outcome.

Two

SURRENDER AS
A POLITICAL CONCEPT

POLITICAL CONSIDERATIONS AFFECTING
SURRENDER

Strategic surrender necessarily involves decisions other than purely military ones based on an appreciation of the trend of attrition. The propensity to offer surrender will be decisively influenced by the nature of the terms the winner is expected to impose after achieving a monopoly of armed strength. The very concept of surrender implies that the loser's life will be spared. But even so, the loser may have reason to think that the new, nonviolent cycle of relationships initiated by surrender will be totally destructive of all his values, including those he holds dearer than life itself. In that case the loser may decide that a last, hopeless fight or even deliberate self-destruction is preferable to surrender.

The earliest surrenders known to history often resulted in the enslavement of the defeated peoples.[1] For groups to which slavery was unacceptable, collective suicide was the only way out when armed resistance became impossible. An example of this is described by Xenophon as follows:

Then there was a fearful spectacle: the women threw their children down the precipice and jumped after them; the men did the same. . . . They [the Greeks] captured hardly any people [in that village]; all they got was cattle, donkeys, and sheep.[2]

On the other hand, the loser's motives for offering surrender may be greatly reinforced if he is optimistic about the use the winner will make of his monopoly of strength. Such optimism may take various forms. We have already referred to the role of personal and social values in influencing surrender decisions. The loser may decide to quit because he feels that his core values will not suffer, even if the winner has his way completely and permanently. Disaffected groups within a belligerent society often feel that it is the enemy's victory, rather than their own society's, that will bring their core values to fruition. It is normal for the members of such groups to surrender spontaneously when the circumstances permit. Extreme war-weariness sometimes leads to such behavior even in groups that were not disaffected at the outset. Such politically motivated surrenders may be partial (tactical) in scope, but if the disaffected or war-weary element seizes political control, it will adopt the policy of strategic surrender.

In certain circumstances surrender may appear advisable as a means of conserving strength for a future encounter under more favorable conditions. In such cases, the loser expects no real peace; he surrenders, not because he considers the winner potentially benign and friendly, but to gain a breathing spell, during which he expects the balance of power to shift in his favor.

Political considerations may overrule military ones. In extreme cases they may rule out surrender altogether, regardless of whether defeat can still be warded off, or they may rule out continued resistance, regardless of whether it could ensure victory. Suicidal resistance has seldom, if ever, occurred in history except in primitive societies. Eagerness to surrender, which can be found in both early and modern war, may be the result of disaffection, war-weariness, or a generally unwarlike orientation.

In modern war, extreme language is often used in propaganda dealing with the problem of quitting or continuing to fight. Propagandists tend to speak as if the question ought to be decided on moral or political grounds, independently of the military situation. Hence the occasional vogue of such slogans as "No surrender in any circumstances," or "Better death than dishonor," in belligerent societies doomed to defeat. Counterpropaganda or "psychological warfare," on the other hand, sometimes proceeds on the assumption that antiwar arguments can sway the enemy in the direction of quitting, regardless of the military trend. The record of modern wars indicates, however, that modern belligerent nations, unlike small primitive groups, do not willingly commit suicide in defeat. The warring societies are too large and too heterogeneous for that. Defeatist behavior, on the other hand, can become generalized in a losing society, as it did in Russia in 1917 and in France in 1940, but this is likely to happen only in conjunction with overwhelmingly strong military pressure. In modern times societal decisions about surrender tend to reflect both the military rationale of avoiding superfluous losses and the participants' expectations about the political aftermath of surrender. When the actual decision has to be made, it does not present itself to the loser in all-or-nothing terms. The question is not merely whether or not to surrender, but on what political conditions the surrender is to be based.

Even if the loser knows that he cannot escape total defeat and that prolonged resistance can only make his losses heavier, he cannot give up without satisfying himself that there is some political justification for surrender beyond mere survival and loss-cutting. For losers who identify themselves with the winner's aims and who therefore count on benevolent treatment, this is not difficult. They offer and expect friendship (and more often than not are rebuffed). Losers who have no such expectations (or illusions) at least make an attempt at bargaining as long as they believe that they have even a minimum of bargaining power left. But then it may happen that the winner refuses to enter into bargains of any sort. For the prospective winner of a war of attrition, the central aim is the monopoly of strength that he feels he has the power to achieve. This, he is apt to think, will enable him to dictate any terms he pleases. At the same time, the prospective loser takes refuge in the thought that his residual strength still gives him a bargaining asset that he can exploit before he becomes completely defenseless.

This discrepancy of views—the winner's conviction that the loser's bargaining strength is nil, the loser's conviction that it is real—regularly arises at the end of wars of attrition. And the curious fact is that it is not always the loser who is deluded. Losers sometimes succeed in establishing a final bargaining position, even in the teeth of the winners' explicit refusal to enter into anything smacking of concessions or negotiation. The Allies' policy of unconditional surrender in World

War II, which will be discussed below, led to some striking situations of this sort.

TOTAL AND NONTOTAL WAR

A military calamity, whether it takes the form of a rout in the field or of surrender due to exhaustion, need not always have disastrous political consequences. To be sure, moderate peace settlements are more likely when war ends in stalemate than when one side achieves decisive military superiority. But even in the latter case the peace settlement may fail to reflect the winner's military dominance. In the Austro-Prussian War of 1866, Austria's army in the field was routed, but the peace imposed by Prussia was extremely moderate. In other cases, however, such as the American Civil War and World Wars I and II, military defenselessness had catastrophic political consequences for the loser. These three wars were far costlier in terms of human life and material resources than the Austro-Prussian War or the other limited wars of the nineteenth century. We might say that they were more "total." The losers acknowledged defeat and offered strategic surrender only when they were close to total exhaustion; and the winners, too, were obliged to assume enormous losses and to expend a considerable portion of their national resources before they could win.

The above remarks suggest that wars may be classified according to three criteria: (1) the symmetry or asymmetry of the final military outcome, i.e., the degree to which one belligerent succeeds in enhancing his military position at the other's expense; (2) the degree of "totality," which may be defined as the proportion of a belligerent's total human and material resources mobilized, consumed, and destroyed in war; and (3) the symmetry or asymmetry of the political outcome, i.e., the degree to which one belligerent succeeds in enhancing his political position at the other's expense. This last criterion may also be described in terms of advantage and disadvantage: the question is whether the political advantages accruing to the winner, and the political disadvantages accruing to the loser, are large or small.

It is clear that the first criterion is independent of the second: total and nontotal wars alike may end symmetrically or asymmetrically. One of the fundamental conditions on which the degree of totality depends is the belligerents' willingness or unwillingness to end hostilities while their losses have not yet exceeded a certain moderate level, no matter which side has the military advantage at the time.

The degree of totality of a given war depends in part on technological and organizational conditions. Where only a small proportion of national resources can be made available for military use, and where no highly destructive methods and instruments for waging war exist, wars necessarily remain nontotal. Conversely, highly developed techniques of destruction and capabilities for mobilization tend to make war more total. But within the limits set by these underlying conditions, the degree of totality is a matter of choice for the belligerents. To the extent that such choices exist, wars become more total when belligerents who are militarily frustrated at a given stage, either by defeat or by stalemate, refuse to consider a peace settlement that would reflect this disadvantage and continue the struggle in the hope of a more favorable outcome. Such conduct is likely when the belligerents' estimate of the political gains and losses involved in an asymmetrical outcome is very high, supposing that they have not lost all hope of reversing the trend of war. If a frustrated belligerent feels that he can expect nothing but more defeats, he will end the war rather than make it more total, even if he sees in a losing peace a great disaster.

If, however, the belligerents' estimate of the political value of the asymmetrical military outcome is low, the losing side will not try to reverse an early defeat or to break an early stalemate. Thus wars in which the political values at stake are given a relatively low estimate tend to remain nontotal, even when possibilities exist for committing or mobilizing fresh forces in order to achieve something better than defeat or stalemate. The risks, costs, and losses involved in further fighting will then appear to outweigh the advantages of the better political outcome that a prolonged war might be expected to achieve. Conversely, such costs and risks will appear worth while if the "political stake" is very highly valued. Getting victory rather than defeat or stalemate, or stalemate rather than defeat, will then seem worth any cost.

It is not suggested here that decision makers, frustrated by the early military outcome, can make a neat comparison between two well-defined quantities: the political stake on the one hand and the additional cost of a possible better outcome on the other. No such comparisons can be made because war costs and political stakes cannot be measured in homogeneous units. Rather, the weighing is done in an instinctive and reactive fashion; the ultimate decision depends on the emotional impact of the alternative courses. In tense war situations, the decision maker is likely to feel that he is acting from necessity rather than from deliberate choice. (This consideration applies not only to decisions about ending wars but also to decisions about starting them.) By the same token, the course that is rejected appears to be impossible, unfeasible, or unthinkable. In nontotal conflict, it is the continuation of hostilities beyond a certain point that is likely to appear unfeasible for political or economic reasons. On the other hand, if the political stake is high enough, making peace might appear unthinkable and the war might become total.

The point to be stressed in this connection is that the terms "victory," "defeat," and "stalemate," when used to characterize the *final* outcome of wars rather than the outcome of military engagements, are not absolute, but relative, concepts. If a war ends asymmetrically, this is because the loser regards as final the asymmetrical outcome achieved at a certain time. The same applies to stalemate. The decision to accept a given military outcome as final is not necessarily imposed by the nature of the outcome as such. It also depends on political constraints.

It is obvious that, other things being equal, a winning peace is better than a compromise peace or a losing peace. But depending on the over-all political and military circumstances in which a war is being fought, the optimal final outcome for a belligerent may be one that falls short of the best military outcome he could achieve. It is possible to pay too much for victory and even for stalemate. One may safely say that the maxim that "in war there is no substitute for victory" is totally erroneous.

Decisions about ending or continuing wars may be said to depend on the belligerents' evaluation of their "political stake" and on their appraisal of military prospects and the cost of prolonged warfare. These factors are subject to re-evaluation as the war proceeds. It is obvious that estimates of military prospects (e.g., of the likelihood that a better final military outcome is attainable) must be revised in the light of developing experience. But the political factor is also variable. War events may induce belligerents to modify their estimate of the political advantages of various military outcomes. In coalition war, for example, it may happen that the weakening of the enemy gradually becomes less attractive to a coalition partner as he becomes aware of conflicts of interest with another partner. In such cases, one or the other member of the winning coalition may revise the estimate of his political stake more or less drastically, possibly to the extent of withdrawing from the war or even changing sides.

TOTAL WAR AND STRATEGIC SURRENDER

When the loser in nontotal war acknowledges defeat, his military position is not necessarily hopeless. He may have additional potential resources that he could press into combat if he were really desperate. In total war, on the other hand, defeat is acknowledged only when all possibilities for reversing the trend by the mobilization or commitment of fresh resources are exhausted. This is to say that strategic surrender is characteristic of total wars in which the final outcome hinges on divergent attrition of the belligerents' mobilizable potentials, rather than on disruptive military action. A war must end in strategic surrender if (a) the warfare is total, (b) resources are mobilized progressively, and (c) a final asymmetrical outcome is brought about not by disruption but by attrition.

On the other hand, total wars need not end in strategic surrender. If the loser of a crucial engagement in total war cannot fall back on uncommitted forces or fresh resources, that engagement will end the war without formal military capitulation. In the past, total wars were often decided early by battles in the open field, since the possibilities for raising fresh forces were limited or nonexistent.[3] "Classical" strategic theory, based on the Napoleonic experience and worked out by Clausewitz, was dominated by the concept of the battle as the primary means whereby total war could be decided.[4] Decisive superiority was achieved by "total" mobilization at the beginning of the war, and the superior side could thus smash and "disrupt" the forces of the inferior side.[5]

In modern times, however, inequality of initial mobilization has no longer represented decisive, strategic asymmetry. The significant relationship has been that of *total* resources. Hence, the outcome of battles has tended to become less important than the security of the belligerents' mobilization bases.

These generalizations apply with particular force to World Wars I and II. The existing German (and Japanese) armed forces were so tough that the Allies found it extremely difficult to disrupt them. Depriving them of resources was relatively easier, although the Allies, too, had to absorb enormous attrition of manpower and economic resources in the process of wearing down the enemy. Both sides persisted because of their high estimates of the political stakes in the war; both pushed on until there was no longer any doubt about whose force level would sink to zero first. At that point, even the losers had to admit that their residual forces could escape superfluous losses only by capitulation. That is the pattern of strategic surrender in total war.

These basic considerations, however, determine only *whether* surrender will be offered. *How* this is done depends on a set of different factors, to which we now turn.

POLITICAL INTERACTION DURING THE TERMINAL STAGE OF TOTAL WAR

When a war is in its terminal stage, factors that make it more or less total are no longer dominant. It is understood on both sides that further efforts can no longer change the outcome, and that the losing side cannot avoid accepting the political cost of defeat. The motive of cutting losses, rather than that of securing the best possible military outcome, therefore becomes dominant. As surrender nears, even total wars become nontotal, and the final act of capitulation itself is a completely orderly and nonviolent one.

During the terminal stage of total war, the political process shows great variation in detail from one case to another, but some of its aspects are fairly constant. For one thing, the basic total-war orientation of the belligerents usually changes in an asymmetrical fashion: it is the loser who reorients himself first. The winner moves straight on toward his objective, the final achievement of a monopoly of strength that can be used to dictate terms. The loser, however, goes through a process of political reorientation. He gives up his total-war objective as unattainable and sets himself more modest aims. He adopts a new basic policy, the central element of which is the decision to "disarm" the winner's hostility by a thorough political reorientation, setting the stage for mutual adjustment.

This revision of policy may be imposed by a complete collapse of the loser's authority structure: the war must come to a stop because the rank and file no longer obey orders. In such cases strategic surrender, the orderly capitulation of residual forces, represents no problem for the winner.

More interesting cases are those in which channels of military authority are not dissolved, and in which cohesive residual forces remain on the losing side. This condition was fulfilled in every defeated country in World War II: it was characteristic of that war that defeat was not associated with the breakdown of military discipline and the revolutionary disruption of the social fabric. But there did occur, as in most presurrender situations, a split within the political leadership of the losers, with "defeatist," prosurrender elements removing the war-committed leaders from their positions of authority. The French surrender in 1940, as well as the later Italian surrender, was preceded by political reshufflings amounting to a *coup d'état*, even though the forms of legality were observed. But these surrenders were nonrevolutionary in the sense that they were adopted and carried out, not by counter-elites surging from below, but by decision makers who had occupied positions of authority during the war. The German and Japanese surrenders of 1945 were not preceded by any change in the political complexion of the two governments.

These nonrevolutionary surrender situations created a dilemma for the winners. The survival of the loser's authority structure was a necessary condition for the orderly surrender of his remaining forces. No radical political transformation had taken place in the losing countries, however, and consequently the winner could achieve a substantial abridgment of the closing stage of hostilities only if he did not insist on immediately im-

posing his ideological and political war aim, the removal
of the enemy's "evil" authorities and their replacement
by ideologically acceptable ones.

To be sure, there was no reason to assume that recognizing the enemy's war regime for the purpose of obtaining its surrender implied *lasting* renunciation of the
winner's ideological war aims. The winner could wait
until surrender was accomplished and then use his monopoly of strength to transform the loser's political and
social order according to his wishes. This is how Soviet
Russia handled the surrender of the satellite states, Rumania and Hungary. The Russians had no compunction
about concluding armistice agreements with representatives of the King of Rumania and the Regent of Hungary. In their eyes, these acts in no way compromised
their ultimate objective, the sovietization of the losing
countries. To the Western Allies and the United States
in particular, however, even temporary dealings with
spokesmen of enemy regimes were a serious stumbling
block. All such acts seemed to compromise the political
objectives for which the war had been fought.

This difference in handling surrender situations may
be traced to different fundamental attitudes toward the
role of power in international politics. The traditional
American view is that in the normal, healthy state of
international affairs there is no need for the actual or
threatened use of coercion. All issues that arise can be
settled by negotiation between equals or by judicial pro-
cedures. The use of coercion is justified only when the
international system is not in a healthy state, i.e., when
someone commits aggression; in that case, the upholders
of a peaceful world order must use force until the roots
of aggression are destroyed. Wars against aggressors

have but one political objective, the elimination of all political forces responsible for aggression; and this task must be completed before peace is restored. To obtain this political objective in peacetime by the use of coercive methods would be a contradiction in terms. At the same time, noncoercive methods may well be ineffective against germs of aggressiveness that have survived in the postwar situation. The only safe and legitimate policy is to destroy these germs before the conclusion of hostilities.

Wars waged in the spirit of the traditional American approach, as outlined above, are essentially crusades. The conflict is seen as one of good pitted against evil. The enemy is the very personification of violence and strife, whereas one's own side fights for universal peace and harmony. This crusading concept of war has been vigorously criticized in recent years as lacking in realism. Indeed, it is easy to see that the two total wars of the twentieth century have failed to banish the danger of conflict and aggression, although the particular aggressors have been defeated. It must be recognized, however, that the concept of war as a crusade is particularly adapted to the mentality of the public in modern Western democracies. Democratic cultures are profoundly unwarlike: to them, war can be justified only if it is waged to eliminate war. It is this crusading ideology which is reflected in the conviction that hostilities cannot be brought to an end before the evil enemy system has been eradicated.

Soviet Russia's attitude toward the termination World War II was in sharp contrast to that of the Uni States. Her war aim, of course, was also an ideologic political one: expanding communist rule as far as po sible. The Soviet doctrine, however, was far from excluding the massive use of coercion once the international war was over. According to the Soviets, political ends can be pursued by the methods of the "class struggle," for which international war creates favorable conditions, but which can also be carried on in peacetime. In fact, according to the Soviet view, the class struggle is the normal state of all societies until socialism is achieved. Hence it was easy for the Russians to deal with the dilemma created by a nonrevolutionary surrender situation. To them, the temporary survival of "reactionary" authorities constituted no serious political threat, since they felt free to use their vastly superior power against them later.

The German attitude toward power was similar to the Russian. When France offered surrender, a pro-fascist *coup d'état* was in the making, but it was by no means completed. Still, the Germans did not insist on complete Nazification before accepting surrender. They had the necessary coercive instruments to effect it, once monopoly of military strength was achieved.

Part Two of the present work contains four case studies dealing with major strategic surrenders that occurred in World War II: those of France (1940), Italy (1943), Germany (1945), and Japan (1945). These provide factual illustrative material relating to the theoretical points set forth in the preceding pages.

Part Three is devoted to an analysis of the policy of unconditional surrender as applied by the Allies in World War II.

Part Four deals with the problem of strategic surrender under conditions of nuclear warfare.

Three

THE FRENCH SURRENDER
June 1940

THE STRATEGIC BACKGROUND

When Marshal Pétain became head of the French government and sued for an armistice, the Allied forces fighting in France were completely routed, so that the military developments leading to France's strategic surrender did not correspond to the strategic model set forth in the foregoing introductory analysis. The "Battle of France" of May–June, 1940, was not waged according to the formula of divergent attrition. It was a campaign of disruption, conceived and conducted along classic, Clausewitzian lines. Hitler's grand strategy was oriented toward disruption. Hitler did not plan for the kind of total war that World War I had been, and World War II was to become. He expected to reduce his enemies to defenselessness by routing their armies. The blitzkrieg strategy did allow for field operations of the siege type—i.e., for battles of encirclement, which were supposed to culminate in mass surrenders like the Belgian capitulation of May 1940—but not for the strategic surrender of cohesive residual forces as an essential final objective.

There had been no final act of strategic surrender at the end of the Polish campaign of 1939. Surviving elements of the Polish army dispersed, or fled into neutral territory, or surrendered individually or in small groups. Conditions were similar in France. British elements surviving the rout were evacuated across the Channel without their equipment, and the French armies lost their cohesiveness and became incapable of mounting any significant terminal operations.

Had the war been a pure land war fought only on the Continent, and with Germany and France the only major antagonists, the stoppage of military resistance after the rout in the Battle of France would not have represented an important service by the loser to the winner, and France could not have expected to receive political counterconcessions. But the war was a coalition war, and the resources of the Franco-British coalition included, in addition to the forces engaged in the Battle of France, navies and vast overseas territories. Hence rout in the ground battle did not automatically reduce Germany's adversaries to defenselessness. Since the Franco-British coalition conserved latent, mobilizable strength after the rout of its land forces in being, the "relativity of victory" asserted itself: the coalition had a choice between acknowledging defeat and making the war more total.

In Britain, there was no controversy about the choice; the political leadership did not split over the question of ending or continuing the war, and no peace party arose among the rank and file. In France, however, the war was unpopular, and the impact of defeat extremely strong. Even before the disastrous events of May 1940, when the land front was dormant, there had been a latent split between the "hard" and "soft" factions in France, with the "hards" resolved to fight the war in earnest and the "softs" hoping to wind it up before serious damage was done.

The defeat convinced the soft faction that they had been right all along: the war was a wrong war, started at the wrong place and at the wrong time. All one could do was liquidate it on the best possible terms. The coalition situation offered opportunities in this connection. If France quit the coalition before Britain, too, was defeated, France could hope to receive a political payment for the service from Germany. By reorienting her policy, she could "disarm" the winner, in the sense of making the Germans less willing to use their armed superiority to impose extreme terms upon her. Such elements of residual French strength as the overseas territories and the undefeated navy could be expected to reinforce the disarming effect by adding to the cost to the winner of any prolongation of hostilities. France had to act quickly, before her bargaining assets dwindled away. Sticking with the coalition until Britain was forced to her knees could only result in a worse settlement for her.

The French "war party" argued, against this, that the outcome could be reversed by making the war more total. By continuing the war overseas, France could keep the final outcome open until the Anglo-Saxon democracies developed new strength in being, great enough to re-engage and defeat the Germans. This policy had a strong patriotic appeal: from the point of view of national self-esteem, aiming at victory is the only acceptable position, and arguing for the acceptance of defeat is invidious.

Yet the position of the war party was politically weak. The hope it held out of a total and successful

Anglo-Saxon war effort was precarious in itself; America, whose contribution was essential, was still officially neutral, and nobody could predict with certainty that she would intervene. Moreover, the victory that the war party contemplated could only be achieved by the efforts of coalition partners. The policy of continuing the war was seriously compromised by the fact that it entailed French dependence on foreign powers. The French surrender party successfully exploited these weaknesses of the prowar policy. It gained the ascendancy in the internal French debate, so that the only remaining question was whether it could "disarm" the Germans sufficiently to carry out qualified surrender.

In view of this strategic-political constellation, the Germans had to take France's residual bargaining assets into account in winding up hostilities. The rout of the French armies did not decide the matter all by itself; the German victory was total victory in the Clausewitzian sense, but it did not dispose of the problem of obtaining surrender and granting political incentives to that end. The Germans did not hesitate to offer the necessary incentives. Their political objectives in the West implied nothing like unconditional surrender; they did not even aim at total victory in the war against the Anglo-French coalition. They hoped to end the war with Britain by a negotiated peace. Total victory in France was a means to that end. But to be politically effective, the French victory had to be exploited quickly, before Britain could build up new strength in being. Hence speed in winding up hostilities with France was essential, and the Germans were ready, in the interests of speed, to meet France's minimum conditions in arranging a strategic surrender.

THE POLITICAL STRUGGLE IN FRANCE

The Antiwar Party at Work

The question of starting negotiations to end the war was raised for the first time at the meeting of the French War Committee on May 25, 1940. There "General Weygand, supported by Marshal Pétain, sought to obtain a decision authorizing immediate discussions with the British government on the question of continuing the war."[1] On March 28, 1940, representatives of the British and French governments had signed a common declaration pledging both governments not to conclude a separate armistice or a separate peace, and to discuss peace terms with the enemy only after having reached a mutual accord.[2] Hence France could not start armistice negotiations with the Germans without a previous consultation with the British. Immediately, therefore, the question of France's coalition obligations became the nucleus of the issue separating the prowar from the antiwar group.

To Premier Paul Reynaud, who was the main exponent of the prowar position in the government, the fulfillment of France's coalition pledge was absolutely imperative; nothing could void the obligation. The British could oblige France to continue the war as long as physically possible, provided they themselves remained at war. Weygand and Pétain found this thesis unacceptable. According to them, the military situation *in France* could nullify France's obligations. Pétain said at the meeting that "France had no duties toward England except in the measure of the help received, and this help had been very weak."[3] Later Weygand told Reynaud: "The country will not forgive you if, in order to remain faithful to England, you reject an opportunity for peace."[4] Pétain, in a discussion with Reynaud, found a classic formulation of this idea: "You put yourself on the international plane, and I on the national plane."[5]

Reynaud's answer was that France's "independence and honor" were primarily "national" questions. He explained during a later discussion that once France had violated the pact of March 28, she could no longer count upon British diplomatic support; she would be isolated— "bound hand and foot and delivered to Hitler."[6] Of course, that argument could have no force if it were assumed that Britain, too, would be defeated, for then British "support" would have no value. What Reynaud had in mind was that it was extremely dangerous for France to desert a potentially *winning* coalition. (He was thinking of a later American intervention that would reverse the situation.) For, if the British and their allies should win the war after France had capitulated, her interests would not be considered in the peace settlement. To Weygand and Pétain, however, it was far more important to settle with Germany before the end of the war with Britain, thus assuring France a good position at the peace table facing a victorious Germany.

According to Reynaud, Weygand's calculations during the period preceding the armistice were based on the assumption that Britain could not long survive the loss of the Battle of France. He recalls the dictum widely attributed to Weygand (but later disavowed by him) that "in three weeks, England will have her neck wrung like a chicken," adding that it was "very much in character."[7]

Weygand, Reynaud says further, told Jean Borotra, who came to see him after the armistice to announce his intention of going to England to continue the struggle:

"No use, England will capitulate in two months." And in July 1940, at Vichy, Weygand told an automobile manufacturer who asked him whether he should start manufacturing *gazogène* apparatus (for converting automobile engines to charcoal fuel): "I guarantee to you that in two weeks England will sue for peace."[8]

In his testimony at the Pétain trial, and in his autobiographical book, *Rappelé au service*, Weygand denied that his stand on the armistice had been based on an expectation of British defeat. His theory was that the armistice was necessary not only in the French but also in the Allied interest. It stopped the Germans at a line far from the Mediterranean and gave the Allies time to organize the North African invasion. The Allies could not have defeated Germany, said Weygand, if France had refused to conclude an armistice.[9]

It seems improbable that Weygand, Pétain, and the other exponents of the antiwar policy had the interests of the Anglo-French coalition primarily at heart in the summer of 1940. They did not then seem to have expected Germany's final defeat. Under the impact of military catastrophe, Germany's victory loomed large, and Britain's continued belligerency seemed just one factor among others that France could utilize to get better conditions from the German victors. Pétain certainly did play this card after the armistice.[10] But the antiwar party ruled out continuing hostilities after the collapse of the front in France. It challenged the prowar party on this issue, and won its point.

The positions were defined at the dramatic cabinet and Supreme War Council meetings in June, after the government had left Paris, which had been declared an open city. The Supreme War Council met twice at

Briare, on June 11 and 12, and a third time at Tours, on June 13. Reynaud, Pétain, Weygand, General Georges, General de Gaulle, and two other officers were present on the French side, and Britain was represented by Churchill, Eden, General Sir John Dill, and General Sir Edward Spears. From the accounts given by the participants, the discussion seems to have been tangential rather than straightforward. The French military leaders insisted on the hopelessness of the military situation, but Reynaud did not pose the question of a separate armistice. Churchill stressed that Britain would continue the struggle even if the country were invaded, but at the same time gave only vague assurances about continued aid to France. Four divisions could stay in France, and if the French army could hold out until spring, twenty to twenty-five British divisions would be available.[11]

In view of the critical position of the Allied forces, this promise of later aid did not impress the French military leaders. They saw no possibility of stopping the Germans anywhere in France. Eden and Dill suggested that French and British forces might retreat to Brittany and try to hold a bridgehead there until Britain could send substantial reinforcements. Weygand rejected this plan out of hand as impracticable. According to Spears, de Gaulle also was a proponent of the "Brittany redoubt" and considered the plan feasible. He gives the following report of a talk he had with de Gaulle on June 13:

> De Gaulle was angry. He had been in Brittany the day before, had seen General Altmayer, and was convinced Brittany could be held. It was evident from the way he spoke that his hope of defending the peninsula was meeting much opposition.
>
> He was suffering from frustration and exasperation. His criticism of Weygand was devastating.[12]

In any case, Weygand's position made illusory any further planning for stabilizing the front in France. According to the French version of what happened at Tours, Churchill finally seems to have understood that it was useless to count on maintaining any front in France. He immediately raised the question of the French fleet: "I understand that you may be obliged to yield. But if the French army found itself compelled to break off fighting, what would happen to the navy? This is a real nightmare."[13]

The British records differ on this point. According to Spears, Baudouin[14] twisted the sense of Churchill's statement that he "understood" that France might be obliged to sue for a separate armistice. When questioned about what he said, Churchill categorically confirmed that "at no time had he given to anyone the least indication of his consenting to the French concluding a separate armistice."

"When I said '*Je comprends*,' that meant I understood. *Comprendre* means understand in French, doesn't it? Well," said Winston, "when for once I use exactly the right word in their own language, it is going rather far to assume that I intended it to mean something quite different. Tell them my French is not so bad as that."[15]

The point is that Churchill, according to his own interpretation, merely indicated that he understood what Reynaud was telling him about the possibility that France might not be able to go on fighting, without implying approval, or "understanding" in the sense of sympathy, for such a course. But there is no doubt that Churchill did gather, from what Reynaud and the other Frenchmen were telling him, that the French land forces might have to be written off, and that he immediately focused his attention on the possibility of salvaging the French fleet.

Armistice or Exodus?

Another issue soon crystallized within the French war leadership. The main question was whether the government should quit metropolitan France and continue the struggle in North Africa (or, possibly, as a government-in-exile), or whether it should conclude an armistice and thereby cease to be a belligerent. At the cabinet meeting at Cangé, on June 12, Reynaud advocated "war from bases in the Empire"; Pétain and Weygand rejected this with the utmost vehemence. They declared that an armistice, concluded with the Germans while the French armies still had some sort of cohesion, was the only solution. Weygand said that "unless France asks for an armistice without the slightest delay, disorder will engulf the armies and the civilian population as well as the refugees. After this, the armistice would no longer do any good, since the damage would be done."[16] But the cabinet supported Reynaud's position.

On the following day, the cabinet met again at Cangé, and Weygand defended his thesis with extraordinary vigor. He heaped scorn upon the "verbal heroism" of the Premier and his civilian supporters in the cabinet. It is easy, he maintained, to speak of resistance from a safe refuge in provincial chateaux or overseas. The cabinet's place was in Paris: it should have stayed there to receive the German victors; that is what the Roman senate would have done.[17]

Pétain also declared that it was the government's duty to stay in France, whatever happened. To go abroad, even to the colonies, would be "desertion"; it would "kill the soul of France." Also, the country would not recognize a government-in-exile. The government had to share the sufferings endured by the people. At any rate, he, Pétain, would not leave.[18]

In this discussion, ultimate political attitudes played a decisive role. Weygand insisted on the importance of quick action, because to him the conditions that the Germans would impose were not the main threat; social chaos and the possibility of a communist seizure of power were the real dangers. Pétain also appears to have been thinking in terms of domestic policy: a government that stayed in France and worked out a *modus vivendi* with the Germans could go about the task of reforming the French "soul." Defeat and the acceptance of defeat were the conditions for moral regeneration.

The war party did not see things in this light. To those who wanted to transfer the government to the colonies to continue the struggle, acceptance of defeat was the thing that would "kill the soul of France"; the chief moral values at stake could be defended only by combating the national enemy and all he stood for.

It seems in retrospect that Weygand's preoccupation with the communist danger was unfounded. Although the agreement between Germany and Soviet Russia was firm at that time, and the Communists did everything in their power to impede the French war effort, it would still have been impossible for them to turn French defeat to their advantage; the German conqueror would not have stood for a communist regime in a defeated France. The Communists probably had some illusions on that score, but they were quickly dissipated.[19]

On the other hand, a counterrevolutionary overturn

of the institutions of the Third Republic was indeed an inevitable consequence of the acceptance of defeat. Not only was the domestic and foreign policy of the republican regime discredited by the defeat; it was also certain that Nazi Germany, installed as the supreme power in Paris, would effect a political reorientation by which French institutions would acquire a basically fascist tinge. Since the French political scene had been "polarized" for some time, with an influential rightist group clamoring for "salvation" along fascist lines, it was obvious that the profascist element would rally behind the peace movement and use defeat to impose its domestic conceptions on the nation.

What the war party wanted to avoid was, among other things, the emergence of an indigenous French fascist regime supported by German bayonets. Hence its efforts to transfer all the elements of legitimate authority—the President, the government, the legislative bodies—to territories not invaded by the German army. If the Germans could not be prevented from overrunning and controlling France, they should at least find a political vacuum there. If they then imposed their own methods and principles in administering France, they would do so as foreign conquerors, without legitimate political authority. "France," as represented by her lawful authorities, would still be at war with them.

In order to clear the way for such a solution, Reynaud tried to liquidate military operations by a purely military capitulation. After the government had moved to Bordeaux, he gave orders to Weygand to arrange a military cease-fire—a *de facto* capitulation—with the German armies, as the Dutch commander-in-chief had done after the Queen and the government had left Holland. But Weygand flatly refused to consider capitulation "à la Hollandaise." That, he said, would be an intolerable blot on the army's honor. Reynaud decided to take the issue before the cabinet.

At the cabinet meeting held on June 15 at Bordeaux, Reynaud's majority collapsed. Vice-Premier Camille Chautemps proposed an "exploratory" course: the Germans, he said, should be asked to make their armistice conditions known; if those conditions—as expected—turned out to be unacceptable, the people would "understand" that the government could do nothing but leave French territory. Of course, Britain should also be asked to relieve France of her obligations and to authorize a French request for a separate armistice. This proposal was favored by thirteen cabinet members, with six opposed. Reynaud offered his resignation, but President Lebrun persuaded him to yield to the majority of the cabinet. Reynaud thereupon decided to ask for Britain's authorization to request an armistice. The British answer arrived on June 16, refusing authorization unless the French fleet was sent to British waters, and the French undertook to consult again with Britain after the German terms were received. At the same time, Britain proposed a federal union of Britain and France.[20] According to a French historian, that plan was suggested to Churchill by General de Gaulle and two members of the French Economic Mission in London, René Pleven and Jean Monnet.[21]

The French cabinet was never officially informed of the British answer to Reynaud's query; the British Ambassador, Sir Ronald Campbell, took back the telegram that he had handed Reynaud (probably under the impression that France would not ask for armistice terms) when Reynaud told him that it had been decided that the President and the main body of the cabinet would go to Africa, leaving Pétain behind with a committee charged with liquidating military operations within France. In those circumstances, it would not be necessary to send the French fleet to Britain.

At the cabinet meeting on June 16, the discussion centered on the union plan. It was supported by Reynaud and the most resistance-minded ministers (Mandel, Marin, Dautry, Rio, and Georges Monnet), but the majority was against it. Ybarnégaray argued that the plan showed Britain's intention to reduce France to the rank of a second-rate power,[22] and Pétain declared that France could not merge "with a corpse." Chautemps renewed his plea for an "exploratory" request for armistice terms. Reynaud held out for the union plan, but was outvoted. Thereupon he resigned and recommended that Lebrun appoint Pétain as his successor. Pétain was appointed, despite the advice of the Presidents of the Chamber and the Senate, Herriot and Jeanneney, who were consulted, as required by tradition.[23]

Reynaud later explained that he had preferred Pétain to Chautemps because Pétain had assured him that he would not accept "dishonorable" armistice terms, and particularly that he would in no circumstances agree to surrender the fleet to Germany. Reynaud was convinced that this was a condition on which Germany would insist, since she wanted to invade Britain. Thus, in Reynaud's mind, Pétain, while asking for terms, would not actually conclude an armistice, whereas Chautemps would.[24]

Late at night, immediately after the formation of the

Pétain cabinet, the Spanish Ambassador, Lequerica, was asked to transmit the French demand for armistice terms to Berlin.

FRANCE AND HER ALLIES

The internal French debate ended with Reynaud's resignation. After that, the French surrender became mainly a diplomatic problem debated among France, Britain, and the United States. Britain sent a note asking that the French fleet be handed over for safekeeping (June 17). The United States associated itself with that demand in the most forceful fashion. On June 18, United States Ambassador Biddle was instructed to tell Admiral Darlan and the new French Foreign Minister (Baudouin)

. . . that in the opinion of this Government, should the French Government, before concluding an armistice with the Germans, fail to see that the fleet is kept out of the hands of her opponents, the French Government will be pursuing a policy which will fatally impair the preservation of the French Empire and the eventual restoration of French independence and autonomy. Furthermore, should the French Government fail to take these steps and permit the French Fleet to be surrendered to Germany, the French Government will permanently lose the friendship and good will of the Government of the United States.

This note was handed to Admiral Darlan as he was on his way to a meeting of the Pétain cabinet; Foreign Minister Baudouin was called out of the meeting and given a copy of the note. Baudouin was greatly irritated by its tone, but he laid it before the cabinet at once. It was decided that the fleet would not be turned over to the Germans; should they insist, the armistice would be refused.[25]

On the other hand, the French leaders were also opposed to sending the fleet to British waters for safekeeping. At the Tours meeting of the Supreme War Council, on June 13, Pétain and Darlan had already vetoed that measure, arguing that the Germans would refuse to conclude an armistice unless the fleet remained under French control.[26] For Pétain, Darlan, and the antiwar group, the question was whether a "common basis" could be found for an armistice agreement with the Germans. They felt that, if the Germans demanded the fleet, France could not sign an armistice, whereas if the fleet were turned over the British, the Germans would not grant one. This reasoning seems to have been realistic. In fact, the value of an armistice with France would have been critically lessened in German eyes unless the French could guarantee that their naval potential would not be used against Germany, while outright surrender of the fleet to Germany would have been incompatible with French "honor"[27] and would have exposed France to political reprisals on the part of the Anglo-Saxon powers.

Everything depended on whether the Germans would push France into continued belligerency by insisting on the surrender of the fleet. To everybody's surprise, they did not. Their armistice terms expressly stipulated that the warships of the French fleet, disarmed in their home ports, would not be used by the Germans for their own ends. Article VIII of the Armistice Convention read as follows:

The German Government solemnly declares to the French Government that it intends to make no use for its own ends of the French war fleet stationed in ports under German control, save for units necessary for coastal patrol and minesweeping operations.

Furthermore, the German Government makes the solemn

and formal declaration that it does not intend to present any claims regarding the French war fleet at the conclusion of peace.[28]

The French leaders thought that this made it possible for them to conclude an armistice without antagonizing Britain and the United States, since the "nightmare" of an active French fleet operating on the Axis side was thereby dissipated.

But Churchill did not see it in that light. He was so convinced of the importance of naval strength as an element of victory that he could not imagine that Hitler had sincerely renounced the objective of enlisting French naval cooperation sooner or later; to him, the armistice stipulations were a smokescreen and a ruse, not a real reassurance. The result was the attack on the French warships at Mers-el-Kebir. Actually, however, the armistice stipulations were genuine. Strange as it seems, Hitler did write off the possibility of seizing the French fleet. He seems to have known that the French would reject the armistice unless surrender of the fleet was omitted from the terms; and he was interested above all in a quick armistice with France, without further complications.

Ribbentrop, in fact, indicated this to Ciano, whom he met at Munich on June 19 while the French request for an armistice was under consideration. Here is Ciano's account:

He [Ribbentrop] said that it was the Führer's intention to avoid putting conditions to the French that might lead to a refusal to conclude the negotiations and to the transfer of the Pétain government to England or Algeria, where it could proclaim a "holy war" and continue hostilities for an indefinite period. He was particularly concerned over the French fleet, an unseizable unit [*elemento inafferrabile*] which would certainly go to England or America, from where it could again enter action at the opportune moment, rather than let itself be handed over to the enemy.[29]

Hitler did not relish the prospect of an indefinite prolongation of the war. He preferred to think that, with the victorious conclusion of the French campaign, the entire conflict would be liquidated. Ciano was struck by the change he noticed in Ribbentrop's use of words: the expressions used were "mankind's need for peace," "necessity of reconstruction," "necessity of a *rapprochement* of the peoples separated by the war," and so on. "I asked him point-blank: Does Germany prefer peace or the continuation of war at this moment? Without hesitation, Ribbentrop answered 'Peace.' "[30]

Ribbentrop, it is safe to assume, did not indulge in giving vent to his own preferences: then, as always, he was nothing but a mouthpiece for the Führer, a mirror of Hitler's moods.

GERMAN MOTIVATIONS

At the time of the French armistice, the German war leadership acted on the assumption that large-scale military operations were over.

After the collapse of France the German Army relaxed with a happy feeling that the war was over and that the fruits of victory could be enjoyed at leisure. Blumentritt's account of the sequel conveys a vivid impression of the prevailing attitude. Immediately following the armistice with France, orders came from O.K.H. to form the staff for the victory parade in Paris, and to dispatch the troops that were assigned to take part in the parade. Spirits were high, as everyone counted on a general peace. Preparations for demobilization had already begun, and we have received a list of the divisions that were to be sent home for disbanding.[31]

Britain, of course, was still at war; but Hitler considered it unthinkable that Britain would not listen to a reasonable peace offer. He sent such an offer through the Swedish legation.[32]

After the victory in France, Hitler believed that he had attained his goal. The invincibility of the German war instrument seemed to have been demonstrated. Once more, as after the Polish campaign, Hitler attempted to get into a talk with Britain. "At this hour," he said in his Reichstag speech on July 19, "I feel bound in conscience to appeal to the good sense of the British people. I see no justification for the continuation of this struggle." At the same time, German propaganda was indefatigable in proclaiming, through official announcements as well as in the newspapers and over the radio, that the British had lost the war. All they had to do was to recognize this and draw the necessary conclusions.[33]

When Hitler made this public offer to the British, however, he knew it would be rejected and that the war would go on. As early as July 7, he told Ciano that he was sure the war with England would continue, and that the German General Staff was working on the plans of attack.[34] The feeler put out through Sweden before the French armistice had produced no results; and although Hitler still believed in the eventual possibility of liquidating the war by some sort of a compromise with Britain, he came to the conclusion that military action, including an invasion, was necessary to "bring the British to their senses."

The Germans realized that control of the Mediterranean would be essential for successful operations against the British. On July 16, Hitler demanded a modification of the armistice agreement with France, providing for "eight bases for the Luftwaffe in Morocco; the railway from Tunis to Rabat to be placed at the service of the German army; the right to use the Mediterranean ports of metropolitan France, as well as those of Morocco, Algeria, and Tunisia; and the requisitioning of French merchantmen with their crews to transport to North Africa the air force units and their accessories, as well as their protecting troops."[35]

When Weygand informed Baudouin, then Foreign Minister in Pétain's cabinet, of these German demands, they were "at once agreed that these demands must be rejected, whatever might be the consequences of this refusal." According to Baudouin, not only Pétain but also Laval adopted the same view when the question was put to them.[36]

When Vichy gave a dilatory answer amounting to a rejection of the German demand, Hitler did not press the matter further. He could only have made things worse by precipitating a break with the Vichy government, for Pétain would then have declared the armistice agreement void and ordered the resumption of resistance in North Africa.[37] And in order to occupy North Africa in that event, Germany would have needed Spain's cooperation. But diplomatic efforts to persuade Spain to enter the war on the Axis side had not disclosed any great Spanish willingness to help Germany without considerable rewards. This was confirmed in October, when Franco promised intervention but posed stiff conditions before he would move.[38]

EVALUATION OF THE ARMISTICE

Evaluation of the French armistice policy involves a moot problem, since nobody can say what would have happened if the policy of the war party had prevailed. The critics of the armistice maintain that it prolonged the war; Hitler, they say, could have been defeated more quickly and at less cost if the French fleet had continued the war at Britain's side, and if the French government had retreated to fight the Axis from North Africa. The fullest exposition of this thesis is found in the memoirs of J. Paul-Boncour. He argues that the continued participation of the French fleet in the war would have been very effective, since the sea was the main theater of war for several months after the fall of France. Further, according to Paul-Boncour, the French military leaders would not have advocated the armistice had they foreseen that Britain would not be crushed and that both the United States and Russia would be at war with Germany by the end of 1941.[39]

The main argument of the defenders of the armistice is that it stopped the German armies at the French demarcation line, thus giving Britain the breathing spell she needed to consolidate her Mediterranean position and making the North African invasion possible. A defender of Marshal Pétain, du Moulin de Labarthète, puts this thesis in the following terms:

We thought that, if Paul Reynaud had not resigned on June 16, the Wehrmacht would have crossed Spain within a week, got a foothold in Spanish Morocco, destroyed our North African divisions overnight, and rounded up our Senegalese troops in six more weeks. All these "redoubts" would have disintegrated in the hurricane one after another.[40]

It must be admitted that, had these things happened, the Allied position would have been placed in extreme jeopardy. But the question is whether these things would have happened if the French had decided to continue the war.

According to the advocates of the war policy, the

French and British fleets together could have prevented a German descent in force on North Africa, even if Spain had made common cause with Germany. This view, however, probably overestimates Allied naval capabilities. Baudouin notes on June 13, 1940:

In fact I have asked Admiral Darlan if the French warships and the English ones at Gibraltar could stop a German force, moved rapidly to the Cadiz area in the south of Spain, from crossing the sea and reaching Spanish Morocco. The Admiral told me that his staff had already examined the problem; their definite conclusion was that ships based on Gibraltar would at this time of year only be able to make the enemy pay a certain price for crossing these thirty kilometres of sea, for in the daytime he would be covered by an air force which was mistress of the sky, and at night he could slip across from one shore to the other. He added that both in Norway and at Dunkirk the British Admiralty had had cruel experience of the considerable losses inflicted on its ships by the Luftwaffe. It had decided to equip its fleet with a great many more antiaircraft guns, but until this had been done, the ships would be exposed to attack from the air. Furthermore, the British aeroplanes at Gibraltar were negligible.[41]

These conclusions seem sound enough, but would Spain have allowed the German troops to pass, thus becoming a belligerent against Britain? We know from the documents made public since the end of the war that Franco had declared his readiness in principle to join the Axis powers as a belligerent. Franco would have justified his intervention by Spain's historic grievance, British control of Gibraltar: entering the war would have served to expel the foreigner from Spanish soil. Expansion of Spanish holdings in Morocco was another of Franco's war aims.

As mentioned earlier, however, Franco's decision to enter the war was not unconditional. He intimated in Berlin that, in order to subdue Gibraltar, he needed heavy artillery; he also foresaw that the British navy would throw a blockade ring around Spain, and he asked for grain supplies and other strategic materials to enable Spain to hold out. Hitler thought that Franco's demands were excessive, and he failed to give Spain immediate satisfaction.[42] The discussion was resumed in October, when Hitler met Franco at the Spanish frontier. Franco then was presented with a bill of particulars, about which he again refused to commit himself. As the Allies grew stronger and stronger, Franco's diffidence increased, and intervention was finally shelved for good.

This sequence of events can be interpreted in various ways. To advocates of continued French belligerency it proves that Hitler would not have been able to overrun Gibraltar and enter Africa. They argue that there was no reason to fear Spanish intervention, since Spain did not have the means required for success, and Germany was not in a position to grant the necessary help. But this conclusion is by no means inevitable. It is not at all certain that Hitler turned down Franco's demands because he could not spare the war matériel and the grain. Had he considered Spanish intervention necessary to win the war, he could have found a way to make the necessary supplies available. But, after the fall of France, he did not think that such additional costs were unavoidable. North Africa, he believed, was effectively neutralized: he was the master there by remote control, since he had the French government under his thumb.

Furthermore, he did not like Franco's bargaining for territorial expansion. He wanted to take certain territories for himself, and the problem of getting enough for Germany—while also satisfying Italy without thoroughly alienating France—seemed arduous enough without the further complication of Spanish demands. It is probable, therefore, that Hitler said no to Franco primarily because he did not think Spanish help was really necessary.

But the whole situation would have appeared in a very different light if France had not concluded an armistice. It seems altogether likely that in that case Hitler would have complied with Franco's demands in order to liquidate French resistance in North Africa, and it is by no means fantastic to assume that the German-Spanish forces could have taken Gibraltar. That would have changed the Mediterranean situation radically, and it is extremely doubtful that the French fleet's continued participation in the war would have overbalanced the loss of Gibraltar. We cannot assume that Allied naval superiority would then have been sufficient to prevent the Germans from landing their troops and equipment in North Africa. The landing itself would not have presented a problem; ports in Spanish Morocco would have been available. It would also have been easy for the Germans to establish complete air superiority.

Continued French resistance would have been extremely unpalatable to Hitler, and he decided on lenient armistice terms precisely to forestall this. This fact strengthens the case of the critics of the armistice: if continued French resistance was "bad" for Hitler, then it was "good" for the Allied cause. But the argument is not decisive. It seems likely, after all, that Hitler wanted to avoid further operations against the French not because he despaired of getting the better of them after they retreated to Africa, but because he thought there was no need to incur the costs of such a campaign in order to bring Britain to terms. In other words, he thought that a cheap victory in the Western war was possible, and he preferred that to a costlier victory. He wanted to show the world (and in particular his "timid" generals) not only that he could win, but that he could win in "lightning" fashion, without total mobilization. He staked his prestige and his reputation as a politico-strategic genius on the proposition that Western resistance was not a serious thing, but only a bubble that he could prick with one deft stroke, to the plaudits of his amazed and enraptured audience.

Hitler's political thinking was a curious mixture of uncanny political insight and immature adolescent fantasy. He knew that victory was not the only thing that mattered in war, and particularly in a war unleashed in cold blood. What mattered was the *cost* of victory and the stability of the peace founded on military success. His *real* interest was in German domestic policy, i.e., in the establishment of his own image as the infallible leader and sole arbiter in all matters. With his real instinct for the realities of political power, he knew that the best way to achieve his supreme ambition was to offer the Germans victory and domination at little cost, i.e., without total mobilization and without the radical interruption of peacetime patterns of life. The more quickly he could send his soldiers home and point to cloudless skies, the greater would be his prestige and authority.

This seems to have been a sound conception. The domestic position of a war leadership after the war depends not only on whether victory has been won but also on whether the sacrifices made for victory are felt by the people to have been bearable and commensurate with the success achieved. Victorious war leaders are likely to be repudiated by their people if they have achieved victory

only at the price of total exhaustion. Such revulsion from
costly heroics could be observed, for instance, in the victorious countries after World War I, particularly in
Italy, but also in France and even in the United States.
(Churchill's electoral defeat in July 1945 was another
dramatic illustration of the same tendency.)

Hitler knew why he had to produce a lightning victory. He wanted to return to "business as usual" quickly,
and to give the Germans tangible proof that they could
cash in on the fruits of the efforts he had forced them
to make. It is erroneous to think that "guns instead of
butter" was an absolute principle with the Nazis. It was
a *prewar* maxim; it was valid for the period when the
capability necessary for winning a lightning victory was
being assembled. But there was nothing wrong with the
butter acquired by using the guns.

The adolescent, immature streak in Hitler's thinking
consisted in his lifetime daydream that such success was
indeed attainable. He believed that only he and his gang
were "men," that all the others, and particularly those
who opposed him, were either contemptible nobodies or
degenerate madmen. The Polish, Norwegian, and
French victories seemed to confirm this assessment of
the value of Western resistance. What did the West
oppose to him? Words, empty words. The guarantee
to Poland was not worth the paper it was written on.
And were not the German generals ridiculous who trembled for the Ruhr when the German front-line divisions
wheeled through Poland? Had there been any risk in
snatching Norway from under England's nose? Had
the French army proved to be a serious military force?
These lessons, Hitler thought, were surely sufficient to

convince England that the "reasonable" Englishmen, those who preached nonresistance, had to be recalled from political exile. When the bubble of Western resistance was pricked, the "strong man" would be recognized for what he was: deadly when opposed, benevolent when appeased. This would be the triumph of the adolescent, the rejected son, who finds the secret of invincibility and returns from his labors to receive the homage of those who have despised him.

The defenders of the French armistice policy argue that concluding the armistice was a blunder on Hitler's part.[43] French agreement to the armistice, then, was simply a shrewd move to exploit the blunder, whereas, by going to Africa, the French government would only have rescued Hitler from the consequences of his mistake.

This last point has some merit. What is not established, and seems indeed doubtful, is that the French peace party acted chiefly on this premise rather than from other motives. Pétain, Weygand, and their supporters seem to have been convinced of Germany's final victory and the inevitability of Britain's surrender. They thought it urgent for France to surrender while she could obtain something for not using her residual capacity. To them, the chief value of the armistice lay in its being a *separate* arrangement, predicated upon the rupture of the coalition. There was a great deal of cold calculation in this, but also a certain amount of emotionalism: resentment against the earlier orthodox coalition policy that led France into an impasse; hope for the "rebirth" of the French nation once it could turn its back on the left-wing, revolutionary, progressive, and secular currents of its historic tradition.

THE PSYCHOLOGICAL BACKGROUND OF THE
ARMISTICE POLICY

It is not easy to separate the realistic and the emotional strands in the French peace party's policy. Its apologists today stress the realistic element in Vichy's thinking and action and minimize the spontaneous ideological element. Its critics, on the other hand, see only the political preferences of the Vichy group and call the armistice policy treasonable; they see it as deliberately sacrificing national independence for the sake of political transformation along fascist lines:

For a long time past the fifth column had been firmly entrenching itself in France. . . . The traitors did not show themselves, they worked in the deepest shadow, so that the eye of justice should not surprise them. . . . One common thought possessed them: *"The Christian regeneration of impious France."* This purpose involved the destruction of the existing political regime, and to attain it any means would be justified, whatever they might be. Even defeat? Yes. Without defeat could the goal be reached? [44]

There is some evidence that the French Right was lukewarm in its determination to push the war effort and to win at any price. Moreover, the feeling that "Hitler was better than Blum" was widespread among the French bourgeoisie. The more the ideological component of France's war policy—antagonism toward Nazism as such —was stressed in war propaganda, the more the French bourgeoisie felt alienated. They could see some sense in a nonideological war (Germany, of course, had to be cut down to size), but they found no justification for a war waged in order to consolidate the rule of the Left. In many bourgeois quarters, the struggle against the Left with its "creeping socialism" ranked higher than the struggle against Germany. Such feelings were no

doubt treasonable and incompatible with French patriotism. But the bourgeoisie was not alone in putting particular group interest above the national interest in winning the war.

The most extreme antiwar stand was taken by the
Communists: to them, fighting was a sacrilege once Moscow had hurled its anathema against the "imperialist"
war.[45] In the French Socialist Party, too, there was a
strong faction, led by Paul Faure, which opposed the war
on pacifist and Marxist grounds. This group believed
that the war would arrest social progress and enrich the
bourgeoisie while placing all the burdens on the lower
classes. The domestic class struggle was an absolute; to
suspend it in favor of the war effort was to betray the
workers. Here, too, domestic political objectives took
precedence over the patriotic motive of winning the war
at any cost.

This cleavage along class lines prevented real national unity behind the war effort. On the international
plane, the situation was no better. To Frenchmen who
had lived through World War I and its aftermath, it
was obvious that France was unable to withstand another
massed German onslaught alone. Only a coalition could
save France. But where was the coalition in 1939?
Britain, of course, could still be counted on; she was the
only great power who had an active interest in support-
ing France. But this also meant that France became more
and more dependent on Britain; and British support and
solidarity, as the interwar years had shown, were by no
means complete. Britain was willing to stand by France
if Germany attacked her directly. But further than that
she was unwilling to go.

The Locarno treaty amounted to a British guarantee

of assistance to France against Germany. By concluding that pact, Britain had abandoned her traditional policy of avoiding unconditional commitments to continental powers. But the Locarno pact guaranteed France's western frontiers only. It was in no way connected with France's treaty commitments to East European powers.

In order to neutralize a possible German military threat, France had also concluded alliances with Poland, Czechoslovakia, Rumania, and Yugoslavia, and had vetoed the absorption of Austria by Germany. But these alliances and guarantees could be made effective only by a united Franco-British stand, and Britain refused to be drawn into a conflict with Germany simply in order to protect France's eastern allies. The result was the disintegration of the eastern flank of France's system of security. Deserted by Britain, France had to look on as Poland drifted away from the coalition, as Austria was absorbed, and as Czechoslovakia was dismantled.

By the middle of 1939, the coalition was reduced to its western core; and even so there was a critical gap, since Belgium refused to join the western security system. A last-minute attempt to enroll Soviet Russia as a substitute for the lost eastern allies had failed, and France was in a precarious position indeed. If Germany wanted to go to war, she could throw her undivided strength against the West. This meant a single front, manned by France virtually alone, since Britain had neglected to build up a peacetime army.

In these circumstances many Frenchmen could see hope only in appeasing Germany. The entire logic of the British policy had pointed in that direction. As the French saw it, Britain had hoped to buy peace at the price of sacrificing Austria and Czechoslovakia and letting the other East European countries slide into the German orbit. The logic of this policy was that a conflict between Germany and the West could be avoided if the West did not hinder Germany's eastern rampages. But Britain suddenly reversed her position. She made it clear in the spring of 1939 that further German expansion in the East, at the expense of Poland, would mean war. In this way, the French decided, Britain made the worst of two worlds. The chance of buying peace through appeasement (if it existed) was thrown away, as had been the chance of containing Germany by means of an East-West coalition. It is small wonder that many Frenchmen were utterly critical of British leadership of European coalition affairs. From the French point of view, that leadership was shortsighted, egotistical, and reckless. First it forced France to abandon the eastern power position which, inadequate as it was, gave her a measure of strategic security, and then it forced her to forgo the only possible benefit that such a policy might have secured, the avoidance of a large-scale conflict.

What made things worse, Britain's policy of appeasement did not apply only to German eastern expansion. Britain was also complacent about Germany's growing military strength. Hitler's unilateral repudiation of the disarmament clauses of the Versailles treaty in the spring of 1935 had drawn no protest from Britain; the British government pointedly sanctioned the German policy of nullification shortly afterwards by concluding a bilateral treaty with Germany on naval armaments (June 1935). In the following year, when Germany put garrisons in her western frontier provinces in open defiance of the Locarno pact, the British flatly refused to intervene. Thus British policy had made it more and more certain that the West would not have a decisive military superiority if and when a showdown with Germany became inevitable. From the French point of view, a policy that had such implications was suicidal.

From the British point of view, of course, things looked different. Britain, though disarmed, had vast mobilizable resources. The British people had been averse to continental entanglements: a conflict "for the sake of" allies would have had no popular support. On the other hand, there was no doubt that, in case of a German westward thrust, the people would be rallied to the cause of resistance. It made sense to the British to see if Hitler could be appeased by "reasonable" concessions, and to make a stand against him if he could not. Such a detached, experimental attitude was impossible for the French. Their sense of security could not be bolstered by the hope of falling back on vast mobilizable resources. Their first stand would be the last; and with Germany's full strength hurled against them, the first stand seemed hopeless.

In spite of all that, there was no despair in France when the war broke out. This was due, in part, to ignorance of the true strategic situation. People think by analogies; the French on the whole were confident that, if the worst came, there would be another miracle of the Marne. But they did not believe at first that the worst would come. They believed that this time the war would not cut into the vital tissue of France: the Germans would be stopped on the Maginot Line. There would be no dreadful bloodletting, no close combat, no invasion. The Germans would be strangled by the sheer weight of the Anglo-French coalition; naval blockade would force them to their knees. How could they con-

tinue to wage war without access to key strategic materials, such as oil and iron ore (which, it was assumed,
they could get only by the sea route)? French morale
was maintained during the "phony war" by large pos-
ters showing a map of the world on which British and
French possessions appeared as huge red expanses, con-
trasting with the puny black spot that was Germany.
The legend was "We shall conquer because we are
stronger."

Internal dissension and the frustration of French
coalition policy notwithstanding, morale could be maintained as long as the war involved no mass bloodletting
and no large-scale combat. One may speculate whether
the war could have been won in 1939, had the French
divisions invaded Germany while the German forces
were engaged in Poland. There may have been a
chance;[46] but the French were entirely unwilling to accept big risks and losses. It is also true, of course, that
the Franco-German frontier along which the armies
were deployed offered no suitable terrain for a decisive
attack on the Ruhr. The German industrial region could
be attacked only through Belgium, which was not a
member of the coalition. In effect, the Belgian gap in
the western security system both shielded the industrial
heart of Germany and permitted German forces to be
used elsewhere. Later, when the German armies appeared in the West, they swept through the same gap
into the fields of France.

After the German breakthrough, with mass combat
a grim reality, French morale collapsed quickly. It was
then that the French people realized the unsoundness
of the political and strategic basis on which the war policy of the coalition had been built. The issue was not

simply one between patriotism and treason. It was, rather, that the war itself had become problematic, for it was not what the French had bargained for. It was extremely difficult for Frenchmen, regardless of their various political attitudes, to face another all-out war that would demand the sacrifice of entire generations. If such a war had been unambiguously forced upon them by an out-and-out attack, they might have regarded it as unavoidable. But to wage such a war "for the sake of" treaty obligations, and in Britain's wake at that, made little sense. It became evident during the tragic weeks of May and June, 1940, that the war had not been well prepared either politically or strategically. Resentment on this score led to further discontent with France's dominant political orientation and with her coalition partner.

These "realistic" reasons for the rejection of France's traditional coalition policy reinforced the emotional and ideological disaffection referred to above. Still, the war policy might have withstood the test of the German attack if the Franco-British forces had adopted suitable countermeasures against the German breakthrough. It was not German superiority of manpower and matériel that led to the collapse of the front but bad tactical and logistical planning by the Allies.

The armistice policy of 1940 was the joint product of all these factors. For those who took the lead and supplied the decisive impulse—such military leaders as Pétain and Weygand, and politicians such as Laval and Marquet—stopping a hopeless struggle was not the only consideration. They also wanted to use the opportunities provided by the defeat to take revenge on the political system of the Third Republic, with which they were profoundly disenchanted. For them, *écrasez l'infâme* was a dominant motive, but many Frenchmen who did not share their animosity toward the Republic could go along with the policy of armistice, since it seemed to be the only policy consonant with the requirements of the situation. There is no doubt that the armistice had the support of the great majority of Frenchmen in 1940.

This majority, it must be stressed, was a purely negative one. It was a majority against the continuation of the war, not a majority for the counterrevolution preached by Pétain and Laval. Vichy was never able to work out a positive program and rally the majority of the people to it. It was only able to establish a stably-functioning administrative system, in which the representatives of several radically different ideological currents were yoked together. The authority of the regime, however, was not seriously questioned, since no better alternative was in sight.

The Vichy regime ended France's belligerency and broke with the coalition policy of the Republic, but it stopped short of total commitment to the German side. Avoiding armed conflict with France's former ally and the collaboration with Germany that it entailed were as fundamental to Vichy's foreign policy as was the armistice itself. This policy of neutrality was accepted by the majority of the people. A noisy, radical group of Pro-German extremists, operating under the benevolent eye of the German authorities in occupied Paris, clamored for active French participation in the war on the German side, but there was no popular support for the idea. What mattered to the immense majority of Frenchmen was to avoid fighting; ending hostilities against one side only to resume them against the other made no sense at all. The policy of neutrality was an element of strength for Vichy, in so far as popular acceptance was concerned. But it became increasingly difficult to maintain that line, for the Germans could not be satisfied with it.

THE AFTERMATH OF THE ARMISTICE

Relations between winner and loser were profoundly ambiguous. For the Germans, the armistice agreement was a point of departure. It gave them overwhelming means of pressure against the Vichy government; when it became evident that the British would not make peace, the Reich proceeded to use these means in an effort to obtain France's active participation in the war. The July 16, 1940, note on the North African bases referred to above was the first move the Germans made in this direction. Tenacious efforts in the same direction followed.

In August, the Reich appointed Otto Abetz Ambassador to France. Abetz was an "old France hand" and a specialist in manipulating press campaigns. Immediately on assuming office, he launched a number of press organs in Paris for the purpose of undermining Vichy's policy of neutrality.[47] More than a year later, in January, 1942, Abetz thought that the time was ripe to broach the question of cobelligerency with the Vichy government directly.[48] But Pétain gave a negative response to Jacques Benoist-Méchin, the French secretary of state who had negotiated with Abetz on the problem. "I took France out of the war," he said. "I did not do this to make her reenter the war on the German side."[49]

Thus, as far as Vichy was concerned, the armistice treaty was a terminal point, determining a maximum beyond which collaboration with the Germans could not go. Yet, since the Germans had overwhelming means of pressure at their disposal, Vichy was slowly obliged to retreat. The high point of defiance was reached in December 1940, when Laval was deprived of office and put under arrest. But the Germans quickly forced Pétain to release Laval and patch up relations with him; after a long tug of war, Laval was back in office in April 1942.

During this whole period, however, the policy of neutrality was maintained. Vichy was careful not to cut diplomatic contacts with the Western world. After the attack upon Mers-el-Kebir, diplomatic relations with Britain were severed, but relations were continued with the Dominion of Canada. In January 1941, Admiral Leahy arrived at Vichy as American Ambassador. He immediately established close relations with Pétain and soon became convinced that Vichy by no means had both feet in the German camp.[50]

What enabled Vichy to pursue the policy of neutrality was a covert means of pressure that prevented the Germans from crossing the demarcation line in force. This was the implicit threat that the seat of government would be transferred to Africa. That policy seems to have been laid down in explicit terms in August 1940. According to Baudouin, it was then agreed that, if the southern zone were invaded, Pétain would appoint Darlan as his successor, and Darlan would go to North Africa with the government and the fleet.[51] The agreement was a verbal one, but Pétain considered it binding.

When the Germans did invade the southern zone after the Allied landing in North Africa (November 1942), Darlan was at Algiers. Yet he did not assume governmental functions as stipulated by the decision of

August 1940. He gave orders to resist the landings, and he concluded an armistice only when a new authorization to do so was received from Pétain; even then, the fleet was not instructed to join him, but was scuttled instead. Aron concludes from this that the 1940 agreement was no longer in force in November 1942:

When Pétain gave this instruction to Darlan in August 1940, he meant it as a momentary expedient corresponding to the situation as it existed at that time. It was not a permanent policy that could remain in force for years to come.[52]

An alternative interpretation seems more plausible. The instruction of August 1940 was still in force, but it did not cover situations of the kind that arose in November 1942. Had the Germans crossed the demarcation line at a time when Vichy's sovereignty over North Africa was uncontested, the instruction would have been put into effect automatically. The Allied landings, however, created a new situation. From Vichy's point of view, they constituted an attack on French territory. The official policy for such eventualities was that of armed resistance.[53] The landings in effect deprived Vichy of the only element of political strength it had retained, and thereby sealed the collapse of the regime. The French government that subsisted after the German occupation of the southern zone was an essentially new entity, without any trace of independent political existence.

The political basis of the Vichy regime was inherently unstable. The armistice with the Reich to which it owed its existence expressed a momentary balance of bargaining factors, but that balance was bound to shift in one direction or another. Had the Germans been victorious, Vichy would have been replaced by a French regime fully integrated into the New Order planned by the Nazis. With the Germans defeated, a French regime fully committed on the Allied side was due to take over. None of the three essential elements in Vichy's policy—armistice, collaboration, neutrality—had permanent value. The armistice could not be transformed into a peace settlement. Collaboration compromised Vichy in the eyes of the French without entirely satisfying the Germans. Finally, a neutral position between the two camps could not be indefinitely maintained as hostilities gained momentum.

CONCLUSIONS

The French surrender shows a considerable "disarming" effect resulting both from the loser's "reorientation" and from his latent threat of using elements of residual strength. On the winner's side, it is an example of the importance of political incentives in facilitating and hastening surrender.

When concluded, the French armistice represented a successful bargain for both sides. The French succeeded in surrendering on a qualified basis and salvaging partial sovereignty; the Germans avoided time-consuming terminal operations. The bargain, however, would have produced satisfactory long-term results only if it had been transformed into a permanent settlement. As it turned out, no permanent settlement was possible. The Franco-German war was only part of a bigger conflict, and the later progress of that conflict subverted the basis on which the armistice had been concluded.

In the armistice situation, both sides operated on a predominantly power-oriented basis. Since no permanent settlement could be reached, both sides endeavored to exploit the temporary balance created by the armistice to promote their power objectives. Both were committed to the principle of cooperation, but they could cooperate only with mental reservations, having divergent ultimate goals in mind. This conflict of objectives was never resolved, since the German defeat swept away the actors on both sides.

Four

THE ITALIAN SURRENDER
September 1943

THE STRATEGIC BACKGROUND

The Allied strategy in World War II was predominantly a strategy of attrition. The Mediterranean theater played a peripheral role in that strategy. Mastery of the sea and increasing mobilization of latent resources enabled the Anglo-American coalition to bring overwhelming pressure to bear on the Axis forces operating in North Africa. By May 1943, all German and Italian forces in the African theater had been driven into a small pocket in Tunisia and forced to capitulate. This enabled the Allies to launch an amphibious assault on Sicily in preparation for a landing on the Italian peninsula. From the point of view of over-all strategy, however, the operations against Italy had a diversionary and probing character.[1] No strategic decision was expected from them, since only an assault from the Channel coast offered an opportunity to engage the bulk of the German forces and to paralyze them by strategic attrition.

For Italy, however, the Mediterranean theater was not peripheral. She had entered the war in the hope of profiting from the liquidation of British and French power positions in that area. The German victory in France forced Mussolini's hand in this respect. He believed that it set the stage for a new political settlement in Europe, in which Germany would replace Britain and France as the dominant power in the West. Italy was not prepared for a full-scale war, but intervention appeared to Mussolini to be the only correct decision. He saw no need for a total war effort, since the strategic decision seemed already achieved. On the other hand, he believed that Italy could claim a major part in the spoils only if she became an active belligerent. Intervention was a gamble, but it seemed safe enough.

When the initiative in the Mediterranean passed to the Allies, the war became a defensive one for the Axis; but there was no natural *defensive* partnership between Germany and Italy. The German-Italian alliance had been a purely offensive one, dictated by desires of aggrandizement. The Italian Fascists had believed that the West was weak and decadent and that German "dynamism" would make short shrift of it, and they had engineered the alignment with Germany because it promised considerable profit without total effort. When their calculations were upset by the course of the war, they were not able to demand a total effort from the Italian people for a purely defensive action alongside Germany. The very basis of the alliance had been the belief that Germany was stronger than the West. When it became evident that she was weaker, only severance of the coalition made sense.

With the Allied armies poised for the assault on Sicily and Italy, it was obvious that the Italian armed forces were not in a position to offer effective resistance. As the German Military Attaché in Rome, Enno von Rintelen, put it,

The backbone of the Italian armed forces was broken. The army was in the throes of agony. The best divisions had been lost or routed in Africa and Russia. The metropolis was practically devoid of troops. . . . In Sicily there were four operative divisions, in Sardinia and Corsica another four. In the Apennine peninsula, the number of operative divisions amounted to twelve. . . . The long coastline of the peninsula and of the big islands was unprotected. . . . The navy continued to suffer from lack of oil. . . . The air force had inadequate numerical strength and equipment and could operate only in conjunction with German air units.[2]

The Italian army chiefs desperately begged Germany for reinforcements. On July 15, however, the German Supreme Command informed the Italians that their requests (in particular for air reinforcements) could not be granted.[3] This made it clear to all Italians, including Mussolini and the other fascist leaders, that Italy was not in a position to continue the war.

Mussolini planned to make this clear to Hitler at their conference at Feltre on July 19. But Hitler, apparently sensing Mussolini's intention, did all the talking at that conference. For two hours, he lectured the Italians on the necessity of waging war in total fashion. After the tirade, Mussolini remained silent. On the following day, the chief of the Italian general staff, General Ambrosio, resigned because Mussolini had failed to make the expected declaration that Italy would sue for peace.[4]

The immediate consequence was Mussolini's fall, when the Grand Council of Fascism turned against him at a meeting on July 24, 1943. A resolution was introduced, according to which the King was to resume supreme command over the armed forces (which had been vested in Mussolini since the beginning of the war) and make all political decisions necessary to save the country.

This was tantamount to an injunction to Mussolini to resign. He did so on the following day, convinced that the King would ask him to form a new cabinet. The King, however, told Mussolini that he was dismissed, and that Marshal Badoglio would head the new government. Mussolini was taken into custody "to protect his safety," and the Fascist Party was immediately dissolved.[5]

It was understood that the new government's task was to liquidate the war. Its position was precarious, however, because of the presence of German armed forces in Italy. Hitler, thoroughly mistrustful, ordered preparations for the occupation of Rome and the arrest of Badoglio and the King. The Italians thereupon concentrated five divisions around Rome, and the Germans decided to avoid an open break. Badoglio also was determined to postpone a break until he had come to a definite agreement with the Allies. He announced that Italy would continue to wage war alongside the Germans, and he maintained normal contacts with them.[6]

Simultaneously, Badoglio tried to conclude an armistice with the Allies, who were prepared to accept nothing but unconditional surrender. Badoglio could not treat with the Allies on that basis because it was obvious that a separate capitulation would immediately lead to hostile acts by Germany. He therefore tried to reach an agreement with the Allies on the basis of cobelligerency, but his proposal was rejected.

THE ALLIED SURRENDER POLICY TOWARD ITALY

This stiff Allied stand represented a departure from earlier policy decisions. In his report to the British War Cabinet on the deliberations at Casablanca in January

1943, Churchill wrote that it had been decided to continue the war against Germany and Japan until "unconditional surrender," but not to press the same demand on
Italy; "the omission of Italy would be to encourage a
break-up there."[7] The War Cabinet objected to any exception, however, and the final statement issued at the
conference included Italy among the enemy nations that
would have to surrender unconditionally.[8]

Apparently the Allied decision makers did not understand the hidden implications of the change in the Italian
government. Mussolini's fall caught them unawares.
No plan had been laid down in advance to deal with such
a contingency.

What was the reason for this lack of preparation?
Field intelligence seems to have had some inkling of
the trouble brewing in Italy. Admiral Franco Maugeri, head of Italian naval intelligence, writes as follows
in his memoirs:

Some two months before Mussolini's fall, I had received a
report through my Swiss agents that British and American
undercover operators had been trying to learn who would succeed the dictator when he was overthrown. At first, I did not
take this too seriously. . . . But the inquiries persisted and I
began to realize that the Allied High Command must have
some reason to suspect, if not to know, that a change in the
government might be on the way. . . . If this was true and
the Allies had advance knowledge of Mussolini's downfall,
then there is little excuse for their failure to act immediately
after it took place.[9]

But whether the Allied operatives knew something or
were merely playing hunches, it is clear that no plan was
based on their dispatches. A plan was developed on the
spur of the moment, and the approach that was adopted

was highly characteristic of the political warfare concepts current at that time in the American (and British) leadership.

General Eisenhower's first reaction, as reported by Captain Butcher, was to exploit the news by launching a propaganda campaign, using broadcasts and leaflets, to give "the House of Savoy and the Italian people their obviously much-needed 'white alley' to get out of the war."[10] The General was apprehensive about the necessity of conducting his campaign under the close supervision and direction of President Roosevelt and Prime Minister Churchill:

Ike regretted existence of rapid communications. If we were still in the day of sailing ships, he thought he could deal more quickly and advantageously with the Italians than is possible when he has to communicate to both Washington and London and wait for the two capitals to concur or direct.[11]

Presumably, Eisenhower's uneasiness was due to fear that the "politicos" (Butcher's word) would prevent him from adopting the only approach that, according to him, promised success: giving Italy generous assurances about "peace with honor" in general, and providing as many immediate, positive inducements as possible in particular. As the psychological warfare "operator" in this situation, Eisenhower apparently felt that a psychological appeal could be effective only to the extent that it was positive and steered clear of fundamental quarrels about principles and long-range political considerations. He was aware of the discrepancy between the operator's perspective and the policymaker's, a discrepancy that actually emerged at every point during armistice negotiations.

About the instrumentalities, methods, and immediate objectives of political warfare, however, there was no difference of approach between the operating and the policymaking centers. Overt propaganda appeals to the Italian people were to be the chief instrument used. Eisenhower, according to Butcher, wanted to build up "public opinion amongst the Italians which would encourage King Victor Emmanuel to send an emissary to negotiate quickly for peace."[12] It is characteristic of the dominant American approach that "pressure of public opinion" was deemed necessary and sufficient to push the King onto the right path. One is reminded of Hans Speier's category of the "democratic fallacy":[13] whatever we want to happen in politics can be made to happen if, and only if, public opinion is mobilized behind it.

As we now know, the King and Badoglio did not need to be pushed by public opinion: their minds were made up; what they needed was *physical* protection against the Germans. This does not mean to say that a psychological campaign would necessarily have been futile. In the Italian case, overt appeals to leaders and people could have been more than pointless exhortations to do the impossible, precisely because the political leadership had already, in principle, adopted the policy that the Allies wanted to promote. If such a campaign had been timed correctly and coordinated with a *direct* approach to the elite, its psychological effects might have been very great.

In order to be effective, however, overt appeals had to stress things other than "peace" and "honorable capitulation." The Allies were not in a position to offer "peace" to the Italians; the Germans had seen to that. What the Italians needed was sufficient motivation to make another military effort, this time against their former ally. Such a motivation could have been based only

on Italian national objectives, such as the preservation of
Italy's independence, which was threatened by the Germans. But even an appeal to fight for independence
would not have been enough. It is always a hard problem
of conscience for a military elite, as well as for sublead-
ers and rank and file, to turn against a former ally. In
spite of widespread friendliness toward the Allies and
hatred of the Germans, this problem of honor weighed
upon the Italians' consciences, and the Allies would have
been well advised to provide the best possible psychological support for making the transition. But such considerations were far from Allied minds at that time.

Badoglio—rightly or wrongly—considered that he
could not show his hand until the Allies had fifteen divisions in Italy,[14] which was more than the Allies had in the
entire region. Badoglio's concept of political strategy
was the exact antithesis of the Allied one. He saw nothing to be gained through mass appeals. He thought that
political and military arrangements from elite to elite
had to be completed before it was safe to let the masses
know about any new policy. Fear of German retaliation
played a large part in Badoglio's avoidance of contact
with the public. But its effect was deplorable. Maugeri
depicts in vivid colors the disappointment and despair of
the Italian masses when, following the overthrow of
Mussolini, no clear national policy was announced:

Badoglio was execrated for not coming to terms with the Allies
at once. I must confess that I condemned him as vehemently
as any. I, too, cried out: "Basta! Basta! Enough! Let's end
this senseless struggle! Let's make peace!"[15]

There is no doubt that popular response to the immediate announcement of a break with the coalition
would have been very favorable. Just such a course had

been advocated by the antifascist political leaders with whom Badoglio had consulted before Mussolini's overthrow. These leaders (Bonomi in particular) proposed to enter into the cabinet (with Badoglio as Premier and Bonomi as Vice-Premier) and at once denounce the German alliance. The Germans, whose best units were still tied down in Sicily, could not react strongly, according to this view; moreover, Italy could hope to win the confidence of the Allies and obtain lenient treatment only if she made a complete and voluntary break with the Germans.

On July 14, Badoglio agreed with these arguments and adhered to the plan put forward by the civilian leaders. But the King vetoed the agreement on the following day because he feared German vengeance.[16] Badoglio bowed to the King's decision; he decided to include only military men and functionaries in his cabinet, and his main endeavor thereafter was to lull German suspicions and stall off German occupation in force until his negotiations with the Allies bore fruit. He even went through the farce of a military conference with Hitler at Tarvis on August 6, in which he gave his word of honor that he was not negotiating a separate peace. (This was, of course, literally true at that time, since only "exploratory" contacts had been made.) In his public statements, Badoglio continued to stress Italy's determination to go on with the war.

On the Allied side, the preparatory consultations for the propaganda offensive were completed within a few days; Eisenhower's message, approved by the Combined Chiefs of Staff, was broadcast on July 30. It offered the Italians "peace under honorable conditions," and a "mild and beneficient" occupation regime. A passage, inserted

at Churchill's insistence, demanded that no Allied prisoners of war be turned over to the Germans. Even this
message, although it made clear that the Allies in fact
intended to impose complete surrender, was too "positive" to suit the guardians of the political purity of Allied
goals and methods. As Butcher says, "immediately there
was a murmur in the press corps because the message indicated permission to retain the House of Savoy."[17]

Another Eisenhower message gave offense in high
political quarters. To Eisenhower's dismay, Churchill
complained to Roosevelt about a broadcast sent out in the
General's name, in which a lull in serial bombings was
explained to the Italians as having been designed to give
them a breathing spell during which they could reorient
their policy. (Actually, the pause was for technical reasons.) Churchill was highly incensed by this "psychological" use of military facts: only the political leaders,
he thundered, had the right to make announcements
about such matters.[18]

Apparently, Eisenhower had unwittingly violated
one of the rules of conduct which Churchill had laid
down concerning the Allies' Italian policy; namely, that
until Badoglio showed his hand, "the war should be carried forward against Italy in every way that the Americans will allow."[19] Churchill's wording suggests that he
felt the Americans might slacken the pace of the Italian
campaign as a result of the emergence of the Badoglio
regime; this may have been why he was so sensitive about
what he considered a symptom of the American military
leadership's intention to substitute "psychological" inducements for hard military blows.

Allied political warfare was handicapped by the lack
of reliable intelligence about Badoglio's true intentions.

The Allies apparently decided to wait until the public appeals for "honorable capitulation" (a euphemism for "unconditional surrender") bore fruit. Badoglio, on the other hand, concentrated his efforts on hoodwinking and placating the Germans. He also put out a few cautious feelers to the Allies early in August, but his emissaries were merely charged either to explain to the Allies that his declarations about continuing the war were just a deceptive smokescreen serving to put off the Germans (d'Ayeta mission to Lisbon, August 3) or at most to suggest a negotiated peace rather than surrender (Berio mission to Tangier, August 6).[20] Such feelers, of course, could produce no tangible results. It was only on August 15 that a military envoy, General Castellano, finally arrived in Madrid with instructions to start negotiations for an armistice based on the general idea of surrender.

In the meantime, the Germans had been pouring more and more troops into Italy: Allied intelligence put the number of divisions at thirteen by August 18, fifteen by August 21, and nineteen by September 3.[21]

Badoglio's slowness in acting was due in part to technical difficulties. He was so impressed with the omniscience of German intelligence in Italy that he dared not send a military envoy until a more or less plausible pretext could be found for such a move. The official justification for General Castellano's mission was, in fact, fantastic enough: he was to proceed to Lisbon under a false name, as a member of an Italian delegation welcoming the Italian Ambassador returning from Chile. This cautious, conspiratorial maneuver was both time-consuming and unavailing. By the middle of August, Hitler knew from intercepted broadcasts that Badoglio was negotiating with the Allies.[22]

The Allies, in the meantime, could do nothing but wait. According to the dominant doctrine, public appeals were the preferred instrument of political warfare; they could furnish the essential results all by themselves. Moreover, according to the "rules of unconditionality,"[23] there was nothing to negotiate about. All that was required of the enemy was an act of submission: when the surrender delegation came, its sole task was to sign on the dotted line. The Italian government had to show its good faith by executing the terms imposed, and, above all, by making a public announcement of surrender. Nothing else needed to be considered, according to the Allies, in connection with Italy's severing her coalition ties with Germany.

In the meantime, military strategy was governed by rumor and impeded by political inaction. Air Chief Marshal Tedder called Eisenhower to an urgent conference at Tunis on August 2. He wanted permission to resume the heavy aerial bombardment of Naples and of the marshaling yards of Rome because he had word that "Badoglio was actively trending to the Germans."[24] Whatever military justification there may have been for hitting Naples and Rome at that time, the justification that Badoglio was "actively trending to the Germans" was not valid; an energetic attempt to get in touch with Badoglio and rouse him from his torpor might have produced far better results than the further destruction of Naples and of the railroad facilities in Rome. Given a suitable inducement, Badoglio might have found a way to put Naples and Rome at the Allies' disposal, although that is not certain, since Badoglio insisted on complete protection against the Germans, which the Allies were in no position to provide. But it is not impossible that a better result could have been achieved in Italy if contact with Badoglio had been made earlier, to induce him to help the Allies make unopposed landings in places where he had strong or undisputed control. Bombing as a political strategy, as a means to influence Badoglio's behavior, was clearly pointless.

As time passed and Italy did not send a surrender delegation, Allied headquarters concluded that Eisenhower's propaganda campaign had failed. On August 12, Captain Butcher notes gloomily:

What appeared to be a quick collapse of Italy has disappeared into uncertainty, with the definite knowledge that the Italians are solidifying their opposition to us and are really fighting. Around headquarters, we are inclined to attribute this to the hardboiled attitude of the Prime Minister and the President, who publicly insisted upon "unconditional surrender" as soon as Mussolini was out. No surrender ever was made without some conditions; the main thing is to have the Italians realize, admit, and act as if they've been defeated.[25]

Later developments revealed that this appraisal of the situation was wrong. Granted that a more positive propaganda approach would have produced better psychological results, it is clear now that insistence on unconditional surrender was not responsible for Badoglio's failure to sue for peace. That demand did not deter the Italian antiwar group from going through with its policy; it could do nothing else. The actual explanation for Badoglio's failure to sue for peace was simply that he was unable to solve the technical problem of establishing contact with the Allies.

The Allied headquarters' assessment of the significance of stiffening Italian resistance at the front also seems to have been in error. That stiffening implied, according to Butcher, that the Italians had not recognized that they were beaten, that surrender was out, and that the situation called for a psychological campaign to convince them that they were defeated. What this theory overlooked was that it is possible for a military leadership *both* to plan for strategic surrender and to order and obtain stiffer tactical resistance from its troops. Badoglio probably felt that a systematic slackening and collapse of Italian tactical resistance would merely attract German troops to all sectors manned by Italians, a development that had to be avoided at all cost. But such considerations apart, it is characteristic of military surrender that the loser wants at least to salvage his honor, and to obtain the largest possible compensation from the winner for stopping resistance. For that reason, stubborn resistance, particularly during the closing stages of a war, is a frequent prelude to surrender.

Allied thinking about the problem of surrender overlooked these finer shadings of the problem and treated tactical "resistance" and "will to surrender" as mutually exclusive. Allied leaders apparently expected the Italian admission of defeat and readiness to surrender to take the form of an abrupt stoppage of all resistance and a completely supine acceptance of Allied dictation of no matter what terms. This mechanical application of the "unconditional surrender" formula was faulty, not because it compelled the Italians to fight on (they surrendered in spite of Allied "harshness"), but because a sudden and total transition from fighting to complete nonresistance was technically impossible. Italy could not just subside like a punctured inner tube; her surrender forcibly entailed continued military action against her former ally. Yet the Allied negotiators neither foresaw that the surrender talks would be dominated by this prob-

lem nor were allowed to conduct the conversations on
that basis.

The political-strategic objective of securing the military cooperation of the Italian government was completely outside the scope of Allied calculations at that
time. When the armistice negotiations actually started
at Lisbon, the Allied negotiators, Brigadier General Kenneth Strong and Lieutenant General Bedell Smith, were
apparently taken completely by surprise when the Italian
side offered, not just unconditional surrender, but active
military cooperation against the Germans. They were
not empowered to agree to such an arrangement, and
they had to return to Algiers to consult with Eisenhower.
Butcher noted on the state of negotiations on August 21:
"The main difference seems to be that the Italian General Staff wants to execute a complete flip-flop and join
the Allies to fight the Germans. To this Beetle [Smith]
was not authorized to agree, but he thinks Ike will insist
on collaboration with us."[26]

Eisenhower also, it seems, had not foreseen that the
Italians would propose a "flip-flop," although the situation in Italy was such that they could in fact propose nothing else. But he was in favor of exploiting the opportunity, as might be expected of an "operator" anxious to
achieve the best possible result, and in a good position to
doubt the miraculous virtue of the unconditional-surrender formula. The political center, however, did not
see things in the same light.

The instructions that Roosevelt and Churchill sent
to Eisenhower for dealing with the Castellano mission
at Lisbon enjoined him to accept nothing but uncondi-

tional surrender, and to do so without discussion. "These terms," the orders stated, "do *not* visualize the active assistance of Italy in fighting the Germans."

That statement did not mean that the Allied leaders excluded the possibility of Italian military activities against the Germans. It meant only that such activities were expected to develop automatically *after* the announcement of the armistice, on the sole responsibility of the Italian leadership and population. They were to be a different phase from the surrender as such. The Italians were to be encouraged to hope that, by fighting the Germans after the surrender, they would create a situation in which the Allies would be willing to reconsider and modify the armistice terms. Any agreement that the Italians would fight the Germans in return for Allied concessions was to be excluded from the armistice talks proper. As Churchill wrote to Roosevelt on August 16, immediately on receiving news of Castellano's arrival in Madrid,

We, the Allies, for our part cannot make any bargain about Italy changing sides, nor can we make plans in common at this stage. If, however, serious fighting breaks out between the Italian Army and German intruders, a new situation would be created.[27]

This seems a strange way to conduct a war. Military operations involving Italians on our side were foreseen, but planning for them was strenuously ruled out. Moreover, the Allies insisted on surrender terms designed to break the spirit of the Italian armed forces and deprive them of their effective striking capacity. The Italian war fleet and merchant shipping were to be turned over to the Allies; all military aircraft were to be flown to Allied airfields or destroyed.[28] Surrender of the fleet (for which, characteristically, Churchill began to press the day he learned about Mussolini's fall), although psychologically hard for the Italians to take, at least did not preclude its being used in later naval operations. But taking the air arm away from the Italian army was tantamount to rendering those already inferior and overmatched forces wholly ineffectual.

Thus the Allied political strategy of calling for complete surrender first and cooperation later was obviously ill conceived, for the first stage could only jeopardize successful implementation of the second. A different, more elastic political strategy could not even be envisaged, because any agreement involving military cooperation would have departed from the fundamental principle of unconditional surrender. It would have smacked of "negotiated peace" rather than complete "victory." In the eyes of the Allied leaders, as well as of the public, such an agreement would have seemed an inexcusable compromise, nullifying the supreme goal for which the war was being waged. If any enemy came to us suing for peace, we could only insist on surrender, ruling out negotiated terms. That principle alone could have precluded discussions about military cooperation with the Italian surrender delegation.

But there was, in addition, the fact that the King and Badoglio, along with all the other leading men of the armistice regime, had a record of full connivance and cooperation with Mussolini and fascism. They could not be considered bona fide democrats. Harry Hopkins' reaction, noted down immediately after Mussolini's overthrow, may be considered typical:

I have grave misgivings about both the King and Badoglio. Certainly neither of them, by any stretch of the imagination, can be considered to represent a democratic government.

It is very easy to recognize these people, but it is awfully hard to throw them overboard later. I surely don't like the idea that these former enemies can change their minds when they know that they are going to get licked and come over to our side and get help in maintaining political power.[28]

To people who were thinking along such lines (and that was the dominant mode of thought in the Allied camp), it was imperative that enemies who wanted to come over to the Allied side should still be treated as enemies, no matter what advantages their defection might confer on the Allied effort. The advantages were clear, but to accept them was unthinkable because it was immoral. Sherwood describes the resulting dilemma in the following terms:

The merest suggestion of recognition of the Badoglio government brought down more and more opprobrium on the State Department which by now was regarded in liberal circles as the very citadel of reaction and of the policy of "doing business" with the avowed enemy. However, the State Department was by no means the predominant policy-making instrument in consideration of the new situation in Italy. It was a matter of cold, hard military calculation. General Eisenhower and the Combined Chiefs of Staff were conscious of the enormous possible advantages of having any Italian government, regardless of its political coloration, which would have the authority to deliver an immediate surrender.[30]

That military pressure put Roosevelt and Churchill in a difficult position. They knew they had to "use" the King and Badoglio, and that it would have been supreme folly not to exploit the split within the enemy coalition for all it was worth. At the same time, it was impossible to make an open "deal," with the King and Badoglio as partners. Roosevelt and Churchill solved the dilemma by imposing unconditional surrender upon the Italian armistice regime, and then deciding to give that surrender a maximally elastic implementation. In that way, they felt, it was possible to keep Allied morale high and satisfy public opinion, as well as meet the requirements of the objective situation. This "manipulative" approach, while successful in neutralizing the psychological stresses created on the Allied side by the split in the Axis coalition, was not effective in quickly liberating Italy from the Germans.

Other more immediate considerations also prevented cooperation with the Italian armistice regime. The Allied leadership thought it would be dangerous to trust Badoglio and the King. We could not know, the Allies felt, whether they really meant to play ball with us. We could not confide in them until they gave unmistakable proofs of their sincerity. The act of submission that we demanded was seen as the first and essential proof of trustworthiness: if the Italians went through with it, we could gradually thaw toward them, and perhaps let them in on some of our military plans. Accordingly, the Allies steadfastly refused to reveal to Badoglio the date of the projected landing near Salerno, in advance of which the armistice was to be made public. While Badoglio's own political strategy was firmly rooted in the principle of "no overt clash with the Germans before substantial Allied forces land in Italy," Allied political strategy was equally firm in postulating "no consultation or cooperation with Badoglio until the surrender is sealed and announced." These divergent conceptions finally precipitated a crisis of confidence that had a disastrous effect on the whole Italian campaign.

THE ROME DISASTER

Badoglio, having no information about the Allies' plans, simply did not prepare any military action; he merely watched the German build-up in Italy and the arrival of German units in the Rome area with mounting despair. The Italians managed to assemble six divisions around Rome; the Germans had about two in that region, including an armored one. Badoglio, of course, did not contemplate anything so rash as an attempt to eject the Germans from the Rome area, in spite of his numerical superiority. For that, he needed the presence of Allied troops.

The Allied High Command, in fact, was ready and willing to put some reinforcements at Badoglio's disposal. The final armistice terms, signed at the Allied forward base near Cassibile in Sicily on September 3, contained one term that departed from the integral unconditional-surrender line. This departure satisfied Badoglio's demand that Allied troops be present before he publicly denounced the German alliance and accepted the Allies' surrender terms.

The Allies undertook, as part of the armistice terms, to drop parts of the American 82nd Airborne Division on airfields near Rome. The action was to precede the main landing at Salerno by a day or two; it was to be synchronized with the announcement of Italy's surrender, planned for September 8. But General Maxwell D. Taylor and Colonel William T. Gardner, the American officers charged with arranging the details of the parachute drop, did not arrive in Rome to get in touch with Badoglio until that very day, September 8. It was impossible to work out the details on such short notice.

Contemporary Italian accounts about the Taylor mission are conflicting. According to Maugeri, General Carboni (commander of the Italian troops in Rome), whom Taylor and Gardner met first, "vetoed" the whole plan: the Germans were too strong around Rome, he argued, and they had managed to deprive the Italian forces of ammunition and gasoline. Both the Italians and the Americans would be "massacred" under such conditions. The whole operation had to be called off for that reason, according to Maugeri, but the situation would have appeared to the Italians in an entirely different light if they had been told by the Allies that the main landing at Salerno was to take place almost simultaneously. For then they would not have been afraid of German reinforcements arriving from the south.

But Taylor and Gardner confided nothing. They couldn't. In fact, at no time were we taken into the confidence of the Allies, and General Eisenhower has since declared that this was one of the greatest blunders committed by the Allies in the entire war.[31]

Badoglio's version of the episode is entirely different. He says the American emissaries *did* tell him that the main landing was to take place immediately, and adds that Carboni merely asked for more time to issue ammunition and gasoline to the Italian troops. This would have taken some time; but, according to Badoglio, Taylor and Gardner had indicated that the landing of the parachute troops would take four or five days. Badoglio's understanding was that he would not be required to announce the surrender before the Allied reinforcements had been landed near Rome; hence he sent a telegram to General Eisenhower asking for permission to postpone the announcement of the armistice until September 12 "in the interest of military operations."[32]

The result was an explosion on Eisenhower's part. Badoglio's request, it was felt at headquarters, simply indicated that he wanted to change the signed agreements unilaterally; his trustworthiness immediately appeared highly dubious. Eisenhower decided to crack the whip and sent a blistering telegram to Badoglio, telling him that the Allies would broadcast the surrender agreement, as originally scheduled, at 6:30 P.M. on September 8; that Badoglio was expected to do his part; "and that if Badoglio, or any part of his armed forces, failed to co-operate as agreed, he would publish to the world a full record of the affair." But Eisenhower "agreed" to suspend the airborne operation since it could no longer be launched prior to announcement of the armistice.[33]

Badoglio, of course, had to "go through with his part of the agreement": he announced the armistice, "in fear and trembling," as Eisenhower recorded, an hour and a half after he received the telegram.

The result of the announcement was disastrous. That night, Badoglio, the other military chiefs, and the King and his household withdrew to the Ministry of War. They were awakened at 4:00 A.M. by General Roatta with the news that the Germans were moving into Rome and that it was necessary to leave. Thereupon they all left for the south, hoping to find safety on the Allied side of the front.[34] They thus escaped capture, but their departure ended all chance of organizing any activity against the Germans. There was nobody at the ministries or at military headquarters who could have given orders. Italy's military apparatus just collapsed.

The Germans' reaction was swift and efficient: they simply ordered the disarmament of all Italian military units in the area under their control. This was done in most cases without any resistance on the part of the Italians; only at La Spezia did Italian troops cover the departure of the fleet for Malta. It is impossible to blame the Italian troops and troop commanders for this behavior. They simply had no orders; there was no leadership; the Rome ministries did not even answer the telephone. In his broadcast announcing the surrender, Badoglio inserted a cryptic phrase to the effect that the Italian forces would have to stop hostilities against the Anglo-Americans but should resist possible attacks "from whatever quarter." That was all. The troop commanders were not told what to do if the Germans demanded their disarmament; nor was there anybody to direct their movements if and when conflicts with the Germans developed. Resistance to the Germans under such conditions would have been senseless and suicidal. Moreover, the armistice announcement merely said that Italy had "surrendered" and was out of the war; recognition of Italy as an ally, or even as a cobelligerent, was studiously avoided. All this certainly was not calculated to spur organized military resistance to the Germans after the armistice.

One may ask why Eisenhower was so insistent on publishing the armistice agreement on September 8. According to one theory, he held that the announcement could not be postponed, in view of the possibility that the Germans might succeed in overthrowing the Badoglio regime at the last moment.[35] But this theory does not seem convincing.

The danger that Badoglio would be overthrown (or, rather, captured) by the Germans surely existed; in fact, this danger was rendered acute by the precipitate publication of the surrender agreement. But it was certainly impossible to hold that the agreement would have represented a positive asset in the hands of the Allies, provided only that it was duly published, no matter what happened to Badoglio and his regime in the sequel. Had the Germans overthrown or captured Badoglio and the King, the agreement would have ceased to be of any value, whether it was published beforehand or not.

The real explanation seems to have been different. It was obviously impossible to cancel the Salerno landing when Badoglio's request for a postponement arrived. And in Eisenhower's mind, announcement of the surrender was inseparably tied to the landing; it was inconceivable to him that the landing could take place before the announcement had been made. It was possible to renounce the Rome operation, but it was not possible to postpone the announcement of the armistice until the Rome operation was completed.

Why did Eisenhower consider it imperative to synchronize the landing with the publication of the armistice (in fact, to make the announcement some time in advance of the landing)? This is what Butcher notes on September 2:

If the acceptance is bona fide, the announcement of the armistice following unconditional surrender is to be made 24 to 48 hours prior to our landing in Salerno Bay. This will be the signal for all Italian services to turn against the Germans, to seize and protect aerodromes, to menace and, if possible, stop movement of German troops and for the Italian fleet and probably other vessels to seek safety in ports which we control.[36]

This, in fact, was the whole tenor of the instructions Eisenhower had received from the political leaders. He could not question the correctness of the forecast. The only real problem was whether the Italian acceptance of the armistice was "bona fide."[37] If this were shown by publication of the agreement by Badoglio, all the rest would follow immediately: the Italian troops would start action against the Germans the moment they learned that they had surrendered unconditionally to the Allies. It is easy, then, to see why Badoglio's behavior on the 8th appeared heinous to Eisenhower. The landing was imminent and could not be canceled; this made it imperative for the Italian forces to turn upon the Germans immediately. And yet Badoglio was refusing to do the only thing that was needed to unleash Italian military action against the Germans, namely, broadcast the armistice. It was clear to Eisenhower that Badoglio had to be forced.

It is extremely strange that such consequences were expected from the publication of "unconditional surrender." Even granting that a complex and difficult military action *could* be touched off by a public announcement, without previously worked out plans, what was there in the agreement that would have stimulated Italian belligerency against the Germans? The Allies did not recognize Italy as a cobelligerent; all the Italians were given was a crushing set of terms depriving them of all authority, all independence, and even their basic means of defense. Eisenhower himself had found the terms "unduly harsh"; he suspected that the Allied home governments wanted "to make a propaganda Roman holiday by publicizing to the entire world the stern restrictions of surrender.[38] But then, how could anyone expect that terms good enough for a "propaganda Roman holiday" at home would also be good for Italian morale?

What would have been necessary to get the Italian

troops to initiate resistance against the Germans was, above all, a functioning leadership, giving clear orders. For technical reasons, such a military leadership could operate only from Rome, where all lines of communication were centralized. Hence, the possibility of Italian military action hinged on the preservation of Rome. Eisenhower does not seem to have expected that the "suspension" of the parachute drop would lead to the precipitate abandonment of Rome by the heads of the armistice regime; he knew that the Italians, after all, had superior forces in the area, and he could not imagine that all the military chiefs would simply leave the troops without making the slightest attempt to defend Rome.

One can only speculate about what would have happened if Allied military liaison men had been sent to Rome, not on the eve of the landing, but before, while conversations in Sicily were still going on. It might have been possible then to work out joint operations while there still was time. The Allies' unreasoning refusal even to consider a cobelligerent status for Italy certainly hampered any action toward that end, however. Eisenhower was not permitted to work out a joint military plan; he had to smuggle in a partial, though all-important, detail—the parachute drop near Rome—by way of the armistice negotiations. By the time the parachute drop was approved, it was too late to put the plan into effect.

Badoglio's precipitate flight from Rome dashed all Allied hopes for Italian military cooperation. Italian troops rendered no help whatever to the Allied operation, either in the rear zone or in the invasion battle of Salerno bay (which almost ended in disaster). During the crucial Salerno days the political and military leaders were wandering aimlessly around in southern Italy, out of touch with the military units.

BEYOND SURRENDER

One of the outstanding characteristics of the Italian armistice agreement was that it began to be obsolescent on the very day it was signed. That, of course, was precisely what was intended by the Allies: loyal execution of the terms by the Italians would prepare the way for mitigating them. The surrender was to be nothing but a first step; it would be followed by concessions granted purely as acts of grace; Italy would be restored to a "respectable place in the New Europe."[39]

Clearly, Roosevelt and Churchill interpreted unconditional surrender for Italy in a special sense. For Germany and Japan, the main enemies, unconditional surrender had long-term implications: it had to ensure that these powers were deprived of any chance to commit further aggression. They had to be eliminated for an indefinite period as independent factors in international life. In Italy's case, unconditional surrender had no such implications; it was conceived as a stage quickly to be left behind, but one that had to be gone through nevertheless in order to obviate the psychological difficulties involved in making a deal with the enemy.

In addition, insistence on surrender enabled the Allies to ease the terms in the exact measure that the Italians cooperated with them. In Churchill's phrase, "Italy must work her passage. Useful service against the enemy will be recognized by us in the adjustment and the working of the armistice terms. . . . Our principle will be payment by results."[40]

This way of handling unconditional surrender looks,

at first glance, like a hard-headed, realistic way of exploiting complete victory. Roosevelt and Churchill probably felt that the solution was ideal, since it ensured that any concession granted to Italy would be fully earned by actual services. The Italians would be maximally motivated to render active help to the Allies, and public criticism of concessions granted to them would be disarmed. Actually, however, the conception of paying by results was not well suited to the problem that faced the Allies in Italy.

The premise of the Allied policy was that whether Badoglio and the King were friend or foe remained an open question until Italian behavior settled it. In war, however, such a skeptical, open-minded approach is likely to be self-defeating. If a group is actually friendly, it is to the winner's interest to strengthen it as much as possible; if it is hostile, it is to his interest to weaken it as much as possible. If, during a probationary period, he fails to strengthen a friendly group, or weaken a hostile one, he hurts his own cause. Hence, a wait-and-see attitude is risky, and should be adopted only if there is no alternative.

In the Italian case, there was no reason to consider the friend-or-foe question as entirely open. The very fact of dissolving the Axis coalition placed the Italian armistice regime in the Allied camp. Once that was done, there was no way back for Badoglio; it was impossible for him to double-cross the Allies. By interposing a probationary period between surrender and active cooperation, therefore, the Allies only weakened their own side.

Moreover, the Allies were not right in thinking that holding out hopes for future concessions was the most effective way of stimulating active Italian cooperation. The presence of the Germans in Italy was the deprivation that was uppermost in the Italians' minds; they had to look at the situation, not merely from the point of view of pleasing or not pleasing the Allies, but from that of ejecting or not ejecting the Germans. The military problem implied a community of interests between the Allies and Italy, and the Italians could not therefore be made to feel that pleasing the Allies was their only objective in life. Willy-nilly, they had to criticize Allied moves that in their eyes were not adapted to promoting the common objective of defeating the Germans; and establishment of "good conduct" criteria in the midst of war belonged in that category.

Badoglio's memoirs are full of the traces of Italian bitterness over the treatment his regime received from the Allies. The Italians, he complains, were held to a subordinate role in the war.

We furnished many supply columns which carried munitions and food up to the front lines, many divisions to protect the lines of communications, and more than 100,000 men who served in a "Pioneer Corps," but *we were not allowed to increase our armed forces.*

I said we were not given arms: it would be more accurate to say that many were taken from us to be sent to the Balkans.

It was an extraordinary way to treat us. The Heads of the Allied Governments called on the Italians to increase their forces, suggesting that the mitigation of the terms of the armistice depended on the part we played in the war. At the same time the Allied Headquarters in Algiers and the Allied Command in Italy prevented, by every means in its power, our taking any share in the fighting.[41]

This complaint is psychologically understandable. Since it had been suggested that mitigation of the armistice terms depended on Italy's contribution to the war, the Allied policy of not entrusting any sector of the front to Italian forces looked like a deliberate way of minimizing Allied moral obligations toward Italy. Such a course was not apt to raise Italian morale.

But the Allies could not adopt a different policy after the Italian armed forces were allowed to collapse. The principle of payment by results fully justified their hands-off attitude, because the Italian army had largely been prevented from "earning" any different treatment. It rendered no service either at Salerno or at the rear of the German forces during the crucial period of the invasion. The upshot was that Italy could contribute no battleworthy unit to the Allies. An effective Italian force could only have been raised from scratch and outfitted with Allied equipment. This was clearly impossible while the battle was raging, and thus, objectively, the Allied position made sense. But given the objective situation, it was pointless to impress upon the Italians that mitigation of the terms of surrender depended on their actual contribution to the war.

Granting cobelligerent status to the Badoglio regime was a terrible stumbling block to the Allied leaders, who were afraid of the psychological repercussions of any such move. The King and Badoglio were undesirable partners because of their past roles in the fascist regime. Therefore, the Allied leaders were anxious to put off recognition until the King and Badoglio had built up a record of active repentance. But the war could not wait. Headquarters was pressing for Italy to be allowed to declare war on Germany, and instructions to that effect had actually been drafted prior to September 20. The opponents of recognition succeeded in holding up the decision for several weeks, however, so that instructions to authorize Italy's entry into the war were not sent to

Eisenhower until October 5, and the actual declaration was not made until October 13.[42]

There were obviously very urgent reasons why the Allies had to abandon their opposition to recognizing the Badoglio regime and why they were unable to await "results" before granting it cobelligerent status. The reasons can perhaps be surmised from a memorandum from Hopkins opposing recognition of Badoglio. Sherwood quotes the memorandum in full:

On September 20, Hopkins read a copy of the proposed agreement whereby Italy would be permitted to enter the war not as an "ally" but as a "co-belligerent," and he wrote the following memorandum and sent it to the President:

"I hope you will not encourage Eisenhower to recognize Italy as a co-belligerent. This will put them in exactly the same status as the rest of our allies. Nor do I think there is enough evidence that Badoglio and the King can be trusted for us to arm any of their divisions. I should think that Eisenhower could quietly look the other way if some of the armistice terms are being violated, such as Italian naval ships being used to transport our troops, or Italian bombers from Sardinia fighting the Germans.

"Would it not be better in paragraph 2 to cut out the words 'to wage war against Germany' and substitute 'to assist us in the war'?

"I cannot see that a declaration of war by Badoglio gets us anywhere except a precipitated recognition of two men who have worked very closely with the Fascists in the past. I think we should get every possible advantage out of them, but I don't think we are under any obligation to them. I don't see why, if Eisenhower wants to use Italian crews and ships, he does not go ahead and do it, providing he thinks he can trust them. I simply hate to see this business formalized until we have had a much better look at Badoglio and the King. McFarlane, the British general's report on them was certainly none too good.

"I would not throw out Badoglio but recognition would be an inevitable [?] step. Could you not tell Eisenhower to keep on as he is for the present and make the decision in another week?"[43]

This memorandum clearly suggests one reason why it was necessary to recognize the Badoglio regime as cobelligerent: the urgent necessity of using part of the Italian fleet in actual operations. Hopkins thought Eisenhower could "go ahead" and use the fleet, provided he considered it reliable. What Hopkins overlooked was that something more than Eisenhower's confidence was needed to make the ships move. Naval officers in general will carry out missions only on orders from their superiors, and the Italian naval commanders were no exception in this respect. They needed orders from the Badoglio government before they could engage in operations. That is why the Allies were compelled to "treat" with the Italian government, and to conclude a special agreement about the fleet. This was the so-called Cunningham–de Courten agreement; it was signed at Taranto on September 22 by the Allied naval commander, Admiral Sir Andrew (later Viscount) Cunningham, and the Italian Minister of Marine, Admiral Raffaele de Courten.[44]

This was a stopgap agreement. It was not possible to conclude the agreement with the government as such, because the Allies were not yet ready to recognize the Badoglio regime; even the so-called longer instrument, containing the long-term and nonmilitary clauses of the armistice, was not yet signed. Hence the curious method of making a treaty with an individual member of a government that one did not recognize.

Even so, this agreement made Italy a cobelligerent in fact, and formal recognition of the fact could not be delayed much longer. As soon as ships flying the Italian flag engaged in naval operations, Italy was in a state of undeclared war with Germany—an anomalous situation from the point of view of international law. Full naval cooperation logically demanded a formal declaration of war; it was actually effected only after the granting of cobelligerency. Badoglio writes:

> As soon as co-belligerency was declared the Navy was treated as an Allied fleet. All the light craft and the cruisers (except five, three of which were later returned to us) took part in operations in the Mediterranean and the Atlantic, winning the admiration of the English and the Americans.
>
> Our Air Force was at once used in the Balkan sector where it carried out not only many bombing raids and machine gun attacks but also took orders and supplies to our detachments fighting with the Partisans.[45]

It is impossible to see what advantage the Allied cause gained from strenuously excluding the policy of cobelligerency in August and imposing it in October. It was obviously never necessary to grant the Badoglio regime cobelligerent status unconditionally: the Italian emissaries could have been told that the regime would be recognized as cobelligerent only after having fulfilled certain specific conditions. But it was precisely a "bargain" of this kind that the Allies had ruled out during the armistice talks. By doing so, they maneuvered themselves into a situation in which the granting of cobelligerency necessarily had to appear like a reversal on their part.

That was the decisive defect of the policy of "payment by results": it conveyed the impression that treaties concluded by the Allies, and terms imposed by them, were not to be taken seriously. The chief policymakers on the Allied side did not appreciate the fact that great powers have an overwhelming interest in establishing the inviolability of pledges granted or received by them. Hopkins' reference to "looking the other way" while a treaty imposed by the Allies was being violated indicates a recklessness, a lack of seriousness, which was only too characteristic of Allied policymaking during the war. It was fully realized that the Italian situation called for something different from unconditional surrender, yet concluding a meaningless, obsolescent treaty was deemed better than abandoning the unconditional-surrender fetish.

The hope that such a treaty would at least confer upon the Allies the benefit of complete freedom of action was also futile. The Allies did not achieve complete freedom of action, since they were not in reality free to grant or withhold cobelligerency once Italy had surrendered. It would have been possible to refuse cobelligerency only to an Italian regime that had been completely deprived of fighting potential. The Italian land forces very nearly were in this state by October, thanks to Allied and Italian bungling; addition of the substantial navy to the Allied forces, however, inevitably implied cobelligerency. This could have been foreseen in August, and it would have been if the Allied leaders had not been addicted to the fantasy that military operations could start on a spontaneous impulse at a moment's notice, requiring neither technical staff work nor legal and political allegiance.

SURRENDER OF THE FLEET

The surrender of the Italian fleet immediately gave rise to a myth concerning the efficiency of "psychological warfare" stunts. Wallace Carroll records the origin of the myth:

Messages from Admiral Sir Andrew Cunningham asked Italian sailors to bring their ships to Allied ports. In Algiers, Maurice Pierce, an OWI engineer serving in the Psychological Warfare Branch, shifted the wave-length of one of the Allied radio transmitters to an international distress frequency to which the naval vessels of all nations listen at all times.

Over this station a message was broadcast to the Italian fleet every fifteen minutes for many hours. Three days later, when the Italian fleet from Spezia steamed into the British naval base at Malta, Admiral Cunningham turned to one of his aides and said: "Tell General McClure . . . that they've accomplished in one day with propaganda what I've been trying to do for three years with the Navy." General McClure took this as a pleasantry, but OWI, which was at that moment fighting hard to get enough money from Congress to keep the Psychological Warfare Branch going, decided it should be accepted as the literal truth and inserted it in the records of the Congressional budget hearings, whence it will certainly find its way into every psychological warfare manual of the future.[46]

This myth, too, reflects the feeling that military actions are a matter of impulse and can be unleashed by suitable verbal stimuli from the enemy. Actually, however, the Allied broadcasts had nothing whatever to do with the sailing of the fleet. The fleet sailed on orders issued by the appropriate Italian naval authorities. Samuel Eliot Morison gives the following account in his history of American naval operations:

The procedure for the Italian Navy to follow when the armistice was announced had been carefully worked at Cassibile and brought by General Castellano to Rome. Admiral Sansonetti telephoned instructions to the appropriate naval commanders on the night of 8–9 September. All warships on the west coast of Italy were to proceed to Corsica and pass down its western coast and that of Sardinia; thence sail to Bône in North Africa for orders. Those in Taranto and on the east coast were to sail directly to Malta; those in the Aegean, to Haifa. Merchant shipping was to make for Gibraltar or Alexandria. All were given recognition signals, and assured that they would be received honorably in Allied ports.

The main battle fleet was at Spezia. Admiral Bergamini, the commander, a few minutes after receiving word from Rome, summoned his commanding officers to a conference. "Tell your men," he said, "to accept this great sacrifice. . . . Our ships, which an hour ago were ready to sail against the enemy, are now able, because the country requires it, to meet the victors with the flag flying; the men can hold their heads high. This is not what we imagined would be the end, but this is the course by which we now must steer, because what counts in the history of a people is not dreams and hopes and negations of realities, but the consciousness of duty carried out to the bitter end. . . . The day will come when this living force of the Navy will be the cornerstone on which the Italian people will be enabled to rebuild their fortunes."[47]

For the circumstances in which the order to sail was received and executed at Taranto, we have a dramatic account by Admiral Alberto da Zara, who was in command of the division stationed there.

Da Zara reports that all commanding admirals were called to Rome to attend a meeting at the Ministry of Marine on September 7. They did not know, of course, that the armistice had been signed four days before and would be announced the next day. At the meeting, the Minister, Admiral de Courten, declared that, "in the event of a German attack, we must react as strongly as possible, without pulling any punches." Da Zara continues:

Had I not been so tired from the long and strenuous motor journey from Taranto to Rome, and had I not been obliged to start on my trip back the next day, perhaps I could have pierced the secret of this strange sibyllic utterance before the facts had spoken. At any rate, I was completely taken by surprise on the evening of the 8th, when, coming aboard the [*Caio*] *Duilio*, I heard from the commanding officer, Morabito, that we had asked for [*sic*] an armistice. I immediately called the commander of the "Cadorna" Group on board and listened with him to Badoglio's proclamation: the war was over.[48]

This report casts a revealing light both upon Badoglio's method of operation and upon the state of mind of the Italian naval officers. Even after the armistice was signed, and when it was obviously necessary to prepare for an inevitable clash with the Germans, Badoglio did not disclose the situation to the top officers; he merely handed them the cryptic information that, in case the Germans attacked, they would have to defend themselves. Da Zara was unable to puzzle out what this information meant, nor does it seem that the others present discussed it with him during the evening. Apparently, the idea that Italy might change sides during the war was so remote from the minds of the officers that they could not anticipate such a move even when the signs were there.

After the announcement of the armistice, da Zara tried for hours to get Rome on the phone for explanations and orders. When the call did not go through, he was not too surprised; telephone connections between Rome and Taranto had never been good. On the morning of September 9, da Zara was called out of an officers' meeting; one of his officers was on the phone, telling him of a telegraphic order that had arrived from Rome that morning: all the ships that could sail were to proceed immediately to Malta! Da Zara was not satisfied; the telegram was truncated and could have been forged. He decided to put in another call to Rome (not knowing, of course, that the government no longer was there), and also to wait for a complete duplicate version of the telegram. In the meantime, he made arrangements on his own for the scuttling of the ships. Two of his subordinates tried to argue him out of it; a third pleaded with him to carry out the order. While this discussion was going on, the complete text of the order arrived, signed by de Courten.

It specified clearly and precisely that sailing the ships to Malta meant neither that they would be handed over nor that the flag would be hauled down. In this way, although I did not have the comfort of hearing the chief's voice, my change of mind was quick and complete; I detected in the telegram de Courten's spirit and style. The absurd hypotheses my distracted mind had conjured up suggesting that the telegram might be apocryphal evaporated.[49]

The admiral returned to the interrupted meeting and announced his decision to obey Rome's orders unconditionally.

I detected in my subordinates' eyes a certain amount of doubt and perplexity; I therefore continued my announcement and went on to explain my point of view before asking them to make a declaration of loyalty.

In the end, all gave me what I asked except Giovanni Galati and Alberto Banfi. Among my commanders, these two had the most brilliant professional and military record.[50]

After the arrival at Malta, Admiral Cunningham asked da Zara:

"Do you know the text of the armistice?"

"No," I replied. "I know only one thing: I shall not haul down the flag—or hand over the ships."

"There is absolutely no question of that," he said. "What is more, I'll tell you that I have decided to withdraw our armed guards from your ships. They will definitely leave at sundown this evening."[51]

It is clear from this account that the surrender of the Taranto fleet (the only one that eventually reached an Allied port) might easily have failed to take place. The Italian government was in a state of dislocation when the orders went out, and everything hinged on the arrival of de Courten's telegram to da Zara. Had the telegram been held up or had de Courten's orders failed to make clear that the ships would remain under the Italian flag in spite of the surrender, the ships would certainly have been scuttled.

De Courten apparently knew that it would have been difficult or impossible to induce the naval commanders to carry out the unheard-of order to sail to the enemy's base in the absence of assurances about the fleet's honor. It was possible for de Courten to give such assurances because the text of the armistice contained no clause about the final disposition of the Italian fleet. He was thus able to interpret the order to sail the ships to Malta in a sense compatible with traditional concepts of honor. Had "unconditional surrender" been spelled out in specific terms as regards the fleet, it is doubtful whether the order to sail would have been given, or obeyed if given.

The Italian government knew, of course, that its existence depended on sending the fleet to Allied ports: had this crucial clause of the armistice agreement not been carried out, the Allies would have broken off all contact and treated the King and Badoglio as enemies. Even so, it was touch and go whether the Badoglio government would be able to assert its authority over its naval commanders. As it turned out later, de Courten's interpretation of the terms of surrender was not correct. The Allies did expect that the big Italian units would be handed over to them; only small craft, destroyers, and some of the cruisers would remain under the Italian flag. These demands, however, were not disclosed to the Italians until several weeks after the ships had sailed to Allied harbors; Badoglio protested against the Allied interpretation, but to no avail.[52]

The Allies' "psychological" campaign clearly played no role whatever in the surrender of the Italian fleet. Da Zara does not mention the Allied broadcasts at all; they do not seem to have been intercepted on the ships under his jurisdiction, and one may assume that the ships at the other bases did not listen to them either. This was probably all to the good, for their effect might have been quite unfavorable if they had been received.

The broadcasts amounted to an invitation to Italian crews and commanders to renounce their allegiance to their own government. It is not clear what advantage was expected from such a psychological-warfare objective three days after the armistice. Perhaps the "psychological warriors" on the Allied side believed that it was safer to bank on a wholesale naval mutiny *against* the King and Badoglio than on Badoglio's compliance with the terms he had signed; were the King and Badoglio not eminently "unreliable"? But such a hypothesis could have been seriously entertained only if there had been some evidence that wholesale mutiny was ripe in the Italian fleet; i.e., either that the naval commanders were anxious to renounce their allegiance to the King, or that mutinous crews were prepared to depose their commanders and sail the ships to democratic shores.

But there was no evidence of either tendency. Luckily for the Allies, subordination and discipline on the Italian ships were quite unimpaired. There was no reason to assume that any Italian sailors would heed the broadcasts. As for the officers, they could not but have been very unfavorably affected by the Allied psychological campaign, if they had known about it. Their resentment at the Allied attempt to disrupt the fleet by psychological means would have increased their opposition to orders to sail for Allied ports, and would probably have strengthened their suspicions that the orders to sail, purportedly issued by the Rome government, were not genuine. It is very possible that the Allies were saved additional woe by the fact that the Italians did not listen to broadcasts on the international wave lengths.

The propaganda campaign directed at the Italian fleet was a model of how not to wage psychological warfare. It violated two cardinal principles of the art: (1) feasibility of the objective and (2) coordination with over-all policy. The objective (to make the ships come over without orders) was not feasible, because the target audience had no motivation to engage in the behavior desired by the propagandist. Moreover, the objective was incompatible with the policy pursued by the Allied governments at that time: obtaining the services of the Italian fleet through an agreement concluded with the Italian government.

The incompatibility of the two methods does not seem to have been realized by the Allies. Appeals to the Italian rank and file and a surrender agreement concluded with the Italian government were considered as having independent, mutually compatible utilities. The positive objective of inducing active Italian cooperation against the Germans was to be promoted primarily through appeals to the rank and file; the Allies, preferring to see such action arise spontaneously by impulses working from below, were reluctant to associate the Italian government's authority with these appeals. The agreement with the Italian government, on the other hand, was primarily intended to serve a negative objective: the government's role was to be limited to an act of surrender pure and simple.

If this analysis is correct, it explains why the Allied command authorized a "psychological" campaign to get the fleet to sail to Malta and other ports after having already signed an agreement to that effect with the Italian government. It would have fitted the Allied conception better if the Italian ships had sailed on their own; it would then have been possible to limit Badoglio's role to that of performing a pure act of surrender, without any admixture of cooperation. Actually, however, the psychological conditions for stimulating spontaneous pro-Allied action by the Italian fleet did not exist. The psychological problem was, rather, how to make sure that the fleet would obey surrender orders if and when the government did issue them. The problem was, in other words, how to avoid a conflict between military discipline and patriotism (or sense of national honor). The solution of that problem was not helped by the amateurish psychological campaign initiated by the Allies. By seeking to induce spontaneous action in preference to disciplined action, the Allies risked getting no action at all. This is exactly what happened with the Italian land forces; a similar collapse of Italy's naval potential was just barely avoided.

While the psychological problem of getting the fleet to surrender was thus solved in spite of the exertions of the Allies' psychological warriors, the actual execution of the surrender maneuver ended in disaster. No air protection could be provided for the surrendering fleet, and the main Italian naval force that sailed from La Spezia and Genoa was decimated by the Luftwaffe.

At 0230 Sept. 9 battleships Roma, Vittorio Veneto, Italia, and light cruisers Attilio Regolo, Montecuccoli, Eugenio di Savoia, sortied from Spezia with eight destroyers, just as German soldiers were breaking into the city. Off Calvi in Corsica, they were joined by ships from Genoa—light cruisers Abruzzi, Aosta, and Garibaldi, and two more destroyers. All headed for Maddalena, Sardinia, to pick up other ships. Just as they were about to enter the Strait of Bonifacio, Adm. Bergamini received word that the Maddalena base had been occupied by German troops. He reversed course and headed for sea. He had no air cover; the Italian Navy possessed none and Allied air forces were too busy covering the Salerno landings to furnish any. So, when a heavy squadron of German bombers attacked at 1552, the ships had only their antiaircraft batteries . . . of little use against the new guided bombs that some of the German planes carried. Roma was sunk with a loss of 66 out of 71 officers, including Bergamini, and over 1,300 men.[53]

EVALUATION OF THE ALLIED SURRENDER
POLICY TOWARD ITALY

The progress of the Italian campaign was determined in its essential aspects by the limited means at the Allies' disposal. First, Italy was a secondary theater from the point of view of Allied ground strategy; second, the supply lines were inordinately long. Logistics presented no comparable problem for the Germans. Although their lines of communication were subjected to constant air attacks, there was never a serious interruption in the flow of their reinforcements and supplies. As General Clark put it,

The theory was widely held at the beginning of the Mediterranean campaign that the German armies could not fight effectively in Italy. It was believed that our superior air power could quickly destroy the enemy's supply lines through the Alpine passes and down the long, mountainous spinal column of Italy, and that, being unable to maintain himself logistically, he soon would find it unprofitable if not impossible to give battle.

This was wishful thinking.[54]

Given this situation, it is very likely that Italy would have had to be occupied the hard way no matter how the surrender situation was handled. It would have been hazardous for the Allies to land their main force beyond fighter range, and the Italian forces were not strong enough to secure Italy and hold it on our behalf. Nevertheless, it would seem that the Allies could have achieved a far greater disruption in German defense arrangements than they did if they had handled the problem of taking Italy out of the German coalition in a more efficient way. Even if the main feature of the strategic plan (the landing at Salerno on September 8) could not have been altered, its sequel would probably have been different if there had been a concerted plan for Italian diversionary operations in the German rear.

But the Allies' reluctance to negotiate with the Italians on the basis of cobelligerency prevented such planning. It was believed that the more sensible course was out of the question because of the strength of the moral feelings condemning all cooperation with fascists, but it may be doubted whether the policy of cobelligerency would have led to a serious moral crisis if it had brought tangible results.

The "Darlan deal" in North Africa, which did set off a moral crisis of considerable proportions, is not fully comparable.[55] The situation in North Africa was complicated by the presence of two rival French factions. One had sided with the Allied cause from the beginning, and the other, made up of erstwhile collaborationists, now proposed to leave the German camp. Since the former collaborationists, headed by Admiral Darlan, actually controlled the French military and administrative machinery in North Africa, they alone could render us immediate help, but de Gaulle had much the better claim to our support on the strength of his record. This posed a real dilemma for the Allied policymakers.

In Italy, however, there was no such political rivalry.

The King and Badoglio were not challenged or opposed by the majority of Italian antifascists. It is understandable that the Allied leaders were reluctant to face another Darlan crisis, but if liaison had been established with Italian circles, they could have found out that recognition of the royal regime would not have antagonized the Italian antifascists. Had the Allied policymakers recognized the potential importance of cooperation with the Badoglio regime, they could have disarmed in advance the inevitable attacks on the policy of recognition, not only on the grounds of military expediency, but also with political arguments based on the domestic situation in Italy.

The fact is, however, that the Allied leadership had no high estimate of the military expediency of concerted action with the Badoglio regime. The North African situation had been quite different in this respect. There, the necessity of coming to terms with the people who controlled the local forces was imperious and unmistakable. Whatever "hostility" had existed regarding the collaborationist Vichy regime, the "disarming" factor was stronger. Also, Allied emotions toward the two French factions were by no means neatly polarized. De Gaulle, though committed to the struggle against the Germans, had been a singularly difficult and unmanageable ally for Britain and the United States,[56] whereas Vichy, though committed to collaboration with Germany, also had a record of quiet cooperation with the Allies. This complicated psychological situation, in addition to the imperative military considerations, facilitated the "deal" with Darlan.

The Italian surrender regime lacked the bargaining assets that the Darlan group possessed in Africa. Its past record had been one of unmitigated hostility, and the contribution it promised did not seem indispensable. This resulted in the dominance of "hostility" over "disarming." There was a complete emotional block on the Allied side regarding any *rapprochement* with Badoglio.

The policy of unconditional surrender, applied to Italy, had been based on the premise that it would enable the Allies to preserve their moral integrity without sacrificing military expediency. Its actual result was the loss of both. The neglect of liaison and consultation impaired the military conduct of the campaign without enabling the Allies to avoid entering into partnership with the royal regime. The aftermath has shown that neither damage was irreparable. The Italian campaign was eventually won, and the recognition of the royal regime did not prevent the advent of democracy in Italy. The problem was never expediency versus morality. The more expedient course was also the more moral one, whether we define morality in a broad general sense or in a narrow political sense. It is clear that military expediency, in the sense of reaching a strategic goal with a minimum of loss and destruction, has a high moral value in the general sense of according with the dictates of humanity. But the same conclusion emerges if we identify moral integrity with the promotion of democracy as against totalitarianism. The greater the amount of destruction imposed upon a society, the more difficult it is to establish a democratic regime in it. The long-range stability of Italian democracy is still menaced primarily by the impoverishment of Italian society, in which wartime destruction was a factor. The gradual transition from fascism has not inhibited the emergence of democracy. A full-fledged revolution would have more thoroughly eradicated the "past," but it would also have been most unlikely to produce a democratic order.

The position of cobelligerency finally reached in Italy was as expedient *and* moral as any policy could have been in the prevailing circumstances. What we have to regret is that the position was arrived at in a roundabout way; the policy of unconditional surrender first had to be scrapped before the Allies could proceed in a way consonant with the exigencies of the situation.

CONCLUSIONS

In one respect, the Italian surrender of 1943 was analogous to the French surrender of 1940: in both cases, a subordinate coalition member decided to stop fighting at the side of a coalition leader who seemed headed for defeat. In nearly every other respect, however, the two surrenders were antithetical.

The French surrender was a neat, professional job, transacted by seasoned practitioners of the political power game. It was consummated with a minimum of delay, with both sides showing remarkably good insight into the maximum they could obtain in view of the immediately prevailing distribution of strength. As against this, the initial handling of the problem of ending hostilities between the Allies and Italy was characterized on both sides by bad judgment, misinformation, and blundering. Yet, considered from a broader perspective, the French surrender was a snare and delusion for both sides, whereas the Italian surrender was politically and historically justified. This was true beyond the immediate context of the war. Since the Allies were the final winners, Italy had to surrender in any case, whereas the French surrender was nullified by the final outcome. But apart from that, restoring Italy's traditional ties with the Atlantic powers was the only policy consonant with Italy's geographic and political position, whereas France's alignment with Germany against the Atlantic world had had no basis in French history.

Relations between winner and loser developed in opposite directions in the two cases. Germany was willing to pay a political price for surrender, whereas the Allies adopted an unreasonably rigid and negative position in this respect. After surrender, however, relations between Italy and the Allies moved toward coalescence and harmony; Franco-German relations became increasingly uneasy and ambiguous.

The Italian surrender also permits us to observe the actual working of the unconditional-surrender policy, to be discussed in more detail in Part Three. The demand for unconditional surrender as such did not prolong Italian belligerency, nor did it imply a really destructive attitude on the Allies' part. As a method of handling the terminal phase of the war, however, it was inept. The Allies' refusal to pay any political price for surrender merely made the job of extricating Italy from the German clutches a more expensive one.

Five

THE GERMAN SURRENDER
May 1945

The Allied grand strategy of attrition had achieved decisive "divergence" long before Germany's strategic surrender on May 8, 1945. The fall of 1942, with El Alamein, the Allied landing in North Africa, and the Soviet encirclement of Stalingrad, may be considered the turning point in the war. After these events, the trend went inexorably against Germany. The defeats of 1942, however, did not yet constitute final proof of "divergent attrition." Germany had not yet mobilized her resources on a total basis; her total effort began only in the spring of 1943, after the fall of Stalingrad. The armies lost in Africa and Russia were not irreplaceable. There was a chance of stabilizing the eastern front, and the bulk of the German forces had not yet come into contact with the Allies in the West. It was by no means certain that the Allies would succeed in landing in force on the Continent. Until that happened, the war was essentially a one-front war, if we consider ground operations only. Although the air war impinged on Germany from two sides, she could hope to sustain a prolonged siege as long as she was subjected to pressure by land on only one front.

Her situation took a critical turn only when the

Allies established a second land front in the west, thus setting up a drain upon German manpower and matériel resources that could only result in their total exhaustion within a foreseeable time. After the landing, or at least after the breakthrough at Avranches on July 30, 1944, it was no longer possible to restore equilibrium: victory, or even a strategic stalemate, was beyond hope. After Avranches, military operations could merely result in superfluous losses; strategic surrender was the only rational decision the military leadership could make.

In terms of our theoretical analysis, then, Avranches marked the beginning of the "terminal stage" of the war. During such a stage the only meaningful use that a loser can make of his residual forces is to "disarm" the winner. If his possession of residual assets is to make possible any bargaining, the loser must radically reorient his war policy.

Germany, however, did not take this course after the breakthrough at Avranches. Given Hitler's rigid views, the first step, "reorientation" of war policy, could only occur after a *coup d'état* against the Hitler regime. The celebrated plot of July 20, 1944, occurred after the Allied landing but before Avranches, and moreover it failed. After the loss of France, a second attempt at reorientation was no longer feasible. Hence, German operations during the terminal stage were simply carried along by the momentum built up during the preterminal period of the war. Besieged from all sides, Germany was forced to give up one line of defense after another in both east and west. It was only after the siege perimeter had shrunk to encircle a tiny area in North Germany that the military leadership initiated strategic surrender. This surrender abridged the final stage only in the sense that there was an orderly capitulation of residual forces instead of a chaotic and futile last battle inside the perimeter. Wholesale capitulations of German forces had already occurred several days earlier in northern Italy and southern Germany. They formed part of the process of winding up hostilities and thus were "strategic" in essence if not in form.

Germany's strategic surrender, then, was characterized by a prolongation of the terminal stage until no further coherent operations were possible. It must be stressed, however, that this prolongation of the terminal stage was by no means accompanied by all-out resistance to the limit of the physically feasible. The postponement of strategic surrender until the German "fortress" was stormed and occupied was due to several specific reasons, some of which we shall discuss in Part Three in analyzing unconditional surrender. This delay retarded the formal termination of hostilities, but actual resistance had collapsed in the west weeks before formal surrender. The abridgment of the terminal stage was somewhat greater than the date of the final surrender would indicate.

We shall now take up in some detail several salient aspects of the political process that culminated in the strategic surrender act of May 8, 1945.

THE PRECEDENT OF 1918

The problem of strategic surrender had already faced Germany at the end of World War I. The Allied offensive of August 1918 convinced the German military leadership that final defeat could no longer be averted. From that moment on, the chief concern of General Ludendorff, the "strong man" who wielded decisive influence politically as well as militarily, was that the armistice offer should not be made too late. It was essential for Germany to conclude an armistice while her armed forces still remained cohesive. But time was pressing; any day could bring a catastrophe. Ludendorff said that "he felt like a gambler, and that a division might fail him anywhere at any time."[1]

Ludendorff argued for the utmost speed in the following terms:

The German Army is still strong enough to stand against its opponent for months to come, to achieve local successes and to exact new sacrifices from the Entente. But each day brings our opponent nearer his goal, and will make him less inclined to conclude with us a peace which is tolerable. Therefore, no time must be lost.[2]

Ludendorff, then, realized that Germany was strategically defeated, and that assuming further losses would be unwarranted from the military point of view. Cutting losses, however, was not the chief consideration making him press for utmost speed in initiating armistice talks. Speed appeared to him essential mainly because the maximal political exploitation of Germany's last bargaining asset, the possession of a cohesive residual force, depended on it. The idea of exploiting this residual asset for what it was worth was by no means unsound, but Ludendorff expected too much from it. He believed that the enemy, even after consummating Germany's strategic defeat, could still be expected to conclude a moderate, negotiated peace, if only armistice talks were started while Germany still possessed a cohesive residual force. This was a serious misjudgment of the political bargaining situation between winner and loser during the terminal stage of total war.

As our theoretical analysis has shown, complete victory in total war implies that the winner will end hostilities only after establishing a monopoly of armed strength. In such a situation armistice talks can be conducted only on the principle of strategic surrender. A further implication is that the peace settlement will be essentially a dictated one: the loser, stripped of war-making capability, has no alternative but to accept the terms on which the winner insists. All the loser can do during the terminal stage is to obtain a political payment in return for the service he renders the winner by renouncing the use of his residual strength. Had Ludendorff seen the situation in this light, he would have realized that in forcing the government to act quickly he was not giving it a last opportunity to conclude a negotiated peace but was merely pushing it into surrender. After the war, Ludendorff and the German nationalists claimed that Germany could have ended the war as an undefeated power, if there had been no revolutionary outbreaks in the hinterland before the armistice talks started. This theory was wholly unwarranted: mutiny and revolution were a consequence rather than a cause of defeat. But the legend of the "stab in the back" had considerable success in Germany, since it was flattering to the national *amour-propre.*

The circumstances in which World War I ended were such that neither the leadership nor the people at large came face to face with the problem of defeat in total war and its concomitant, strategic surrender. On the one hand, there were those who, like Ludendorff, admitted only two possibilities—victory for Germany or, at the worst, a negotiated peace. When surrender was imposed, it did not fit into their preconceived scheme,

and hence they blamed it on foul play. On the other
hand, there were those to whom war itself was an abomi-
nation, so that its outcome did not matter to them; they
were impatient to get on with revolutionary socialism,
which would make an end of such horrors as militarism
and war. Both groups refused to recognize the reality
of Germany's defeat or, indeed, that defeat is one of
the eventualities that have to be faced in war.

After the war, the *mystique* of a complete social
renovation, with its gospel of nonviolence, antimilita-
rism, and antiauthoritarianism, flickered briefly and then
died. There was no place for it in the postwar world.
The totally disaffected were won over by the Communists, who profited by the prestige of the victorious Russian revolution, and were quick to develop their own
brand of violence, militarism, and authoritarianism.
This was rejected by the vast majority of the German
people.

The nationalist denial of the reality of defeat fared
much better. Not all Germans accepted the crude alibi
of the "stab in the back," but the legend was believed or
half-believed by many, and its appeal grew as memories
of the war faded away. Hindenburg's election as President in March 1925 manifested the victory of the myth
of an "undefeated" Germany.

To be sure, the supporters of the Republic—Catho-
lics, Social Democrats, and other moderate groups—did
not accept that myth. But they could not combat it
effectively, since they had no counterphilosophy. They
had to compromise with the traditionalists who controlled the army and the presidency, just as the traditionalists had to compromise with the representatives of
republican legality, who were still indispensable in the

making of coalition governments and had a firm control over the administration of Prussia. The existence of the Weimar Republic depended on this balance between a traditionalist and nationalist *mystique*, on the one hand, and democratic and republican legality, on the other. The balance was destroyed by the economic crisis of 1929–33 and the rise of Hitler.

NEGOTIATING FROM STRENGTH

The refusal of the Germans to realize and digest defeat in World War I decisively influenced their thinking about ending hostilities in World War II. There was, for example, the official Nazi doctrine that defeat and capitulation were impossible. But the anti-Nazi opposition, too, started from the premise that the only alternative to victory was a negotiated peace. The opposition, however, rejected not only defeat but also victory. To them, victory was not only unlikely in view of the potential strength of the adversary, but unthinkable on moral grounds.

Among those who regarded a Nazi victory with moral revulsion were General Beck, Ambassador Ulrich von Hassell, Carl Gördeler (the former mayor of Leipzig), and their associates.[3] Early in the war, they desperately sought to establish contact with British (and American) circles, suggesting that they were ready to remove Hitler and then to conclude a moderate peace.[4] Germany was to retain Hitler's "peaceful" conquests such as Austria and the Sudeten region; even the Polish Corridor was to remain in German possession; but the "new" Germany would observe international law and would be a trustworthy partner for the West. The first feelers of this type were put out in the period of the "phony war." Since no trial of strength had as yet taken place between Germany and the Anglo-French coalition, it is doubtful whether the Allies would have negotiated on such a basis, even if the opposition had succeeded in overthrowing Hitler. Neville Chamberlain, who knew about the ideas of the German opposition, expressed his interest in purely academic terms.

More than a year later, after France had been knocked out of the war and Britain isolated, a similar offer was drafted by Carl Gördeler and forwarded through Swiss channels to London. This draft, dated May 30, 1941, contained the following main peace terms: Germany was to keep Alsace-Lorraine, the Corridor and Danzig, Austria, the Sudeten region, and Memel; all other territories overrun by the German army were to be evacuated and returned to their prewar status; Germany was to be given colonies under an international mandate system.[5]

At the time this draft was written, Hitler's position seemed impregnable. He controlled Europe from the North Cape to the Aegean and the Pyrenees, and he was knocking at the gates of Suez. In this situation, Gördeler's proposals were moderate enough.[6] But the war soon took a fateful turn for Germany with the invasion of Russia and the attack on Pearl Harbor, which ended Britain's isolation. A succession of defeats followed the string of early victories, but the opposition's peace platform remained substantially the same.

A second peace draft by Gördeler, written in the summer or fall of 1943 (but presumably never transmitted to the West), has been preserved. Its terms hardly differ from those of the first. Austria, the

Sudeten region, and the Polish Corridor are still to remain German, and even South Tyrol is to be reannexed;
the only major differences are that colonial demands are
dropped and Alsace-Lorraine is to be either divided
along linguistic lines or made independent.[7]

It appears strange that, at a time when Germany was
clearly losing the war. Gördeler still considered it possible that the Allies would accept a "Greater Germany."
The explanation for this lies partly in the Great German
mystique that gripped Gördeler and his generation. To
these Germans, it was axiomatic that no German-speak-
ing population could remain outside the national domain.
But Gördeler's terms are further explained by the fact
that he was convinced that the Reich's political bargaining position was still strong enough, despite looming
strategic defeat, to ensure acceptance of his program by
the Allies. Moreover, a new factor had now gained
prominence in the thinking of the opposition: they believed that the threat of massed Soviet legions in the
east would bring it home to the Western Allies that they
needed Germany as a bulwark against Russian and communist expansion.[8] Now that military strength alone no
longer afforded Germany a strong bargaining position,
Gördeler and his group put their hopes in the latent
tension between Russia and the West.

The logic of the situation made it impossible for the
Western powers to insist on Germany's "unconditional
surrender," once Hitler was removed. If Germany
could not expect a negotiated peace on the basis of military strength alone, she could still reach the same objective as a result of the latent tension within the Allied
camp. But this would be possible only if Hitler were

removed quickly and peace overtures made while the German military position was still outwardly strong.

After Stalingrad, Gördeler circulated a memorandum among the German generals whose support he sought to win for his plans. The main argument of this paper follows Ludendorff's thesis that when victory appears impossible, residual military strength must be used to obtain a negotiated peace, but Gördeler thought that Ludendorff erred in waiting too long. This mistake must not be repeated. Referring to the deterioration of the war situation, Gördeler wrote:

These developments show a fateful parallel with the course of events from the early summer of 1918 onwards. At that time, responsible circles in Germany were slow to take this trend of developments into account. . . . No rationalizations, no moral alibis [this refers to the "stab in the back" theory, which Gördeler discusses in a passage omitted here], can relieve a responsible leadership of the duty to draw the conclusions while there is still time. The example of 1918 teaches us what one must do to avoid missing the right moment. When a conscientious weighing of the facts leads to the conclusion that the war can no longer be won and that a more favorable situation for negotiations can no longer be brought about, then political action must take the place of military effort. If the existing political leadership has blocked all avenues in this direction, it must obviously yield its place.[9]

If peace were proposed immediately, Gördeler assured the generals, Germany could count on retaining "the frontiers of 1914, enlarged by the addition of Austria and the Sudeten region," on recovering South Tyrol, and even on exercising hegemony on the Continent. Only colonies could no longer be bargained for.[10]

In a passionate letter of July 25, 1943, Gördeler implored Field Marshal von Kluge to strike against Hitler:

Obviously the chances [for a favorable peace] are more difficult to realize now than they were a year ago. They can be
exploited only if the politician has sufficient time to act, that
is, if he is not confronted again, as in 1918, with a sudden
military declaration of "no further action possible."

But the chances were definitely not lost.

I have ascertained anew, and assume responsibility for this,
that there is still a possibility of concluding a favorable peace,
if we Germans render ourselves capable of entering into negotiations.[11]

For the circle around Beck and Gördeler, the action
for peace could not start early enough if Germany was
to negotiate from strength. But they were unable to
enlist the active support of the only group that was
strong enough to move against Hitler—the active military leadership. Disaffected as the German generals
mostly were, they simply could not bring themselves at
this early stage to do anything that would diminish Germany's chances of military success.[12] For the old-line
generals, action against the political leadership became
possible only when they had no doubt that the continuation of the war could only lead to strategic defeat.

In September 1943, Field Marshal von Kluge, who
had formerly been reluctant to join the conspiracy
against Hitler, came around to this point of view. The
matter was discussed at a meeting in Berlin between
Beck, Gördeler, and the Marshal. The British, Gördeler
argued, would not insist on destroying Germany's
might; they must be aware of the necessity of stopping
Russian expansion. Kluge agreed: "It is high time,"
he said, "to act so as to exploit the military situation.
. . . If an understanding is reached with the Anglo-
Saxons, it is still possible to stabilize the eastern front

east of the Polish borders and to make it impregnable."
In answer to Gördeler's suggestion that the generals
persuade Hitler to resign, Kluge argued in favor of
assassinating the Führer.

This conversation, however, had no practical consequences. Shortly after his return to the eastern front,
Kluge had an automobile accident that immobilized him
for four months. A number of attempts on Hitler's life
were made during this time, but none of them succeeded.[13]

Readiness for action also crystallized among the military chiefs on the western front during the weeks preceding the Allied landing in Normandy. The landing,
as the generals recognized, would lead to a two-front
war; and in such a war Germany could only lose. To
forestall this, the generals worked out a program for
selective capitulation in the West only.

The details of this venture were described by General Speidel, Field Marshal Rommel's chief of staff.[14]
According to Speidel, in May 1944 Rommel and Generals von Stülpnagel and von Falkenhausen held a series
of conferences at Rommel's headquarters. A plan was
worked out, outlining the following course of action:

In the West: Definition of the premises under which an
armistice could be concluded with Generals Eisenhower and
Montgomery *without* participation by Hitler. Marshal Rom-
mel thought of sending as his negotiators General K. H. von
Stülpnagel, General Baron Leo Geyr von Schweppenburg, Lt.-
Gen. Hans Speidel, Lt.-Gen. Count Gerd von Schwerin, Vice-
Admiral Friedrich Ruge, and Lt.-Col. Cäsar von Hofacker.

The bases foreseen for negotiating an armistice were:

German evacuation of the occupied western territories and
withdrawal behind the Westwall. Surrender of the administration of the occupied territories to the Allies. *Immediate*

suspension of the Allied bombing of Germany. Armistice, not unconditional surrender, followed by negotiations for peace to bring about order and prevent chaos. Field Marshal Rommel expected that the Allies would give them such an opportunity. Appeal to the German people from all radio stations in the Western Command, frankly revealing the true political and military situation and its causes, and describing Hitler's criminal conduct of State affairs. Informing the troops of the measures necessary to avert a catastrophe.

The Home Front: Arrest of Hitler for trial before a German court by the resistance forces in the High Command of the Army, or rather by Panzer forces to be brought up for this purpose. . . .

In the East: Continuation of the fight. Holding a shortened line between the mouth of the Danube, the Carpathian mountains, Lemberg, the Vistula, and the Memel. Immediate evacuation of Courland (Lithuania) and other "fortresses."[15]

The essential elements of this plan closely paralleled Gördeler's conception. Here, too, the basic idea was that, once Germany got rid of Hitler, the Allies would be ready to grant her favorable terms and would welcome active German assistance against the communist peril. On the method to be followed, too, the generals adhered to the Ludendorff-Gördeler line. An armistice was to be proposed before the invasion began. "For all negotiations," Speidel says, "a firm western front was a prerequisite. The stability of the western front was, therefore, our constant concern."[16]

The generals' plan eventually came to nothing; there is no evidence that they even attempted to contact General Eisenhower, and they did nothing to arrest and try Hitler. All Rommel did was to send an "ultimative" memorandum to Hitler on July 15, calling on him to "draw the conclusions" from the fact that the war was lost.[17] Kluge was now in the West, having succeeded Rundstedt as commander in chief. As we have seen, he had actively joined the conspiracy a few months earlier. Summoned by the conspirators to act, he declined, saying that he was not sure whether his subordinates would obey him.[18]

SELECTIVE SURRENDER

The military catastrophes of the summer of 1944 (the Allied breakthrough in France and the simultaneous rupture of the eastern front in Poland) had a shattering effect on the opposition. They destroyed the basis of Gördeler's conception, negotiation from strength. In terms of his theory, it was too late to act. On July 12 Beck told one of the conspirators, Gisevius, that he thought the right moment for attacking Hitler had been missed. Germany's total occupation could no longer be prevented.[19]

Before these military disasters it had been hard for the Beck-Gördeler circle to recognize that hostilities could only be ended on the basis of surrender. This had been clear to Gisevius since long before mid-1944: he did not believe that the Allied demand for "unconditional surrender" could be disregarded. For him, then, the only possibility was to make the surrender as "selective" as possible, by sucking the Allies into German territory before the Russians entered.[20] In the spring of 1944, Beck and Gördeler finally came around to the same position. They tried to find out through Gisevius, who had contacts with Allen W. Dulles in Switzerland, whether the Americans would accept unilateral surrender from an anti-Nazi German government.[21] The conspirators may have thought that the Allies' attitude toward Germany would change after a new German government offered capitulation to them. They contemplated making an offer of active military help to the Allies, including assistance for the landing of parachute troops in Germany. This is how Ritter sums up the situation:

It is clear that the leaders of the opposition were now [spring, 1944] virtually ready to accept the formula of "unconditional surrender" *vis-à-vis* the Western powers, confident, to be sure, that sober political reason would overcome the stark will to destruction in the latter's camp and that the common interest in preserving Western civilization would assert itself and save the German state from total destruction. They evidently had in mind, not an armistice with a shortened western front line . . . but a kind of merger of German and Anglo-Saxon units, or at least immediate occupation of Germany from the west, before the Red armies had overrun Poland and reached the Reich's borders. Peace negotiations were then to follow between victors and vanquished, but with a new German government to whom the victors would owe a substantial shortening of the final phase of hostilities, and whom they had pledged to recognize.[22]

In the end, then, the German opposition did work out a terminal strategy of "disarming" the winner. But the strategy could not be applied because of the failure of the coup against Hitler. Even if the coup had been successful, it is uncertain how much the strategy of "disarming" would have achieved. The Allies were unwilling to recognize any latent conflict of interests with Soviet Russia. Their reaction to the German opposition's earlier appeals, appeals that had made much of the danger of bolshevization, had been completely negative.

AN EASTERN SOLUTION?

Because of this unyielding stand of the Western Allies, the idea of offering selective surrender to Soviet Russia instead emerged in the circles of the German opposition. Adam von Trott zu Solz warned Allen Dulles that the German opposition, if rebuffed by the West, would seek to establish contacts with Russia.[23] Gisevius judged that part of the opposition movement was Eastern- rather than Western-oriented: he considered Stauffenberg, Trott, and some others to be exponents of the pro-Soviet wing.[24] According to Rothfels, however, neither Stauffenberg nor Trott had in mind a *rapprochement* with Soviet Russia. Rather, they were thinking about a natural solidarity between oppressed Germans and Russians, united in a common struggle against their totalitarian masters (and also against the Western bourgeoisie).[25]

On a more practical basis, some of the conservative members of the opposition, such as Gördeler and Hassell, weighed the possibility of playing off Russia against her Western partner. In the autumn of 1943, when Ribbentrop's emissary, Peter Kleist, was having talks with Soviet agents on Russian peace feelers,[26] Gördeler, Hassell, and Schulenburg, the former German ambassador in Moscow, had a conference in Berlin, where the possibility of negotiating with Stalin was discussed.[27] Schulenburg said that the ties between Soviet Russia and the West were not insoluble, and that Stalin was a cold calculator who would decide on the basis of what was offered him. In the end, however, the conspirators rejected the Russian alternative. For one thing, they did not believe in the possibility of permanent cooperation with the Communists.[28] For another, their orientation was basically pro-Western.

In the eyes of the Social Democratic members of the conspiracy, nothing but a pro-Western orientation was acceptable. According to Allen Dulles,

Around Christmas of 1942, Carlo Mierendorff, Theodor Haubach and Emil Henk, Social Democrats of long standing and members of the Kreisau circle met at a spa in the Bavarian mountains. . . . According to Emil Henk, these Social Democrats decided to influence their fellow conspirators to postpone Hitler's assassination until the American and British armies had established themselves on the Continent and at least could compete with the East for the domination of Germany. Mierendorff was delegated to persuade Leuschner [a Social Democrat], and Moltke was chosen to talk the matter over with Beck [formerly Chief of the General Staff]. Leuschner agreed, though he saw the danger of delay. . . . Beck's reaction is not known, but since an attempt was made on the life of the Führer early in 1943, it seems likely that he and Gördeler favored getting rid of Hitler and letting the chips fall where they may.[29]

THE DILEMMA OF TIMING

Looking back on the sequence of events that culminated in the ill-fated coup of July 20, 1944, with its frightful sequel of repression that wiped out virtually the entire group of conspirators, we have to conclude that the original platform of the conspiracy, peace without victors and vanquished, had very little chance of success. When the Reich was winning, it was too early to strike: the old-line soldiers, as well as the bulk of the people, would have been horrified at the idea of depriving the Reich of a possible victory because the regime was morally objectionable. For these people, action to stop the war was thinkable only when there could be no doubt that further military action could not prevent strategic defeat. Moving in this direction while there was still the slightest chance of establishing military equilibrium could only expose the antiwar group to charges of high treason. But on the other hand, if Germany waited until her last chance of averting defeat was gone, it would be no longer possible to bargain for moderate peace terms, and the opposition would be saddled with the odium of having obtained a destructive peace.

The opposition tried various methods to escape this dilemma. The Gördeler-Beck group sought originally to obtain assurances from the Allies that favorable peace terms would be granted to a new German government. Had they been given such assurances, this would have diminished the political risks of turning against the home government in mid-war. But after 1941, the entire nature of the war changed: it became so big that it could be waged only in total fashion, with victory as the only possible objective. One of the go-betweens through whom Gördeler maintained some liaison with British circles, the Swedish banker Jakob Wallenberg, repeatedly told him that it was futile to insist on coming to terms with the Allies before attempting a coup. The only possible course of action was to go ahead and then see how the Allies would act.[30]

An alternative course of action was to argue that in the judgment of the military experts the war was already lost. The Kluge-Rommel combination of 1943-44 was based on this premise. The dissident generals of the western front thought of acting on Clausewitz's advice to avoid a battle that one was certain to lose. But the psychological situation, as Kluge discovered, did not permit such a rational procedure: the army was saturated with Nazi elements who put Hitler's "intuition" above sober military judgment. One could not argue, let alone act, on the premise of defeat until it was an inescapable fact.

The timing of the coup, it seems, was as bad as it could have been. Had the conspirators launched a successful coup before the landing, they would have been more vulnerable to charges of a "stab in the back," but their success might have had a considerable "disarming" effect on the Allies. Had the coup been postponed until after the breakthrough at Avranches, the opposition's bargaining position with the Allies would have been very weak and an armistice could have been negotiated only on the basis of unconditional surrender, but at least it would have been clear to the army and the people that the war was already irretrievably lost.

THE FINAL SURRENDERS

Selective Resistance

Hitler's military orders during the last stage of the war monotonously repeated the same slogan: no retreat, no surrender, fight to the last man from fixed positions. This was extremely galling to the army leaders, whom it deprived of all freedom of movement. Rundstedt's chief of staff described his superior's state of mind in the following terms:

We have seen that Rundstedt, the oldest officer in the Army, by no means possessed freedom of action; nor could he have managed to gain it. Everyone who knew him knows how much suffering this caused him, how it robbed him of rest and sleep to have to stand by in impotent rage while blunder was piled on blunder, while our last powers of aggressive action were wasted in an offensive with the wrong objective. He often trembled with emotion when his proposals, carefully thought out and based on long experience, were turned down by the OKW and he was forced into impracticable and damaging action.[31]

Rundstedt's state of mind was far from unique. Indeed all generals of the old school shared it. Relations between Hitler and the German professional military leaders had never been good. Throughout the war, Hit-

ler had insisted not only on laying down the lines of
Germany's grand strategy but also on prescribing operational and even tactical details. This created a good deal
of tension even while Germany's military situation was
favorable and relations between Hitler and the military
chiefs were outwardly correct.[32] After the attempt on
Hitler's life on July 20, 1944, in which a number of high
officers were implicated, Hitler's hatred of the professional military erupted with destructive fury. From then
on, his attitude, even toward those who had not been involved in the plot, was one of contempt and distrust; all
were incompetent, and potential traitors to boot.

As Germany's strength was ebbing away and enor-
mously superior forces were hammering at the Wehrmacht from two sides, the military leaders found themselves in an unbearable situation. Hitler peremptorily
ordered them to carry out impossible operations with
nonexistent forces. To remonstrate was useless, if not
suicidal. All that the mortally wounded army could do
was to fight on against impossible odds. Even when the
defense lines of the Reich itself were breached in east
and west (January 1945), Hitler would not recognize
that the time had come to liquidate military operations.

The High Command's orders to hold the line at all
costs made no distinction between the eastern and western fronts, and until the end of March the pattern of
resistance was similar in east and west. After the beginning of April, however, the picture changed. The Allies'
advance from the west into southern and central Germany became a walkover, while the battered German
forces continued their all-out effort to stem the advance
of the Russian forces from the east and southeast.

The following excerpts from the U.S. Army's official history of the European theater throw light on what happened on the western front:

> The campaign from 1 April until the end of the war is likely to be cited frequently in the future because it is replete with perfect "book" solutions to military problems. It was possible in most cases for commanders to set missions for their forces, allot troops and supplies, and know that their phase lines would be reached. Only when objectives were taken far before the hour chosen were the timetables upset. By its very nature, therefore, the great pursuit across central Germany may mislead the student who attempts to draw lessons of value for future campaigns. Allied superiority in quality of troops, mobility, air power, matériel, and morale was such that only a duplication of the deterioration of enemy forces such as that which existed in April, 1945 would again make possible the type of slashing attack that developed. . . .
>
> The enemy fell apart but waited to be overrun. A German high command virtually ceased to exist and even regimental headquarters had difficulty in knowing the dispositions of their troops or the situation on their flanks. In those instances where unit commanders still received Hitler's messages to hold their positions, they tended to ignore them as having little relationship to the realities of their situation. Expedients such as the calling up of *Volkssturm* units proved futile. These last hopes of Hitler's army readily laid down their arms except in a few cases where their resistance was stiffened by SS elements. And the general public, which might have furnished cadres for guerrilla warfare proved uninterested in partisan activities. Near the war's end, civilians in many cities sent word that they were ready to surrender and asked that bloodless entries be made into their towns. . . .
>
> In the eighteen days required to close and destroy the Ruhr Pocket the Allied forces north and south of that area roared on to the Elbe, often against no opposition. . . . Apparently feeling that they could not stem the tide, the Germans in most sectors made a half-hearted resistance and then merely waited until the flood rolled over them.[33]

During the same period the situation on the eastern front developed along different lines. The Russians massed strong forces between the Baltic and the lower Neisse for a final breakthrough. On April 15 near Küstrin they began to attack the German Ninth Army, which they hopelessly outnumbered and outmatched in heavy equipment. But the defenders, according to a German war historian, "spent their last ounce of strength to stop the assault west of the Oder." It took the Russians three days to complete their breakthrough. Further south, on the lower Neisse, Konev attacked on April 16; he achieved his breakthrough in one day and moved on to envelop the desperately fighting Ninth Army from the rear. In the north, the German Third Panzer Army, anchored on the lower Oder, was attacked by Marshal Rokossovski's troops on April 21. No breakthrough was achieved for several days.[34]

How can we explain the contrast in German military behavior between the western and eastern fronts? For one thing, the discrepancy in strength between the German forces and their opponents was far greater in the west. There the Allies had an abundance of everything—fresh troops, weapons, transport, motor fuel, air support. The Russian forces were exhausted from the grinding offensives and forced marches of the preceding months; their air arm was far weaker than that of the western Allies. But in addition to this, a psychological factor played a significant part. Russian penetration appeared as the supreme disaster to all Germans, soldiers and civilians alike. Also, whereas at the end German soldiers welcomed rather than feared Allied captivity, they dreaded being taken prisoner by the Russians. As Field Marshal Kesselring put it, "The German frontline fighter, who was always fearless as long as he had weapons in his hands, literally trembled at the thought of falling into Russian captivity."[35]

It was pointless for Germany to continue military operations once her strategic defeat had been consummated. From a purely military point of view, holding actions in east and west were equally irrational. Moreover, it was impossible for Germany to trade the abandonment of last-ditch resistance for political concessions that would make her surrender something less than unconditional. Yet Hitler's orders forced the military to continue resistance as long as the German command structure remained intact. When this structure began to disintegrate in April, military resistance became increasing a matter of the soldiers' and officers' attitudes toward the enemy. Stopping the Russians became a blind, desperate reflex action, imposed by the terrifying image of Russian control. The Germans' image of the Western Allies was not terrifying and hence did not generate such reflexes. This distinction in the minds of Germans manifested itself impressively in civilian behavior. In the west, German civilians begged their military defenders to let the Allies take their towns without resistance. In the east, they fled *en masse* before the approaching Russians. These civilian attitudes influenced local commanders and contributed to the contrast between eastern and western patterns of resistance.

Furthermore, during the terminal stage the highest German officers in the west, the theater and army group commanders, adopted a practice for which there was no parallel in the east: they initiated the liquidation of hostilities, mostly by capitulation agreements.

Piecemeal Surrenders

The first large German force to wind up resistance *en masse* was Army Group B, commanded by Field Marshal Model. This group, with a total strength of over

300,000 men, was located in the Ruhr region, Germany's industrial heart. A double envelopment by Allied forces resulted in the encirclement of Army Group B on April 1, 1945. The German commander, intent on pinning down large Allied forces as long as possible, refused to capitulate, but he offered feeble resistance. On April 14, the American Ninth Army cut the Ruhr pocket in two. The German High Command ordered Army Group B to break out of the pocket, but this was clearly impracticable in view of the military situation. What followed is described in the official United States Army history:

With defeat obviously a few days or hours away, the Germans adopted a novel procedure to avoid formal capitulation. On the morning of 17 April, they announced the dissolution of *Army Group B*. The extremely young and the very old soldiers were dismissed from the service and told to return home. The remaining officers and men were told they could stay to be overrun and then surrender, could try to make their way home in uniform or civilian clothes, and without weapons, or try to break through to another front. Field Marshal Model thus did not have to take responsibility for a surrender. He disappeared from the scene shortly thereafter and no trace of him was subsequently found, although members of his staff testified that he committed suicide.[36]

Even before these events, however, Field Marshal Kesselring, theater commander in Italy, had initiated formal capitulation talks with the Allies. The account he gives of this action in his memoirs shows that he found a way to reconcile the principle of unwavering loyalty to the Führer with the military expediency of capitulating when the situation demanded it. Capitulation, he says, is primarily in the domain of the political decision maker. No army leader has the right to initiate the termination of hostilities as long as he has forces capable of fighting. On the other hand, he, Kesselring, was fully justified in authorizing his subordinate, SS General Wolff, to initiate capitulation talks with American representatives in Switzerland in the autumn of 1944 without informing the OKW (but reporting the step to Hitler after it was made). This had to be done, Kesselring says, since he came to the conclusion that "the war had to be terminated through diplomatic and political channels." Wolff's negotiations were not meant to initiate the surrender of Kesselring's front sector; nothing so crude as that. They constituted "help for the political leadership in getting into a negotiatory situation."[37]

By the end of April, 1945, Wolff's negotiations were concluded, and on the 28th Kesselring, now commander in chief in the West, was summoned by his former subordinates to Innsbruck in order to approve the agreements made. At a conference in the house of Gauleiter Hofer of Tyrol, General von Vietinghoff, commander in chief in the Southwest, and Ambassador Rahn put the question of surrender to Kesselring. Wolff himself could not attend: he had been detained by partisans. Vietinghoff apparently dared not tell the Marshal that the agreements had already been initialed and that the question of capitulation was no longer open; he argued merely that capitulation was necessary. Kesselring, however, not being fully informed about the situation, forbade the capitulation. This led to tragicomic complications. Kesselring relieved Vietinghoff and his chief of staff of their command and ordered their arrest; the deposed officers in their turn arrested their successors. Finally, Kesselring restored Vietinghoff to his position and authorized the signing of the capitulation agreement to take effect on May 2, 1945.[38]

Further piecemeal surrenders on the southern front followed during the next few days. General Schulz, commander of Army Group G, sent General Förtsch to Munich for capitulation talks with Generals Devers, Patch, and Haislip. An instrument of surrender was signed on May 5, to take effect the next day.[39] Also on the 5th, General Brandenberger surrendered his Nineteenth Army at Innsbruck.[40]

Nothing resembling these piecemeal surrenders occurred where the German forces faced Russians. On the contrary, as we shall see, a German army continued to fight in Czechoslovakia even after the official surrender of all German forces on May 7.

Efforts of Nazi Leaders to Surrender

Hitler reportedly told Rommel some time before February, 1944: "The war is lost; nobody will conclude peace with me."[41] Yet he ruled out the possibility of capitulation. He adopted the position that the German people, having suffered defeat, no longer had the right to exist. The only alternative to complete victory was complete annihilation. In his last public speech, on November 8, 1943, Hitler expressed this idea quite clearly.

Accordingly, when the enemy entered German territory, Hitler ordered the total destruction of all installations that might fall into enemy hands. Hitler's Minister of Supplies, Albert Speer, challenged this order. Hitler thereupon summoned him (March 18, 1945) and told him:

If the war is to be lost, the nation also will perish. This fate is inevitable. There is no need to consider the basis even of a most primitive existence any longer. On the contrary, it is

better to destroy even that, and to destroy it ourselves. The
nation has proved itself weak, and the future belongs solely
to the stronger Eastern nation.[42]

Now, it was characteristic of the last stage of the war
that practically nobody in Germany thought either of
putting into effect Hitler's peremptory order of national
suicide or of removing him from authority. The repression after the July 20 coup left the field to the Nazis and
their docile instruments. These people would never
have thought of openly disobeying the Führer, still less
of combating or killing him. Almost to a man, however, they parted company with Hitler on the latter's
policy of national self-destruction. They chose survival.
Speer himself quietly sabotaged Hitler's scorched-earth
order. Others, closer to the center of power, took on
themselves the responsibility for preparing for surrender
behind Hitler's back.

On April 2, SS General Schellenberg, a member of
Himmler's staff, asked Count Folke Bernadotte, head of
the Swedish Red Cross, who was then in Germany in
connection with matters concerning Scandinavian prisoners of war, whether he would transmit an offer of
capitulation to General Eisenhower. Count Bernadotte
was unable to act on this offer because Schellenberg
lacked the necessary authorizations. Later, on April 23,
Himmler himself met Count Bernadotte at the Swedish
consulate at Lübeck. He made an offer of capitulation
on the western front only. The offer was transmitted by
diplomatic channels to Prime Minister Churchill, who in
turn relayed it to President Truman. The President
rejected the offer on the grounds that only unconditional
surrender on all fronts simultaneously was acceptable.[43]

Himmler's independent move for capitulation was

facilitated by the fact that Hitler had retired into the bunker beneath the Reich chancellery in Berlin, whence he could not effectively supervise the dispersed Nazi chiefs. Göring, who left Berlin on April 20 for the Obersalzberg near Berchtesgaden, assumed full governmental powers on the 23rd as Hitler's designated successor. He apparently thought that Hitler himself, in a message conveyed by word of mouth, had expressly authorized this step and empowered him to liquidate the war. But when Göring demanded confirmation of his new status by radio, Hitler exploded and ordered his arrest as a traitor.[44]

The Dönitz Regime and Global Surrender

Germany's global surrender on all fronts was consummated on the basis of Nazi legality. Before committing suicide on April 30, Hitler appointed as his successor Admiral Dönitz, the head of the navy. Receiving news of his appointment on the day of Hitler's death, Dönitz, ignorant of the Führer's suicide, replied by telegram, pledging his unconditional loyalty and promising to continue the war "to an end worthy of the unique, heroic struggle of the German people."[45] On May 1, having been officially informed of Hitler's death, Dönitz addressed by radio a solemn proclamation to the German people. Hitler had "fallen," "fighting at the head of his troops." Dönitz, now commander in chief of all branches of the Wehrmacht, would "continue the struggle against Bolshevism until the fighting troops and the hundreds of thousands of families in Eastern Germany have been preserved from destruction." Against the British and Americans, he said, he "must" wage war "as long as they hinder me in the prosecution of the fight against Bolshevism." The people, then, had to render Dönitz "unconditional service." "He who now shirks his duty . . . is a coward and traitor."[46]

The language used by Dönitz clearly indicates that he, too, had mastered the secret of reconciling impeccable Nazi orthodoxy with a strong resolution to avoid self-immolation. In his proclamation he spoke only of continuing the struggle, but the qualifying clauses he added clearly indicated his real objective: selective surrender to the West.

One of Dönitz's aides, Walter Lüdde-Neurath, has written an eyewitness account of the Admiral's one-week regime.[47] It appears that, on taking office, Dönitz and his associates were thinking about the possibility of ending resistance without a formal act of capitulation. Should one offer surrender or just cease fighting? According to Lüdde-Neurath, this question gave rise to "grave conflicts of conscience." Both unconditional surrender and the cessation of combat without a formal agreement would have the same practical consequences; they would be "frightful."

But was it not possible to avoid giving our assent to what would happen? Was it not our duty to raise a last solemn and emphatic protest against destiny? Had we not cried "Never!" time and again, sometimes with passionate conviction? . . . What did a few more weeks, some additional sacrifices, matter? Would History not render a magnificent and consoling homage —a homage which ultimately would bear fruit—to our refusal to capitulate? . . . Would the signing of the act of surrender not be interpreted as a manifestation of weakness, of personal cowardice? Would the names of the signatories—as had already happened once before—not be forever dishonored in German history?[48]

These questions greatly worried Dönitz; he reached his decision only after a "painful struggle." Lüdde-

Neurath's account of the factors that affected this decision is psychologically revealing. Dönitz, he says, originally thought of seeking death in action. He never thought of suicide; that would have been tantamount to an admission of guilt. Had the end of the war still found him at the head of the navy, he would have managed to die in battle, ordering the fleet to surrender but personally sailing against the enemy and firing away until he was killed, thus expiating the "crime" of surrender. But when he acquired "the right and freedom to decide on general capitulation," he gave up the idea. For then "personal" considerations could no longer interfere with the performance of his duty.[49] Apparently, then, under the code to which Dönitz subscribed, offering surrender, or even the mere thought of it, was a fault for which death alone could atone. But this principle applied only to subordinates. It was not necessary for the supreme leader to propitiate history by death, even when he decided that capitulation was necessary. The leader could determine with impunity that certain national objectives could best be attained by capitulation; in subordinates, such thoughts were criminal.

For Dönitz, the problem was to achieve the painful ascent from the underling's to the leader's mentality. When he finally managed it, he also discovered some national objectives to which explicit capitulation (but capitulation to the West only) was relevant. To be sure, the grand objective, that of splitting the enemy coalition, was unattainable: the Allies would never stand by to let him combat Bolshevism, no matter how hard he fought them. But selective capitulation still offered a tangible advantage. It made it possible for the German soldiers facing the Russians and for the civilians fleeing from territories occupied or threatened by Russian troops to reach a haven behind the screen of the line of demarcation. This salvaging action could be carried on only if hostilities were terminated along the Anglo-American front but not on the Russian front, so that a continuous stream of fugitives could pass across the stabilized Anglo-American lines. Hence, Dönitz hastened to end hostilities with the West by explicit surrender before weapons had to be laid down on the Russian front too.

With this in mind, Dönitz fully approved Kesselring's capitulation talks with the Americans in the southern theater. The U.S. Army history has summed up the Admiral's viewpoint as follows:

Dönitz said he felt the Germans should be pleased every time U.S. and British forces, rather than Soviet forces, occupied a part of Germany. He agreed that the over-all situation demanded capitulation on all fronts, but held that the Germans should not consider it at the moment since it would mean delivering most of the forces east of the Elbe to the Russians.[50]

On May 2, Dönitz took the initiative for the surrender *en bloc* of the German forces facing Field Marshal Montgomery's group of armies in northwestern Germany. Although this was a large-scale capitulation, it was still part of a piecemeal pattern. In keeping with his basic idea of saving as many German troops as possible from Russian captivity, Dönitz wanted to yield to Montgomery a number of German units then fighting the Russians east of the Elbe. Montgomery declined this offer and also refused to grant authorization for civilian refugees to cross the Allied lines. He agreed, however, that German soldiers of any unit would be accepted as prisoners of war if they surrendered individually. Otherwise, the surrender was to be unconditional.[51]

All weapons, including naval ones, were to be handed over in serviceable condition.

Characteristically, General Jodl, chief of staff of the High Command, rebelled against this last provision: it was incompatible with German "honor." He urged the immediate destruction of all equipment. But Schwerin von Krosigk, Dönitz's foreign minister, counseled against the destruction of weapons, arguing that it would cause the negotiations to collapse, invite reprisals, and lead to the closing of the escape routes to the west.[52] In Lüdde-Neurath's words: "With heavy heart, Dönitz decided to accept this condition as well, realizing fully that he alone would bear the responsibility for it before history, and that no subordinate who, contrary to military tradition, surrendered his arms intact would incur any blame."[53]

On May 4 the agreement for capitulation in the northwest was signed, and it took effect the next day. It then became necessary to start talks with General Eisenhower about the surrender of the entire Wehrmacht. Dönitz tried at first to make the surrender selective, affecting only the troops facing the Western Allies. On May 5, his emissary, Admiral von Friedeburg, made a proposal in this sense when he arrived at SHAEF headquarters at Rheims. Eisenhower refused to discuss surrender on this basis. Only unconditional surrender on all fronts simultaneously was acceptable. All arms, ships, and airplanes would have to be handed over intact; the troops would stay where they were. In case of violation, there would be reprisals. Friedeburg, not authorized to treat on this basis, radioed Dönitz for instructions. Dönitz refused to give in and sent a new representative, General Jodl, to continue the talks in Friedeburg's place. Jodl's instructions were unchanged; Dönitz flatly refused to "deliver the troops standing on the eastern front to the Russians."[54] Eisenhower then threatened to break off the talks and seal the zonal frontier against all traffic. There was nothing Dönitz could do but comply with the Allied demands. A capitulation agreement was signed on May 6, with cease-fire fixed for midnight on May 8.

The negotiation tactic followed by Dönitz was mainly designed to gain time for his salvaging operation. Dönitz ordered all commanders on the eastern front to "do everything possible short of violating truce terms to reach the lines of the western powers."[55] Accordingly, the few days preceding the Rheims meeting and the forty-eight-hour delay between the signing of the capitulation agreement and the cease-fire were feverishly exploited on the eastern front. For example, on May 4, General Wenck, commander of an eastern front sector, offered to surrender his troops, 100,000 strong, to the American Ninth Army; he also requested permission for civilian refugees to cross the Elbe. The American commander, General Simpson, refused to sign a formal agreement along these lines, but he agreed to accept German prisoners "individually." With this assurance the main body of Wenck's forces crossed the Elbe and surrendered. Many civilians also were able to cross the lines (the ban was not strictly enforced).[56] All in all, two and a half to three million German soldiers and civilians escaped from the path of the Russians during Dönitz's brief tenure.[57]

No salvaging operation was possible before the cease-fire for the German forces fighting in Czechoslovakia under Field Marshal Schörner because there were no western forces in the neighborhood. Accordingly, these troops continued to fight even after V-E Day. On May 10, General Eisenhower ordered Dönitz "to insure prompt compliance of these commanders [i.e., those in Czechoslovakia] to cease fire." Simultaneously, Eisenhower directed all troops under his command to imprison German soldiers coming from the fighting area and hand them over to the Russians as violators of the Act of Capitulation.[58] Dönitz thereupon had to tell the German commanders involved that the salvaging operation ordered by him could not go on once the capitulation had entered into effect. This being the case, nothing remained for them to do but to surrender to the Russians after all. Schörner, however, "warned that virtually no order would make his troops leave their comrades behind or voluntarily surrender to the Red forces, and that it would also be difficult to control them if they were attacked by Czechoslovak partisans."[59] Prague fell to Czechoslovak partisans and Russian troops on May 12, and after that German military resistance ceased.

EVALUATION AND CONCLUSIONS

Germany's surrender was the only surrender in World War II that was strictly unconditional on the face of it. The Germans were unable to achieve any "disarming" effect during the terminal stage of hostilities. A revolutionary transformation of the German regime might have achieved such an effect, but the Nazi ruling group succeeded in warding off all efforts to this end. Alternatively, the Germans might have tried to obtain political concessions from the Western powers by using their residual strength as a bargaining asset. This, however, was also impossible, not only because of the enormous disparity of force between Germany and the West, but also because the Germans felt compelled to concentrate their last remaining strength on desperate attempts to stem the Russian advance.

There was a third factor from which the Germans expected to derive political advantage: the latent political differences between Soviet Russia and the West. Exploiting these differences remained the focal point of their surrender policy to the end. Their terminal objective was to liquidate hostilities in the west, in the form of unconditional surrender if necessary, but at the same time to obtain the tacit acquiescence of the Western Allies to their continuing resistance in the east. It was expected that the Western Allies would find this policy attractive because they had every reason to oppose Russian penetration into Central Europe.

This calculation by no means lacked foundation in fact. The United Nations coalition *was* heterogeneous, and losing powers facing heterogeneous coalitions sometimes do escape political disaster when the enemy coalition falls apart before the war ends. But in Germany's case, things did not work out this way. In spite of the latent divergence of their interests, the Western powers and Soviet Russia were anxious to maintain their coalition. The Western Allies steadfastly resisted all temptation to countenance Germany's plan of limiting the war to one front. This policy was greatly facilitated by the Allies' ingrained habit of looking at the war from an exclusively military point of view. Nothing was allowed to interfere with the unique objective of defeating the enemy.

If the Western Allies' realization of the latent conflict of interests within the United Nations coalition played any role in the terminal stage, it must have reinforced rather than counteracted their determination to weaken Germany as much as possible. Since each side of the coalition feared that the other side might someday capture Germany as an auxiliary, both sides agreed that the weaker Germany became, the better. The terminal political behavior of the coalition partners suggests a tacit compromise of this kind.

Germany, then, was not able to exploit her enemies' intracoalition difficulties in the grand manner. Yet her attempt to surrender to the West alone had a measure of success. The United Nations' formula that surrender had to be global and simultaneous for Germany's eastern and western forces could not be enforced. Instead, the surrender was carried out piecemeal over a period of weeks and remained one-sided until the cease-fire took effect. The Germans thus succeeded in entering into some sort of political interaction with the Allies during the terminal stage. This interaction took place, not in the form of negotiations, but purely in terms of behavior. From the Western Allies' point of view, the final capitulations of the German forces were a purely military matter, but for the Germans they had political significance. Their purpose was to suck the Allied forces into German territory, denying as much of it as possible to the Russians. Of course, how much German territory would ultimately be occupied by the Russians had been determined at Yalta, and the Germans' military behavior had no effect on this issue. But another political objective of the selective surrenders—the rescuing of German combatants and civilians from Russian control—was largely attained. Unconditional as it was, Germany's surrender did produce a small political dividend.

Six

THE JAPANESE SURRENDER
August 1945

In a war waged according to the formula of divergent attrition, Japan's defeat at the hands of the United States was a foregone conclusion. To such men as Marquis Kido, Keeper of the Privy Seal (who later played a crucial role in bringing the war to a conclusion), this was clear almost from the beginning.[1] For civilian politicians like Yoshida and Kido, the Battle of Midway (June 7, 1942) was already an alarm signal.[2] Later, in 1943, the armed services themselves began to be worried about the trend of attrition. In September, Rear Admiral Takagi, acting on orders, began a systematic study of the war situation based on material in secret army and navy files. The study was finished in March 1944, when Takagi reached the crushing conclusion that Japan could not possibly win. Her losses of shipping, both naval and commercial, were prohibitive. She could no longer import essential raw materials or defend her cities against air attacks. Hence, the only course open to the country was to seek a compromise peace.[3]

Takagi's conclusions, of course, were known only to

a small circle. In July 1944, however, the fall of Saipan convinced even those who had been hitherto optimistic that defeat was inevitable. One of the immediate results of the loss of Saipan was the resignation of Premier Tojo, who had committed himself irrevocably to an all-out pursuit of the war and would not tolerate any talk about peace.

The fall of Saipan marked the beginning of the terminal stage of the Japanese war, for after that event the only question was when and how the war would be liquidated. The process of ending the war, however, was agonizingly long and arduous. The supreme political leadership in Japan, unlike the Nazi leadership in Germany, was willing enough to terminate the war on almost any terms. But its efforts in this direction were constantly hampered by a close-knit and extremely powerful group of prowar fanatics in the armed services, particularly the army officers' corps. Members of this group were determined to remove, if necessary by assassination, any political officeholder who took steps to end the war. The extreme war objectives of the United Nations constituted another formidable difficulty facing the propeace group. The Allies' refusal to offer any political incentive for surrender had a paralyzing effect on the group's policy.

The peculiar relationship between Japan and Russia, too, helped lengthen the terminal phase of the war. The Japanese government hoped to obtain a mitigation of the unconditional-surrender formula from the Western Allies by enlisting the good offices of Soviet Russia, which was not yet at war with Japan. As we shall see, this illusory hope, which the Soviet government deliberately encouraged, had decisive and disastrous effects.

UNITED STATES SURRENDER POLICY
TOWARD JAPAN

The Cairo Declaration of December 1, 1943, stated that "the three Allies [the United States, China, and Great Britain], in harmony with those of the United Nations at war with Japan, will continue to persevere in the serious and prolonged operations necessary to procure the unconditional surrender of Japan."[4] But although "unconditional surrender," the basic war objective of the Western Allies, applied to Japan as well as to Germany, the phrase was not interpreted identically for the two countries.

As we shall see in Part Three, the hallmark of the unconditional-surrender policy in its application to Germany was the avoidance of specific (and therefore limited) peace aims. The political context of the war with Germany made such avoidance necessary. In Japan's case, political necessity worked the other way, and accordingly the Cairo Declaration formulated certain specific territorial provisions:

The Three Great Allies are fighting this war to restrain and punish the aggression of Japan. They covet no gain for themselves and have no thought of territorial expansion. It is their purpose that Japan shall be stripped of all the islands in the Pacific which she has seized or occupied since the beginning of the first World War in 1914, and that all the territories Japan has stolen from the Chinese, such as Manchuria, Formosa, and the Pescadores, shall be restored to the Republic of China. Japan will also be expelled from all other territories which she has taken by violence and greed. The aforesaid three great powers, mindful of the enslavement of the people of Korea, are determined that in due course Korea shall be free and independent.

The situation in the Far East, in fact, required the formulation of explicit territorial peace aims. China,

now recognized as a great power, had territorial griev-
ances and claims that the Western Allies were morally
obliged to endorse. The recognition of these claims implied that Japan would revert to her territorial bound-
aries in the period preceding the Sino-Japanese War of
1894–95. No such procedure was considered feasible
for Germany, since a unified German national state, even
stripped of all Hitler's conquests, appeared potentially
dangerous.

Moreover, Japan's position differed from that of the
European Axis powers in so far as the terminal aspect of
unconditional surrender was concerned. Japan possessed
a capital bargaining asset that Germany and Italy lacked;
a residual force capable of offering very strong resistance to any attempt to invade her homeland. Whereas
the residual strengths of Germany and Italy had been
relatively small after the war reached their home territories, Japan seemed likely to become an extremely formidable opponent in her home islands. The Allies' very
high estimate of Japan's terminal capabilities decisively
influenced their political and military planning during
the last stage of the war.[5]

Our theoretical analysis implies that strong residual
capabilities on the losing side are apt to produce a substantial "disarming" effect on the winning side by in-
clining the winner to make political concessions to the
loser as incentives for surrender. The course of events
in the terminal stage of the war with Japan is fully consonant with this hypothesis. In the end, Japan was able
to trade the surrender of her residual force for a political
concession, the sparing of the monarchy. But this outcome was reached only after a considerable policy struggle in the United States, where for a long time it was

believed that Soviet military help was the best means to overcome Japan's terminal resistance.

In the years after Pearl Harbor, Soviet Russia's forces were fully extended in the war against Germany. In this period, too, the Russians were bitter about the Allies' failure to set up a second front. In view of these facts, the Allies did not press for Soviet participation in the war against Japan. It was Stalin who broached the matter unexpectedly at a banquet that concluded the Moscow conference (October 30, 1943). As Cordell Hull recorded the incident, "Then . . . he [Stalin] did make a statement of transcendent importance. He astonished and delighted me by saying clearly and unequivocally that, when the Allies succeeded in defeat-Germany, the Soviet Union would then join in defeating Japan."[6]

One month later, at the Teheran Conference, Stalin talked to Roosevelt in the same sense:

He said that up to now the Russian forces in Siberia were sufficient for purely defensive purposes but that they would have to be increased threefold before they could be strong enough to engage in offensive ground operations against the Japanese— and he added that when Germany was finally defeated the necessary Russian reinforcements could be sent to Eastern Siberia and then, he said, "We shall be able by our common front to beat Japan."[7]

Later, at the Yalta Conference, it turned out that Stalin had definite territorial and political aims in mind when he proposed joining in the war against Japan. As a counterpart to the Soviet Union's entry into the war "within two or three months after Germany has surrendered and the war in Europe has terminated," the United States and Britain had to agree in advance to the Soviet annexation of Southern Sakhalin and the Kuriles, the internationalization of the port of Dairen with Russia's "pre-eminent interests" safeguarded, the lease of Port Arthur as a Soviet base, and a few other terms.[8]

The American acceptance of these conditions was predicated on the character of American strategic plans for the Pacific war at the time of the Yalta Conference. These plans were settled: after the termination of the Okinawa operation, there was to be an assult on Kyushu and "the decisive invasion of the industrial heart of Japan through the Tokyo Plain."[9] Against this background, the Joint Chiefs of Staff saw the Soviet role as follows:

> Basic principles regarding our policy toward Russia's entry into the war against Japan are:
>
> a. We desire Russian entry at the earliest possible date consistent with her ability to engage in offensive operations and are prepared to offer the maximum support possible without prejudice to our main effort against Japan.
>
> b. We consider that the mission of Russian Far Eastern Forces should be to conduct an all-out offensive against Manchuria to force the commitment of Japanese forces and resources in North China and Manchuria that might otherwise be employed in the defense of Japan, to conduct intensive air operations against Japan proper and to interdict lines of communication between Japan and the mainland of Asia.[10]

Later some American leaders came to doubt the desirability of Russia's entering the war against Japan. Byrnes and Leahy, in particular, went on record against it.[11] The military, however, welcomed a Soviet contribution as possibly indispensable for defeating Japan.[12]

The American planners were much preoccupied with the probable high cost of an invasion of the Japanese home islands, a factor that induced some to look for an alternative course of action. There was some discussion among strategists about whether Japan could be forced to surrender merely by a stepped-up sea-air blockade. The Navy thought that this could be done,[13] but the finally dominant view was that the sea-air blockade could do no more than soften up Japan for the final invasion.[14]

Although the parties to this debate disagreed over the means that would be sufficient to ensure surrender, they shared the belief that surrender could result only from military pressure. The possibility that surrender could be hastened by offering political incentives to the Japanese leaders received little attention. Among strategic planners, it seems that Admiral Leahy alone opposed the invasion. He did so not so much because he believed that less costly and equally effective military strategies were available as because he considered the political approach preferable to the military one and capable of achieving equivalent results. As he reported,

> I was unable to see any justification, from a national-defense point of view, for an invasion of an already thoroughly defeated Japan. I feared that the cost would be enormous in both lives and treasure.
> It was my opinion at that time [June 1945] that a surrender could be arranged with terms acceptable to Japan that would make fully satisfactory provisions for America's defense against any future trans-Pacific aggression.[15]

The possibility of hastening Japan's surrender by political moves came up only as an afterthought at the crucial White House conference of June 18, 1945, called to lay down the main lines of strategy for the final phase of hostilities. The Joint Chiefs of Staff presented their views, after which President Truman rendered his decision. The attack on Kyushu was to take place, but final decision on the invasion of Honshu was to be kept in abeyance. What happened after this was described by one of the participants, John J. McCloy, then Assistant Secretary of War, in the following terms:

> After the President's decision had been made and the conference was breaking up, an official, not theretofore participating, suggested that serious attention should be given to a political attempt to end the war. The meeting fell into a tailspin, but after control was recovered, the idea appealed to several present. It appealed particularly to the President, and to one member of the Joint Chiefs of Staff, who, by the way, was the one member of that body who had no responsibility to a particular service.[16]

The proposal for political action carried the day; it led within six weeks to the Potsdam Declaration, with its implication that the Emperor would be allowed to keep his throne.[17] Those who favored the political approach, however, equated it with the issuance of a public appeal combining military threats with political blandishments. Another form of political action, backstage contacts with the enemy to determine whether there was a mutually acceptable basis for surrender, was never contemplated, since it ran counter to the fundamental American belief that anything smacking of negotiation would fatally detract from the completeness of victory and thereby jeopardize future peace.

The American policymakers were desperately anxious to hasten Japan's surrender and to cut terminal costs as much as possible, but their basic concept of non-negotiation[18] ruled out the one form of political strategy that was best suited to saving time. The only kind of political strategy they would allow was a combination of military pressure and public declarations. In this way, one of the basic corollaries of the unconditional surrender policy, nonnegotiation, interfered with the speedy liquidation of the war.

The other corollary of the policy, nonrecognition of the enemy government as the legitimate custodian of national sovereignty, also caused difficulties. Some American policymakers, particularly Joseph C. Grew, the former Ambassador to Japan, recognized that an orderly capitulation of all Japanese forces could be obtained only through the agency of the Emperor: he alone had the necessary authority to order the soldiers to lay down their arms. Grew writes: "I knew very well that when the time came for Japan's surrender, the Emperor was the only one who could bring it about, and that by issuing an Imperial Rescript, a document sacred to all Japanese, he alone could put it into effect."

Grew argued that the maintenance of civil order in Japan would also require the retention of the Emperor. He wrote in a memorandum to Secretary of State Cordell Hull (April 1944):

If, after final victory, we wish to avail ourselves—as common sense would dictate—of any assets that we find in Japan which can be used for the maintenance of order as distingiushed from the maintenance of the military cult, we would, in my judgment, simply be handicapping the pursuit of our ultimate aims by any attempts to scrap or to by-pass the institution of the Throne. Should we insist on so doing, I can see only chaos emerging from such a decision.[19]

As it turned out, the maintenance of the imperial institution, which Grew held indispensable both for the orderly execution of a surrender agreement and for the preservation of civic order, was precisely the political incentive necessary and sufficient to induce the Japanese to surrender. This policy, however, was bitterly opposed by the American public and by influential political leaders, who believed, often intensely, that a political vacuum had to be created in the interests of a stable peace.[20]

Congress became a sounding board for this belief. Representative Roy O. Woodruff of Michigan inserted in the *Congressional Record* of August 30, 1944, an article by Captain Miller Freeman, U.S.N.R., castigating Ambassador Grew and hinting that the O.W.I. directive stopping personal attacks on the Emperor was "sabotage." The maintenance of the "Emperor myth," the article stated, "means a short-of-victory war with Japan—and that, in turn, means another war with Japan." The article concluded: "We need not fear that war if we follow God and our conscience as to what is right—instead of seeking to uphold a lone human being who is the Japs' incarnation of God."[21]

Senator Russell of Georgia forcefully denounced the "softness" of the final terms on which Japan was allowed to surrender. In a speech delivered shortly after V-J Day, he reviewed the efforts that he had made in favor of a sterner policy. In his view, Japan did not deserve better treatment than Germany; on the contrary, he said, "if there must be a difference in the treatment accorded Germany and Japan we should be sterner with the Japanese." He added:

Holding these views, Mr. President, I was naturally concerned when I read the Potsdam declaration and saw the loopholes which that document knocked in our previously announced and oft-reiterated policy of unconditional surrender. On August 7, before the Japanese ever offered their conditional acceptance of the Potsdam declaration, I telegraphed the President from my home in Georgia to enter my vigorous protest against accepting any conditions offered by Japan in derogation of unconditional surrender which might be likely to allow the well-known aggressive spirit of the Japanese people to retain a breath of life.[22]

In this telegram Senator Russell urged a revision of the Potsdam terms and the continuation of air attacks until the Japanese offered unqualified unconditional surrender:

If we do not have available a sufficient number of atomic bombs with which to finish the job immediately, let us carry on with TNT and fire bombs until we can produce them. . . . Our people have not forgotten that the Japanese struck us the first blow in this war without the slightest warning. They believe that we should continue to strike the Japanese until they are brought groveling to their knees. We should cease our appeals to Japan to sue for peace. The next plea for peace should come from an utterly destroyed Tokyo.[23]

The retention of the Emperor, Senator Russell claimed, was generally disapproved by the people:

When the Japanese finally submitted their counter-proposals and conditions with respect to retaining their Emperor and form of government, the idea was generally disapproved. Reference to the newspapers of those days will show many editorials in leading publications warning against the dangers of keeping Hirohito. Our allies in the struggle, with the exception of England, were quoted as opposing any conditions in the Japanese surrender. The wounded in the hospitals and the men in the service, including many on their way overseas, were interviewed by newspapermen, and the majority were opposed to accepting the conditions. Here are a few headlines taken at random from a daily newspaper of August 11, just after the Jap offer was announced:

"Russia and China Frown on Jap Offer."
"Australians Oppose."
"Romulo Calls for Elimination of Hiro."
"Servicemen Want Emperor Hirohito Deposed."
" 'Blast Him Off Throne,' Say Wounded."

Admiral Halsey was quoted as saying that the terms of the

peace were a political question on which military men should keep quiet, but that it was his own personal view that it would be a mistake not to hang the Emperor.[24]

In the view of Senator Russell and the other opponents of qualified surrender, the prospects for future peace were directly proportional to the harshness of the terms on which hostilities were ended and of the deprivations meted out to the enemy:

The question of whether or not we can permanently preserve the peace of the earth will be largely determined within the next five years, even though the outbreak of war may be postponed for a generation. . . . Nearly every report, whether over Radio Tokyo; through the Domei News Agency; from American newspaper correspondents on the scene, or from our returning military men, seems to indicate that the people of that country, of all classes and positions in life, regard the present situation as a mere armistice or interlude in warfare rather than the utter defeat calculated to convince them of the necessity of forever abandoning their dreams of world domination . . . the Japanese are acting as though this were only a recess between two antagonists who will resume the fight—presumably when and if Japan obtains the secret atomic bomb or other equalizer. . . . Our present policy of politeness and respect for the individual's property and security of person, while admirable, is tending to confirm the Japanese belief that they have not been conquered . . . I am thoroughly convinced that unless the Japanese people—all of them from top to bottom—are shown beyond question that they have really lost the war and that the way of the aggressor is hard this time and will be much harder in the case of future aggression, we shall lose the peace in the Pacific. . . . If we follow the easy course of a soft peace, we are simply courting the disaster of a more terrible war in the future.[25]

Although Senator Russell was convinced that softness toward Japan would breed a war of revenge and that harsh terms would ensure peace forever, he was against assigning large numbers of American troops to the occupation of Japan. Prompted by Senator Wherry, he confessed that he found "startling" General MacArthur's statement about the need to keep 200,000 American troops in Japan. Then there was the following exchange:

Mr. Wherry. Will the Senator agree that the occupation probably could be carried out by policing by Chinese soldiers and the soldiers of other of our Allies, just as well as by our own soldiers?

Mr. Russell. I am in favor of using other soldiers so far as possible, because any member of the Senate cannot fail but be impressed with the overwhelming desire of the people of this country to get the boys back home, and any member of the Senate can tell from his mail each morning that the boys themselves are just as enthusiastic as are their families, if not more so, that they be returned home.

Mr. Wherry. I thank the Senator.[26]

Senator Russell's speech and the exchange that followed vividly illustrate a basic postulate of the doctrine of unconditional surrender: that there is a causal connection between maximum destructiveness in war and the perpetual peace that is to succeed it.[27]

Such an idea strongly militated against offering a political incentive to the Japanese in order to hasten surrender, but it was not the only argument used by American policymakers in opposing political incentives. Secretary of War Stimson was at once in favor of moderation in dealing with the Japanese Emperor and opposed to letting the Japanese know it:

In the view of Stimson and his military advisers, it was always necessary to bear in mind that at least some of Japan's leaders would seize on any conciliatory offer as an indication of weakness. For this reason they did not support Grew in urging an immediate statement on the Emperor in May. The battle for Okinawa was proceeding slowly and with heavy losses, and they feared lest Japanese militarists argue that such a statement was the first proof of that American fatigue which they had been predicting since 1941. It seemed possible to Stimson, in 1947, that these fears had been based on a misreading of the situation.[28]

In May, indeed, American government officials were not yet in a position to know what was the prevailing state of mind in leading Japanese political circles. Had they been, they would have known that the Emperor himself and his close political advisers were ready to capitulate on terms very severe to Japan,[29] and that in fact surrender negotiations could only be conducted with this circle. Ironically enough, it follows that what to do about the Emperor was not an open question at all if the United States was interested in the orderly capitulation of the Japanese forces. Without prior assurance to the Japanese on this point, no surrender talks could have been initiated at all.

This is not to say that a *public* statement about the Emperor, delivered in May 1945, would have been enough in itself to bring surrender. Although the Emperor and his advisers would have been encouraged by such a statement, they had to reckon with fanatical officers who were determined to use every means, including assassination, against anybody who talked about capitulation. It seems that a moderate American statement would not have been sufficient to enable the circle around the Emperor to force the military group to give up its opposition to the peace policy. On the other hand, such a statement would not have been altogether useless, as withholding it certainly was. It was illusory to believe that extreme verbal intransigence, together with maximally destructive military blows, was needed to break down the Japanese die-hards' desperate will to resist.

Peace Efforts Before V-E Day

Robert J. C. Butow, in his *Japan's Decision to Surrender*, has traced lucidly and painstakingly, using all the available documents, the history of the long and arduous efforts for peace on the part of a group of Japanese statesmen whose central figure was Marquis Koichi Kido, Keeper of the Privy Seal. In what follows we shall follow Butow's account.

According to Butow, the idea of a "peace mission" was first discussed in this circle just four days after the Battle of Midway, i.e., on June 11, 1942. On that day, Shigeru Yoshida, the former Japanese Ambassador to Britain, who was to become Premier after the war, called on Kido to discuss a scheme that involved sending Prince Konoye to Switzerland. The prince was to have no definite mission other than to keep in touch with influential leaders of various nations so as to ensure that Japan would not miss any opportunity that might lead to a termination of the war.[30]

Nothing came of this particular idea, however, and a long time was to pass before Japan actually put out peace feelers. But the topic of ending the war never disappeared from the consultations that members of the inner circle around Kido and the Emperor continued to have among themselves, and as time went on, the theme acquired greater and greater urgency.

The entries in Kido's diary relating to this period (early 1943) reveal that he knew that the war was going against Japan and that Konoye and Shigemitsu shared this view. Early in February, 1943, for instance, Kido had a three-hour discussion with Prince Konoye, who was extremely pessimistic about the war situation. In Butow's words:

During the course of this long conversation . . . Konoye repeatedly spoke of the necessity of terminating the conflict as soon as possible lest unsettled internal conditions lead to an intensification of Communist activity within Japan. The issue, in Konoye's mind, was clear-cut: end the war now or be prepared to see communism emerge as the ultimate victor.[31]

Talk along these lines, of course, was one thing, and political action against the die-hard war party another. General Tojo was still Japan's Premier, and he ruled with an iron fist. The cabinet consisted entirely of Tojo supporters, men who did not share the misgivings of the Kido circle and were determined to fight on to victory. The first overt political move of the peace party was to break up the monolithic unity of Tojo's cabinet. They succeeded in having Mamori Shigemitsu, one of their number, appointed Foreign Minister in the Tojo cabinet. This occurred a short time after the conversation related above.

Plans for ending the war took on a more specific shape after the Cairo Declaration, which called for Japan's "unconditional surrender" and for her expulsion from all continental and island territories other than the home islands. Shortly after the Declaration was issued, Marquis Kido worked out a territorial plan on which a peace settlement might be based: the Pacific areas under Japanese occupation were to be placed under a joint commission in which Japan, the Soviet Union, China, the United States, and Great Britain would be represented. Apparently Kido thought that the Allies would moderate the Cairo terms if Japan came forward with a peace offer soon enough, i.e., before Germany's collapse. Kido aired these ideas to Shigemitsu and found him more pessimistic: "Shigemitsu . . . spoke of a need for 'great determination' and frankly declared 'unconditional surrender, in essence, will be unavoidable.' "[32]

It appears, then, that at least one responsible Japanese statesman stated explicitly, as early as January 1944, that Japan would have to surrender unconditionally. Many other members of the peace group seem to have felt the same way, even if they did not say so.

Among the experts of the Japanese Foreign Office the prevailing tendency was not to take the Cairo Declaration at face value. Toshikazu Kase, a high official of the Foreign Office, whose *Journey to the Missouri* is an important source for the history of the period, describes the official reaction to the declaration in the following terms:

Upon word of the Cairo declaration a special conference was held in the Foreign Office to study its significance. I listened in silence to the discussion. The participants, without exception, appeared shocked by the severity of the terms. But most of them did not take them too seriously, regarding them as only an inducement offered Chungking or as a diplomatic gesture to forestall China's defection from the Allied camp. China was then in a serious plight since the Allies, preoccupied elsewhere, could not help her effectively. There was a precedent in April, 1915, during the First World War, when the Allies secretly promised Constantinople and the Dardanelles to Russia in order to prevent her from deserting them. Russia at that time was reeling from a shattering defeat inflicted by Germany. The Allies did not desire to pay such an exorbitant price and keenly regretted it soon afterward but they thought it essential at that critical juncture. Such was generally the tone of the argument.

I myself thought, however, that there was more than that in the Cairo declaration. While in World War I the United States offered Germany the Fourteen Points as an inducement for peace, this time the Allies announced the Cairo declaration as terms to be meted out to Japan. . . . This I believed was because of the unique character of the second World War, which unlike the first was being fought on the basis of unconditional surrender. There was to be no halfway compromise, no negotiated peace.[33]

Admiral Toyoda, former chief of the Japanese Imperial General Staff, told the U.S. Strategic Bombing Survey (USSBS):

We looked upon [the Cairo declaration] as a declaration but not as one whose terms would actually be applied to us. By way of possibility of reducing these terms, if you should continue pushing the war, we would demand of you the heavy sacrifice when your landing operations should commence in Honshu.[34]

Apparently many Japanese leaders believed either that the United States was not sufficiently interested in crushing Japan to enforce the Cairo terms or that she would be deterred from doing so by the heavy losses involved in a landing operation. At any rate, they were consistently thinking in terms of a negotiated peace.

In any case, the antiwar group was powerless to act during the months immediately following the Cairo Declaration, since it did not control the key political positions. No action for peace was possible as long as Tojo remained Premier. Tojo's cabinet, however, finally fell on July 18, 1944, under the crushing impact of the loss of Saipan, an event which brought home the irrevocable loss of the war even to those who had been hopeful up to then.

When Tojo fell, it was generally understood that the next cabinet would have the task of paving the way for peace.[35] The first solution considered was the curious one of a cabinet headed jointly by General Koiso, military governor of Korea, and Admiral Yonai, an outspoken antiwar man. The plans for a joint premiership, however, did not work out, and, after a series of chaotic consultations, Koiso emerged as sole Premier, with Yonai as Navy Minister. Shigemitsu remained Foreign Minister.

The Koiso cabinet was willing enough to explore all avenues that might lead to ending the war. But that was more easily said than done. Blocking the way from the outset was the Cairo Declaration, a document so worded as to rule out its voluntary acceptance by any Japanese government no matter how few illusions it had about the ultimate outcome of the war. The Declaration termed all Japanese territorial acquisitions since 1895 as "theft" pure and simple. This was an apt characterization, perhaps, from the point of view of a Chinese patriot; but the Japanese could not help remembering that the Japanese procedure before 1914 was by no means out of keeping with the international mores prevailing at that time, particularly in dealings between the great powers and China. According to Butow,

. . . the tenor of the Cairo Declaration as a whole was unacceptable to the Japanese and was considered by many as a purposeful distortion of historical fact. The net result was that the declaration immediately became a serious hindrance to those who wished to exert themselves toward bringing the war to an end.[36]

Furthermore, the temper of the junior officers of the army, a formidable group of fanatics, could not be overlooked. In the fall of 1944, according to the USSBS, a threatened revolt of the military prevented the Koiso cabinet from making a move to end the war.[37]

The only concrete action for peace of which we have a record from this period was a curious, half-private venture. A prominent Japanese journalist, Bunshiro Suzuki (not to be confused with Kantaro Suzuki, the last wartime Premier), approached the Swedish minister to Tokyo, Widar Baggë, on behalf of Prince Konoye, asking him to transmit Japanese peace overtures to London. The purpose of this move appears to have been exploratory. The Japanese leaders wanted to obtain some clarification of what "unconditional surrender" actually meant. For them, the paramount problem was to discover whether there was a possibility of ending the war—on the Allies' terms, to be sure, but without complete self-abasement and without the disruption of the imperial institution on which all social order in Japan seemed to rest.[38]

As time went on, Japan's military situation grew more and more hopeless: the war fleet all but ceased to exist, devastating air raids got under way, and in December Leyte fell to the American forces. All the same, it was impossible for the Japanese government simply to throw in the sponge and accept the Cairo Declaration as the basis for surrender. Had such a move been made, the extremist elements of the Army, among whom the *mystique* of the "holy war" for Japan held unlimited sway, would have staged a *coup d'état*. In this situation, the antiwar circle reached the conclusion that the only hope for ending the war lay in enlisting the good offices of some third power for a "negotiated" peace. Even this approach was fraught with danger, and people like Kido and Konoye soon recognized that only the Emperor's personal intervention could steer it through without a violent explosion. But the chances for obtaining mediation were slim, and it was very doubtful whether the Allies would grant Japan any concessions even if some third power transmitted a Japanese offer for peace talks.

The first tentative move through Baggë had fizzled out. Another attempt to use this channel was made in March 1945, when Baggë was about to return to Sweden. In a conversation with a Japanese diplomat shortly before his departure, Baggë remarked that in his opinion the Allies would not insist on removing the Emperor if Japan made an offer to surrender. This was reported to Shigemitsu, the Foreign Minister, who immediately got in touch with Baggë. In the ensuing conversation, the Foreign Minister avoided making a specific, official request for good offices. Instead, he remained on the plane of generalities. He emphasized in the strongest possible terms the Emperor's desire for peace, adding that the Emperor had always been opposed to the war, and stressed that he himself entertained the same feelings, along with the entire diplomatic corps of Japan. He concluded by requesting Baggë "very earnestly" to do whatever he could to determine Japan's chances of obtaining a "negotiated peace."[39] The impression Baggë gained from this was that Shigemitsu meant business; it seemed to the Swedish diplomat that the Foreign Minister was willing to end the war "even at great sacrifice to his country."

This action for peace through mediation, however, eventually bogged down. The Koiso cabinet fell on April 5, 1945, and in the new cabinet, headed by Admiral Kantaro Suzuki, Shigemitsu was replaced as Foreign Minister by Shigemori Togo. Togo was an extremely clear-sighted man, fully committed to the antiwar policy of his predecessor, but he was not conversant with what went on between Shigemitsu and Baggë immediately before he took office. When he learned about it on April 11, he wanted to see Baggë, but a meeting could not be arranged because the Swedish diplomat was leaving.

Baggë thus returned to Stockholm without any official communication from the Tokyo government on the basis of which official action could have been taken. In Stockholm, Baggë talked with the American minister, Herschel Johnson, giving him a full account of his explorations in Tokyo and of the prevailing state of mind in the Japanese Foreign Office. He also got in touch with the Japanese minister. The latter, however, had no formal instructions to press the peace action. When Togo was asked to send formal instructions, he gave a noncommittal reply. The Japanese government had apparently decided to try a different approach.

The Suzuki cabinet in fact was skating on thin ice. On April 15, shortly after it took office, the Minister of War, General Anami, ordered the arrest of four hundred persons suspected of harboring antiwar sentiments, including Yoshida. Suzuki, though hand-picked by the antiwar leaders, seemed anxious above all not to provoke the extremists, and his first official statements after taking office were warlike in tone. He spoke in terms of "fighting to the very end," and avoided making any reference to peace or mediation.[40]

The diplomatic approach to the problem of ending the war, temporarily suspended, was soon revived in a new and fateful direction. The new diplomatic formula saw a *rapprochement* with the Soviet Union as the most promising method for getting Japan out of the impasse in which she found herself.

The Road to Moscow

This disastrous "Moscow policy" went through two stages. The first was an attempt to improve Japan's diplomatic position by negotiating a new, favorable pact

with Soviet Russia after Stalin had denounced the
Soviet-Japanese Neutrality Pact in April 1945. The
second was a determined effort to enlist the Soviet
Union's good offices to obtain favorable surrender terms
from the Allies.

Neither move had the slightest chance of success.
When the policy of trying the Moscow channel was initiated in April 1945, Japan's position was hopeless, and
there was no valid reason for assuming that the Soviet
Union could be tempted to make common cause with a
power that had nothing to offer. The Japanese policymakers, however, were hypnotized by the idea that it
was possible to exploit the "friendly" relations that still
existed between their country and one of the great
powers. One cannot blame the Japanese for trying this
approach; anyone in their desperate position would have
grasped at a straw. It is difficult, however, to understand the obstinacy with which the Japanese government
clung to the mirage of a *rapprochement* with Moscow
and later to that of mediation by Moscow, even when it
became obvious that the Soviet Union did not have the
slightest interest in helping Japan out of the war.

The policy of seeking a *rapprochement* took its departure from an event that in ordinary logic would have
implied that Moscow was the last place from which
Japan could expect support. On April 5, 1945, the day
on which the Koiso cabinet fell, Stalin denounced the
Soviet-Japanese Neutrality Pact. Even though Molotov
subsequently assured the Japanese Ambassador that neutral relations would continue during the remainder of
the pact's life (it was to run for another year), the gesture itself was plainly a hostile one. It indicated nothing
but Soviet Russia's desire to regain a free hand vis-à-vis

Japan at the earliest moment permitted by the existing treaty. Actually, Stalin at Yalta had assumed a commitment to enter the war against Japan within two or three months after Germany's surrender, a commitment incompatible with Soviet Russia's observance of even the year's grace provided by the pact. To the Japanese, however, the denunciation of the pact seemed to open up marvelous prospects. If Japan were to offer a new pact on terms more attractive than the old, they thought, Soviet Russia might well be willing to take Germany's place as an effective ally. Japan would obtain political and material help (for a hefty payment, to be sure), enabling her to put up stiffer resistance to the Allies. Should the Russians prove unwilling to go that far, however, Japan could at least try to enlist their help in negotiating peace on a basis better than the Cairo Declaration. Mediation was to be sought only if *rapprochement* failed.

This diplomatic approach toward the problem of ending the war was quite acceptable to the armed services. In fact, it was first suggested (shortly after the denunciation of the pact) by two military die-hards, Army Chief of Staff Umezu and Vice-Chief of Staff Kawabe, who were joined later by Vice-Chief of the Naval General Staff Ozawa.[41] It is a sign of Togo's diplomatic astuteness that he was pessimistic about the policy's chances of success from the very beginning: he suspected that Soviet Russia already had committed herself to enter the war against Japan.[42] But Togo, having no evidence except the logic of political analysis to support his hunch, was not in a position to go against the army's wishes. While the sands were running out, Japan was forced to embark on a hopeless pilgrimage to Moscow.

The "Moscow policy" was discussed in detail by the Supreme Council for the Direction of War, an inner war cabinet consisting of the Premier, the Foreign Minister, the War and Navy Ministers, and the Army and Navy Chiefs of Staff.[43] It was characteristic of the situation then prevailing in Japan that even this body could not discuss the situation openly, since its meetings were ordinarily attended by junior staff officers who were quick to seize on "defeatist" talk and reveal it to likeminded comrades, with disastrous results. Togo finally succeeded in having the Council meet without the junior secretaries, but even then he did not succeed in injecting his own sober realism into the debate. The Council developed fantastic schemes, such as the plan, suggested by Yonai, to offer Japanese cruisers to the Soviet Union in exchange for Soviet oil and airplanes.

When the deliberations of the Council reached that stage, Germany had already surrendered and Japan was alone facing the most formidable military coalition in all history. If her leaders had immediately decided to try their luck with the second plank of the "Moscow policy," mediation, that would have been understandable in the circumstances, though still hopeless. But the Council (in which the heads of the military services had a very strong position) was not even in favor of seeking mediation at once. Germany's surrender seemed to mean to them, not that everything was irretrievably lost, but that it was necessary to acquire a new ally in Germany's place, that ally being Soviet Russia. This at a time when Moscow's main worry was how to get into the war against

Japan before the latter had a chance to surrender, in order to participate in the making of the peace as a belligerent rather than as a neutral.

The first tangible move to put the "Moscow policy" into effect came about the middle of May. Togo asked Hoki Hirota, a former Premier and Ambassador to Moscow, to see Soviet Ambassador Malik and make overtures for a *rapprochement*. Hirota was instructed to suggest talks for a renewal of the Neutrality Pact or for the conclusion of a new pact, emphasizing Japan's desire for friendship and good relations. The good offices of the Soviet Union in ending the war were to be solicited only if the suggestions for a *rapprochement* yielded no results.

Not until June 3 was Hirota able to see Malik, whose response to his offers of friendship was decidedly sour. The more Hirota talked about "friendly relations," the more Malik harped on the "anti-Soviet" feelings of the Japanese. Hirota was dismissed from Malik's presence without the slightest encouragement.[44]

This was the end of the *rapprochement* policy for all practical purposes. The next logical step would have been to try mediation. That step, however, could not be taken immediately, for the army went over to the counterattack and by a swift move torpedoed the peace policy of the circle around the Emperor. The army's stratagem consisted in calling, on June 6, a full meeting of the Supreme Council, with the junior secretaries present. At that meeting, the chiefs of the armed services introduced a Fundamental Plan for the further conduct of the war, calling for a *levée en masse*. A hundred million Japanese were to rise from the ground and strike the invader dead.[45] In support of this plan the army also submitted memoranda giving facts and figures about the world situation and the situation within Japan. The facts and figures contained nothing to prove that the plan would have a chance to succeed; in fact, they demonstrated beyond doubt that Japan lacked all essential means for continuing operations. Nevertheless, Togo was the sole member of the Supreme Council who dared to oppose the army's appeal for last-ditch resistance. The Fundamental Plan was adopted as Japan's policy. On the following day the Cabinet rubber-stamped it, and on June 8 it was imposed upon a silent Emperor at an Imperial Conference. The peace group had to begin again from the beginning.

It was the indefatigable Kido who again set the ball rolling. On June 9, the day after the Imperial Conference, he saw the Emperor and suggested that the Cabinet be sent an Imperial Letter, instructing it to take the necessary steps to put the mediation plan into effect. Kido would have preferred the direct approach to the United States and Britain (obviously the only practical method), but in view of the attitude of the army he had to settle for the revival of the attempt to secure mediation by Moscow. In eleven days of arduous discussions with cabinet members (June 9–19), Kido secured their agreement, including that of the War Minister, General Anami. Thus the stage was set for another showdown. This time the full Supreme Council with its eager young war hawks was bypassed. After a restricted meeting of the Council on June 18, at which "mediation" was endorsed,[46] the initiative was again put in the Emperor's hands. An imperial conference was called on June 22. The Emperor indicated that the decisions of June 6–8 had to be reconsidered. Togo thereupon moved to send a representative to Moscow to ask for mediation before the Potsdam Conference convened. He stressed the need for quick action. After some subdued opposition from the army representatives, the proposal was carried: Togo obtained the green light for approaching Moscow.

The execution of the plan, however, again miscarried. Instead of sending a mission to Moscow immediately, Togo decided to try the Hirota-Malik channel again. On the day following the conference he saw Hirota, informed him of the decision, and instructed him to resume his talks with Malik. Hirota called on Malik on the 24th and again on the 29th. On neither occasion, however, did he mention mediation, nor did he bring up the proposal to send a special envoy to Moscow. He talked exclusively about a new pact and the concessions that Japan would make in order to obtain it. In the second talk with Malik, Hirota handed him a written proposal: Japan would be ready to recognize Manchurian independence, to renounce fishing rights in Soviet waters, and to consider any other Soviet proposals, if Moscow were willing to enter negotiations for a new pact. Malik pocketed the proposal, promising to send it to Moscow, and that was the last Hirota heard from him. For two more weeks Hirota tried again and again to see Malik, but in vain; the Soviet diplomat was too "sick" to receive him.[47]

While Hirota's ill-fated venture was under way, the problem of the special embassy to Moscow was further debated by the Emperor and the members of the Supreme Council. On June 29 the Emperor called together the six members of the Council and "stated that, while it was of course necessary to keep on pushing the war, it was necessary at the same time, in view of the domestic situation, to consider the possibility of bringing the war to a conclusion. What did the members of the Council think of that idea?"[48]

The Emperor finally having uttered the fateful word, the ministers eagerly concurred. "Then the Emperor in turn asked when the Ministers expected to be able to send a special Ambassador to Moscow. The reply given was that the date was not certain but it was hoped that he would be sent before the Potsdam Conference should be held."[49]

This decision again produced no immediate results. It was only on July 7—after the Emperor had summoned Premier Suzuki and prodded him into action—that Togo first got in touch with Prince Konoye, who had been chosen to undertake the mission. And five more days passed before Konoye was officially appointed and a note was sent to Moscow informing the Soviet government of Tokyo's decision to send the special envoy. Moscow was informed that Konoye would carry with him a personal letter from the Emperor, stressing the latter's desire for a speedy termination of hostilities and proposing immediate negotiations to that effect. The note, radioed to the Japanese Ambassador in Moscow, Naotake Sato, for transmittal to the Soviet government, expressly repudiated "unconditional surrender," adding that if Great Britain and the United States were to insist on it, "Japan would be forced to fight to the bitter end with all her might in order to vindicate her honor and safeguard her national existence, which, to our intense regret, would entail further bloodshed."[50]

In spite of its insistence on "negotiation," the note clearly envisaged last-ditch resistance in certain circumstances, i.e., if the United States and Britain refused to make concessions that would safeguard Japan's "honor" and "national existence"—in other words, the imperial institution itself. Japan was not to budge from this stand to the very end, and the final surrender was actually made on this basis. Japan's diplomatic approach, however, was fundamentally vitiated by the delusion that the Soviet Union would lend a hand to help Japan get out of the war on these terms.

Having received the message, Sato, who himself had no hope that the action would succeed, immediately went to the Kremlin (July 13) but could not see Molotov. He was received, instead, by Vice-Commissar Alexander Lozovsky, who merely told him that Stalin and Molotov were about to leave for Berlin and that no answer could be given before their departure. An answer was promised as soon as the Soviet leaders could be reached in Berlin. Lozovsky accordingly received Sato again on the 16th, but only to ask for clarification of the exact mission entrusted to Prince Konoye. The clarification was sent on July 21: Konoye would "solicit the good offices of the Soviet government with a view to obtaining terms of peace other than unconditional surrender."[51] This telegram was delayed, and Sato could not proceed to the Kremlin before the 25th. But the Soviet government still gave no clear-cut answer. Sato continued to press, explaining that all Japan wanted was to terminate hostilities on an "honorable" basis, avoiding the formula of unconditional surrender.[52] But in spite of the most urgent appeals, no answer came from the Kremlin. After his return from Potsdam on August 6 (the day the atom bomb was dropped on Hiroshima), Stalin did not receive Sato, but he did see the Chinese Ambassador, T. V. Soong. In Kase's words,

When Sato again requested an interview with Molotov he received an appointment for 5 p.m. on August 8. At this meeting, without allowing Sato to state his case, Molotov abruptly notified him that the Soviet Union would be at war with Japan as from the following day.[58]

It is clear from this sequence of events that the Soviet government never had any intention of mediating between Japan and the Western Allies. At the same time, Moscow did nothing to enlighten the Japanese on the futility of their hopes. Moscow's objective apparently was to let the Japanese dangle at the end of the Moscow wire as long as possible. This is understandable: had Moscow let Tokyo know that it was not willing to mediate, the Japanese might have approached the Western powers with a direct offer to surrender. Moscow, however, had every interest in not letting this happen as long as the Soviet Union was not at war with Japan. It was essential for the Soviet Union to claim belligerent status at the moment when the Japanese empire was liquidated. After Yalta, the Soviet leaders were satisfied that the Western Allies would not move to end the war with Japan before the Soviet Union joined them. Even after Japan's position had become desperate, Soviet procrastination in replying to Tokyo's request for mediation offered a reasonable guarantee that Japan would not surrender prematurely.

It would not be true to say that Stalin kept the Japanese peace feeler hidden from the Western Allies. As Butow tells us,

On July 28, . . . Stalin personally told President Truman, Secretary of State Byrnes, and Prime Minister Attlee, that the Japanese had requested Soviet mediation and proposed sending Prince Konoye to Moscow. As if to allay any misgivings which might otherwise have appeared, the master of the Kremlin quickly explained that Japan's approach did not show a willingness to surrender unconditionally but was, instead, a calculated endeavor to obtain Soviet collaboration in the furtherance of

Japanese policy. The Japanese had even indicated, Stalin said, that although they wanted to end the war they would fight on with all their strength as long as the Allies continued to adhere to the unconditional surrender formula. As a result, the Soviet government had unhesitatingly informed Japan that it could not give a definite reply to her request in view of the fact that the imperial message was general in form and lacking in any concrete proposals.[54]

Actually, Stalin's communication was by no means the American government's first inkling of the Konoye mission. American intelligence with its customary prowess had intercepted and deciphered the coded messages passing between Togo in Tokyo and Sato in Moscow from July 21 on; Secretary Forrestal entered copious extracts from them in his diaries for July 13, 15, and 24.[55] The exchange revealed that the Japanese Emperor had authorized the mission because he was extremely anxious to end the war as soon as possible; it also contained a poignant debate between the Ambassador and the Foreign Minister. The former argued that it was illusory to expect anything from Russian mediation and that the only course open to Japan was to take direct steps toward unconditional surrender; the latter insisted that the decision to seek Moscow's good offices could not be changed and that Japan would be compelled to fight to the last unless she could get better terms than unconditional surrender. Although Japan's minimum terms were not spelled out in so many words, the entire drift of the communications strongly suggested that Japan, though unwilling to surrender unconditionally, was prepared to surrender on terms.

When Stalin brought up the Konoye mission at the Potsdam Conference, Allied policy toward Japan had moved away from strict unconditional surrender. The Potsdam Declaration, issued two days before, made it clear that the Allies would not demand the removal of the Emperor. It restricted the demand for unconditional surrender to the Japanese armed forces, stipulated temporary occupation of the home islands while recognizing Japanese sovereignty, and called for punitive measures only against war leaders other than the Emperor himself. The Declaration, which purported to give the full extent of Allied armistice conditions, remained silent about the Emperor and the imperial institution, thereby implying that the head of the state would not be touched.[56]

At that stage, the American government could have decided to explore whether any substantial gap remained between the surrender terms as laid down at Potsdam and the terms of reference of the Konoye mission. A channel for sounding out the Japanese was available: Allen Dulles's group in Switzerland had been in contact for months with the Japanese military attaché at Berne, General Okamoto, and a representative of the Japanese navy, Commander Fujimura.[57] No exploratory steps were taken, however, either when the first reports about the Konoye mission reached Washington or after the drafting of the Potsdam Declaration. The American position seems to have been that nothing was needed besides the Declaration itself, broadcast *urbi et orbi*. If the Japanese were ready to surrender on the Potsdam terms, they were free to say so. If they did not accept the ultimatum as it stood, this merely proved that they preferred last-ditch resistance. In that case, only increased military pressure could convince them that they were beaten and had to accept the Potsdam terms. Since the Declaration itself expressly ruled out any bargaining, confidential contacts were deemed superfluous.

According to this reasoning, there could be only one conceivable reason for a Japanese failure to surrender without delay on the terms proclaimed at Potsdam, namely, Japan's hope that prolonged resistance would force the Allies to make further concessions. The Allies ruled out the possibility that the Japanese might refrain from bowing to the Potsdam ultimatum for a different reason. Actually, such a reason did exist: the Japanese expected last-minute diplomatic help from Soviet Russia. As we have seen, the American government was fully informed about Japan's move in this direction, the Konoye mission. American policymakers did not, however, reckon with the possibility that the Japanese might still be waiting for Russian mediation even after the Potsdam Declaration had been issued. They assumed that the Konoye mission was dead and buried, in so far as the Japanese government was concerned, and Stalin's statement about the Japanese feeler and the Soviet response to it confirmed them in this belief.

What Stalin disclosed to Truman and Attlee was the Soviet government's reply to the first communication received from Tokyo: the imperial message was too general in form and the Soviet government could not act on it unless more specific proposals were made. But Stalin failed to tell Truman and Attlee that when a clarification was supplied by Tokyo on the 25th, the Soviet government still did not tell the Japanese whether it would or would not act as a mediator, but promised to give a definite answer on this point later. According to President Truman's account, a summary of the clarification, trans-

mitted by Sato from Moscow, was read to Stalin in Truman's presence on July 28. Having listened to it, "Stalin
declared that there was nothing new in it except that it
was more definite than the previous approach and that
it would receive a more definite answer. . . . The
answer would be in the negative, he said."[58] Stalin said
nothing about having encouraged the Japanese to wait
for an answer.

Even so, it is somewhat strange that the Western
leaders did not press Stalin for further details about what
he had told the Japanese. Had they been more alert,
they would have noticed that the information relayed
by Stalin did leave open the possibility of a deliberate
Russian tactic serving to keep Japan's hopes for mediation alive. But they paid no attention to this aspect of
the matter; they seem to have been satisfied with Stalin's
assurances that Russia was in no way interested in helping the Japanese escape unconditional surrender and left
it at that. Stalin thus was able to keep the Western leaders convinced of his loyalty as an ally without giving
away his own diplomatic game.

Stalin's strategy was entirely successful: both the
Japanese and the Western Allies were hoodwinked. The
Japanese assumed that immediate acceptance of the Potsdam ultimatum was not justified as long as there was a
chance that Moscow would obtain a mitigation of its
terms. The Allies remained in the dark about the fact
that Moscow deliberately confirmed the Japanese in this
belief. The result was that the Japanese still were tem-
porizing after the Potsdam Declaration had been issued,
and that the Americans attributed this to an unimpaired
Japanese will to fight.

Things were made worse by Premier Suzuki's incredibly inept handling of the situation. When the Potsdam ultimatum was received in Tokyo, the Vice-Minister of Foreign Affairs, Shunichi Matsumoto, favored immediate acceptance.[59] Foreign Minister Togo, although opposed to outright rejection, advised that, before Japan accepted the terms, one more attempt should be made with Moscow's help to obtain a clarification and, if possible, a mitigation of them.[60] The representatives of the army urged outright rejection of the ultimatum. The cabinet, after listening to all these opinions, decided on July 27 to give no answer for the time being but to ascertain Soviet intentions. Since it was impossible, however, to withhold the Potsdam Declaration from the public, the cabinet decided to publish it without comment, pending further contact with Moscow.

After the meeting, Premier Suzuki proceeded to inform the journalists of the cabinet's decision. He did not content himself with saying that the Japanese government would abstain from making any comment for the time being. He used, instead, a colloquial expression, *mokusatsu*, the literal meaning of which is "to kill with silence."[61] This Japanese term carries a special connotation: contemptuous dismissal of something as not worthy of any attention whatever.[62]

On July 28, "mokusatsu" got into the newspapers on instructions from the government. At the same time, War Minister Anami and his clique redoubled their efforts to have the ultimatum rejected, and Premier Suzuki at a press conference used the same expression again, adding that Japan would "press forward to carry the war to a successful conclusion." This did not correspond to the decisions made by the cabinet. Suzuki apparently had decided not to divulge these decisions but to mislead the public. Such behavior has been frequent in analogous situations: Badoglio also talked in public about continuing the war when his real intention was to get out of it, and Dönitz did the same. It is a delicate matter for a government to tell the people that it has decided to capitulate, for this involves the danger of an immediate collapse of discipline. Moreover, an open announcement that Japan was about to surrender, before the step was accomplished and supported by the Emperor's authority, would very probably have provoked a revolt by the extremists who headed the army, thus nullifying the government's peace policy. The Allied statesmen, however, were not in a mood to make allowances for the difficulties in which the Japanese government was entangled. Suzuki's statement was taken at face value and led to the decision in Washington that Japan would be brought to her knees by the "full application of military power," meaning the dropping of the atomic bomb.[63]

The Atomic Bombs and Surrender

The two atomic bombs that the United States had available were dropped on August 6 and 9 on the cities of Hiroshima and Nagasaki, respectively. Japan's surrender offer, on the Potsdam terms interpreted as implying that the Emperor would not be removed, followed on August 10. Thus Japan surrendered without a final battle on the beaches involving large Allied and Japanese casualties, and, since the surrender occurred within a few days after the atomic bombs were dropped, it seemed plausible enough to assume that the saving of these lives was due to the use of the bomb.

Several high United States officials stated after the

war that the atomic bombs, by ensuring Japan's quick and virtually unconditional surrender, shortened the war and saved many lives that otherwise would have been lost during the last stage. According to a British writer,

President Truman stated in a speech on August 9, 1945, three days after the first bomb was dropped: "We have used it in order to shorten the agony of war, in order to save the lives of thousands and thousands of young Americans." Then, on October 3rd, in a message to Congress, he said: "Almost two months have passed since the atomic bomb was used against Japan. That bomb did not win the war, but it certainly shortened the war. We know it saved the lives of untold thousands of American and Allied soldiers who otherwise would have been killed in battle."[64]

James F. Byrnes, who was Secretary of State at the time of the Japanese surrender, also suggested that it was necessary to drop the bombs in order to induce the Japanese to surrender. He wrote:

Had the Japanese Government listened to Sato and surrendered unconditionally, it would not have been necessary to drop the atomic bomb. But his advice was ignored as the militarists clamored for a negotiated peace. . . . The Japanese Cabinet did not decide to surrender until the atomic bomb had been dropped on Hiroshima.[65]

In his article published in *Harper's Magazine* for February, 1947, dealing with the same question,[66] Secretary Stimson similarly argues that the bombs had to be dropped in order to overcome Japanese reluctance to surrender. His main point is that before the dropping of the bombs the Japanese leadership's behavior did not suggest any readiness to renounce the use of Japan's still formidable fighting capacity in a last, desperate struggle. The Potsdam ultimatum was flatly rejected by the Japanese. The United States government could not know how firm that attitude was or whether the Japanese would have shown themselves more tractable without additional military pressure of a dramatic kind. According to Stimson, in order to ensure Japan's "quick and complete surrender," it was necessary to give the Japanese an object lesson in what was involved in the rejection of the Potsdam ultimatum:

On July 28 the Premier of Japan, Suzuki, rejected the Potsdam ultimatum by announcing that it was "unworthy of public notice." In the face of this rejection we could only proceed to demonstrate that the ultimatum had meant exactly what it said when it stated that if the Japanese continued the war, "the full application of our military power, backed by our resolve, will mean the inevitable and complete destruction of the Japanese armed forces and just as inevitably the utter devastation of the Japanese homeland." For such a purpose the atomic bomb was an eminently suitable weapon. . . .[67]

This theory, however, was challenged by the report of the USSBS team that interviewed many Japanese policymakers after the war in an effort to determine the role played by the bombs and the Russian declaration of war in precipitating Japan's surrender. The Survey's conclusion is presented in the following terms:

Based on a detailed investigation of all the facts and supported by the testimony of the surviving Japanese leaders involved, it is the Survey's opinion that certainly prior to December 31, 1945, and in all probability prior to November 1, 1945, Japan would have surrendered even if the atomic bombs had not been dropped, even if Russia had not entered the war, and even if no invasion had been planned or contemplated.[68]

The Survey's conclusion was based on evidence dealing with the gradual strengthening of the peace trend among Japanese policymakers. According to the Survey, the composition of the successive Japanese cabinets after 1944 clearly revealed such a trend, and Suzuki was appointed Premier on April 7, 1945, for the sole purpose of ending the war. The attempts to "negotiate" undertaken by the Suzuki cabinet were mere pretense, the Survey suggests. Since there was a large contingent of die-hards in the armed services, the cabinet was unable to offer surrender openly, but would have agreed to it *in extremis* if nothing better could be obtained. The policy-makers were afraid of the die-hards, but they knew that Japan no longer had the means to continue resistance and had to end the war on whatever terms she could. The atomic bomb was not needed to bring the hopelessness of the situation home to them. Even without such an "argument," they would have admitted defeat.

This analysis, though correct in its main outline, fails to mention an important point: although Japan's political leaders were willing to capitulate, they neither could nor would do so unless the United States *expressly* agreed to spare the imperial institution. Kido, the "senior states-man," the civilian members of the cabinet, and some navy chiefs had long recognized defeat as an accomplished fact, and they were anxious to end the war on almost any terms. Yet even this group recognized no alternative to a suicidal last stand within the home islands should the Allies prove unwilling to spare the imperial institution. As to the military extremists around Anami, the War Minister, they talked until the very end as if they thought that the "last battle" in the islands would turn the tide. This seems to have been empty rhetoric: when pressed, the military chiefs could offer no hard facts to back up their claim. While talking about "victory in the last battle," they quite probably knew that the "last bat-tle" would be a quixotic, suicidal venture. But they were absolutely determined to lead their army into such a holo-caust if the Emperor gave the word, and as we shall see, they were trying to the last to persuade the Emperor to do that very thing. Thus the decision lay with the Emperor and his advisers. And, for this group, "admitting defeat" was not the crucial factor on which their decision depended. The decisive question was, rather, whether the Allies would modify "unconditional surrender" to the extent of sparing the imperial institution. This concession required that the Emperor himself choose surrender and rule out resistance at the beaches, something which, as we have seen, he was very willing to do. The American policymakers unfortunately were not aware of this and therefore thought that the solution of the problem lay in increased military pressure. This miscalculation was well-nigh unavoidable under the circumstances. Everything conspired to mislead Washington on the real nature of the problem of the Japanese surrender. The Japanese government gave the impression of rejecting the Potsdam Declaration, and the United States government could hardly guess that the failure of the Japanese to accede immediately to the Potsdam terms meant simply that they were maneuvering to surrender through a circuitous route.

Secretary Stimson, writing in 1947, admitted that, since "a large element of the Japanese cabinet was ready in the spring to accept substantially the same terms as those finally agreed on," an early and unequivocal announcement of the concession dimly adumbrated at Potsdam might have been sufficient to ensure surrender.

It is possible, in the light of the final surrender, that a clearer and earlier exposition of American willingness to retain the Emperor would have produced an earlier ending to the war; this course was earnestly advocated by Grew and his immediate associates during May, 1945.[69]

Curiously, however, Stimson asserted in the same article: "All the evidence I have seen indicates that the controlling factor in the final Japanese decision to accept our terms of surrender was the atomic bomb."[70] In other words, the Japanese would have surrendered without being bombed, if the United States had clearly declared its readiness to retain the Emperor; in the absence of such a declaration, the atomic bomb was needed to make them surrender on the same basis.

Stimson argues, too, that the very nature of the conflict compelled the United States to persevere in the most destructive warfare possible, including use of the atomic bomb, as long as the Japanese failed to announce their readiness to surrender. To be sure, there had been reports about Japanese peace feelers.

But such reports merely stimulated the American leaders in their desire to press home on *all* Japanese leaders the hopelessness of their cause; this was the nature of warmaking. In war, as in a boxing match, it is seldom sound for the stronger combatant to moderate his blows whenever his opponent shows signs of weakening. To Stimson, at least, the only road to early victory was to exert maximum force with maximum speed. It was not the American responsibility to throw in the sponge for the Japanese; that was one thing they must do for themselves. Only on the question of the Emperor did Stimson take, in 1945, a conciliatory view; only on this question did he later believe that history might find that the U.S., by its delay in stating its position, had prolonged the war.[71]

This argument suggests a very serious misconception of the "nature of warmaking." It is true that exerting "maximum force with maximum speed" is necessary in order to reach a strategic decision. But once the strategic decision has been reached, the "nature of warmaking," or, if you like, a rational economy of warfare, prescribes the quickest and least costly transition from violence to nonviolence, and this aim is not likely to be achieved by intensifying the destructiveness of the war during its terminal stage. In this context the analogy with a boxing match is quite misleading, for a boxing match lacks anything comparable to the "terminal stage" of such a war as World War II. A boxer who is behind on points still has a chance of knocking out his opponent with a lucky blow, and the stronger boxer has good reason not to relax lest his opponent take advantage of such an opportunity. During the terminal stage of war, however, the loser cannot change the strategic outcome. The victor's problem is to induce him not to engage in operations that are strategically meaningless and will merely inflict superfluous losses on both adversaries.

That this was the problem facing the United States in the summer of 1945 was clear to the American policy-makers. They were not concerned that Japan might find an opening and knock out the United States. Their objective was to avoid a last battle whose outcome was a foregone conclusion but which would have been extremely costly. The problem was not whether and how Japan could be defeated but how she could be induced to capitulate before an invasion battle.

There might well be differences of opinion about the best method for achieving this objective. It was not absurd to suppose that more devastation of their homeland might induce the Japanese die-hards to change their minds about the final battle, even though it could be doubted that more devastation would have a decisive effect on people so desperate that they were ready to sacrifice themselves anyway. But the human and material cost of persevering in a maximally destructive form of warfare during the terminal stage could be justified only on the assumption that this course *alone* could lead to surrender before invasion. Once it was recognized that another method, that of accepting surrender on minimal terms, could achieve the same objective, the principles of strategy did not dictate the continuation of a maximally destructive form of warfare. The victor would incur no risk by exploring the possibility of obtaining capitulation without an invasion by political concessions, or by forgoing attempts to achieve the same result by maximal destruction.

Now the path of maximal destruction was not the only one open to the United States. On the contrary, the data that have come to light since the war indicate that it was the nonviolent method *alone* that could lead to capitulation without invasion, and that the alternative method, that of stepped-up violence, could not do so. The American government could not know this: the Soviet maneuver of deception about the Japanese peace mission, together with the inept Japanese reaction to Potsdam, thoroughly confused the picture.

Now that the facts are available, there can be no doubt that the American readiness to spare the Emperor's position alone induced the Japanese to surrender. The note conditionally accepting the Potsdam terms, sent by the Japanese on August 10, after the bombs were dropped and after Russia entered the war, still reserved last-ditch resistance as the only course open to Japan unless the Allies explicitly agreed not to remove the Emperor. True, the note was sent the day after the second atom bomb attack, but it would have been sent on or about August 10 even if no atomic attacks had taken place. The main factor that determined the timing of the surrender note was the Soviet declaration of war. It finally dispelled the illusions the Japanese leaders had entertained up to that time concerning Russian mediation. We may say in this sense that the Soviet declaration of war played a bigger role in triggering Japan's final move to make a direct offer of surrender than did the atomic bombs.

Not that the intervention of the Soviet armies was needed to convince the Japanese that their situation was militarily hopeless. The point is that until Russia's declaration of war the Japanese government, anxious to obtain the best possible surrender terms from the Allies, preferred acting through the Moscow channel to approaching the Allies directly. After the sudden closing of that channel, the only possibility still open was to ask Washington directly whether the Potsdam terms actually implied sparing the Emperor. Japan finally surrendered when Washington gave a favorable answer on this point.

The "end-the-war group," to use Butow's apt phrase for the Emperor and his circle, obviously did not need the stimulus of the atomic bomb to offer surrender on the Potsdam terms. But what about the military extremists? Did they not need the atomic flash over Hiroshima to see the light? Did they not finally abandon their uncompromising stand because the atomic bomb softened their dour spirit? And was it not such a change in the army's attitude that finally enabled the Emperor to offer surrender?

We are now in a position to answer these questions unequivocally. We know the details of the policy discussions that immediately preceded the sending of the surrender note. After the dropping of the bombs the discussions show no manifest change in the attitudes held by either the end-the-war group or the military extremists. The deadlock in the Supreme War Council and the cabinet persisted after Hiroshima and Nagasaki, and even after the Soviet declaration of war. It was not a change in the attitude of the military leaders that enabled the Emperor to offer surrender, but the fact that the Emperor was the strongest factor in the political setup then existing. He was not obliged to defer to the military.

The decision to send the note offering conditional surrender was made at an imperial conference[72] that convened shortly before midnight on August 9, after Soviet Russia had declared war. At that meeting Foreign Minister Togo proposed that a note *conditionally* accepting the Potsdam terms be sent immediately to neutral capitals for transmission to Washington. The military chiefs, asked for their opinion, passionately rejected this proposal. Anami advocated continuing the war and fighting a "decisive" battle in the homeland, in order to force the enemy to grant Japan better terms than those of Potsdam. The Army Chief of Staff, Umezu, spoke in the same vein, and so did the Navy Chief of Staff, Toyoda. In the course of the discussion, the question of the military significance of Soviet Russia's entry into the war was touched on, and Umezu said that even that event could not change his mind. The atomic bombs were also mentioned only in passing, with an army spokesman suggesting that further bombings could be stopped by antiaircraft defense.[73]

Stimson tells us that "all the evidence" he had seen indicated that the atomic bomb was "the controlling factor in the final Japanese decision to accept our terms of surrender." (It would be interesting to know what that evidence was.) Had this been true, the advocates of capitulation presumably would have made much of the atomic bombings in their arguments. In such a case we can imagine either Togo or the Emperor himself (who carried the ball for the antiwar group) arguing with the military in some such terms as these: "Up to now, a reversal of the unfavorable military situation, though we did not really believe in it, has been at least conceivable. But now that the Americans are dropping atomic bombs, even you must admit that resistance is futile. We must surrender, and we must do it at once, before they drop a third bomb on one of our cities." This argument, however, was conspicuously absent from the Emperor's case for surrender. What he said was something entirely different. He argued with the military on their own level. "There are those," he declared, "who say that the key to national survival lies in a decisive battle in the homeland. The experiences of the past, however, show that there has always been a discrepancy between plans and performance. I do not believe that the discrepancy in the case of *Kujukurihama* [the "national redoubt" the army said it was readying] can be rectified. Since this is the shape of things, how can we repel the invaders?"[4] And that was that. The Emperor made the army "lose face" once and for all, by using the stock argument of the antiwar group that army performance never measured up to army talk. The Emperor's specific point about the "redoubt" had been served up to him by Kido in a memorandum submitted on July 25, nearly two weeks before the first atomic bomb was dropped. This strongly indicates that the political strategy by which the army was to be outmaneuvered had firmly crystallized before the bombs fell. The only reason this strategy was not applied earlier was that *direct* conditional surrender could not be envisaged before Moscow gave an answer, one way or another.

It cannot be said, of course, that the atomic bombing of Hiroshima and Nagasaki played no role whatsoever in the Japanese deliberations leading to the decision to offer surrender. Togo, who reported to the Emperor on the Hiroshima bombing two days after the event, "impressed upon the Emperor the urgency of the situation and the necessity of terminating the war at once on the basis of the Potsdam Proclamation."[75] The Emperor concurred. According to a statement by Kido, the Emperor said on hearing the news of Hiroshima: "Under these circumstances, we must bow to the inevitable. No matter what the effect on my safety, we must put an end to this war as speedily as possible so that this tragedy will not be repeated."[76]

Since the Japanese could not know that only two bombs were available, they had to reckon with the possibility that more bombs would be dropped, and this probably contributed to the extreme haste with which the surrender note was prepared and debated. Had the threat of further bombings not hung over Japan, the imperial council might have been convoked at a more convenient time than midnight. But this effect on the timing was trivial. In fact, even the speedy Japanese answer involved a gamble, for the surrender offer was still only conditional, and Tokyo could not be sure that the United States was still willing to treat on the basis of the Potsdam concession. Had Washington changed its mind, the conditional Japanese offer would have ensured further bombings, supposing that more bombs were available. But the Japanese government took this risk because it could not do otherwise. The atomic bombs, far from being the "controlling" factor, caused no significant reorientation of attitudes, no manifest change in points of view.

Can it be said that the atomic bombs made a difference

to the outcome of the final debates, in the sense that they decisively weakened the moral position of the military group? Butow suggests that this factor did play a part:

It was not that the military men had suddenly become reasonable in the hours following the Hiroshima and Nagasaki disasters; it was rather that they . . . had momentarily been caught off balance. They were also at a loss for words which could make any lasting impression upon the end-the-war faction. Prior to the dropping of the two A-bombs they had been able to pledge their belief in their ability to meet effectively any action taken by the enemy, but now whatever they said made them look foolish and insincere.[77]

It may well be that the impression produced by the bombings contributed to pointing up the emptiness of the army's pretensions, even though, as we have seen, the clinching argument used by the Emperor made no reference to it. It is impossible, of course, to ascertain what the attitudes of the military would have been if the atomic bombings had not taken place. Nevertheless it seems unreasonable to suppose that the imperial council, had it been faced with the Soviet declaration of war but not with atomic bombings, would have decided against the direct approach and in favor of a last-ditch battle.

Another "if" question may also be considered. What would have happened if the bombs had been dropped on August 6 and 9 but no Soviet declaration of war had occurred? Would the Japanese government then have decided in favor of the direct approach without waiting further for Moscow's mediation? This question is more difficult to answer than the preceding one. It may be argued that the bombs would have provided a sufficient stimulus for direct surrender, but the contrary assumption seems more probable to the present writer. As long as the hope for mediation by Moscow was not dead, the Japanese government would probably have clung to it.

Speculations about the timing of the surrender, however, are quite irrelevant. After all, the vital question from the American point of view was not whether the Japanese government surrendered in August or in September, but whether it could or could not be induced to surrender without offering last-ditch resistance. From this point of view, it was not the exact timing of the surrender that counted, but the nature of the final choice. The evidence shows that the final decision for or against a last-ditch battle did not hinge on the atomic bomb or any other military consideration. It was a political matter.

The army chiefs were by no means as strongly committed to the last battle as may appear from what has been said above. At bottom they recognized the futility of such an operation, and those among them who still possessed a scintilla of realism and a sense of responsibility looked upon all-out resistance not as an end in itself but as a means to get the best possible terms. In this respect, the gulf separating them from the end-the-war group was not very wide. The latter, too, saw no alternative to a suicidal last stand in case the United States refused to guarantee the Emperor's tenure. The militarists' last argument against capitulation was that the American guarantee was not clear and unequivocal enough.

After the American answer to Japan's surrender note was received, the army chiefs made a last, desperate effort to drop the surrender policy and revert to that of last-ditch resistance. But the argument they used was not that surrender was unthinkable in principle. They maintained, rather, that the American answer of August 11 did not meet Japan's minimum condition, the retention of the imperial institution.[78]

The American answer, indeed, conceded the Emperor's tenure only by implication, stating that "from the moment of surrender the authority of the Emperor and the Japanese Government to rule the state shall be subject to the Supreme Commander of the Allied powers," and even adding that "the ultimate form of government of Japan shall, in accordance with the Potsdam Declaration, be established by the freely expressed will of the Japanese people.[79]

The crisis caused by the American answer was once again solved by the Emperor's direct intervention: at another imperial council meeting, on August 13, he "commanded" the cabinet to accept the American answer as satisfactory.[80]

As we have seen, the last supporters of last-ditch resistance took their stand because they doubted whether Japan's minimum terms for capitulation had been met. This had been the crucial issue all along, and it remained an issue after the dropping of the bombs. Whatever effect the bombing of Hiroshima and Nagasaki may have had on the thinking of the Japanese political and military leadership, the choice between last-ditch resistance and capitulation did not depend on it. That choice was governed by the political payment on which the Japanese insisted and had to insist—the retention of the Emperor. Had this not been conceded, the chances are that the Japanese would have felt compelled to resist to the last. This concession, rather than the dropping of the bombs, saved the lives that would have been lost in the invasion of Japan.

EVALUATION OF THE UNITED STATES SURRENDER POLICY

Could the Japanese surrender have been brought about before August 10-14 if the United States had applied different methods of political warfare? Stimson, as we have seen, thought so after the war: he believed that the American failure to offer assurances about the Emperor resulted in a prolongation of the war. According to the present analysis, this view oversimplifies the matter: the war would have been prolonged until Soviet Russia's entry into it even if the American concession had been formulated unequivocally earlier, since the Japanese were angling for still better terms as long as the illusory Moscow channel was open.

Had direct and confidential channels of communication been established with the Japanese government, it is conceivable that the United States would have been able to clarify the situation and to disabuse the Japanese of their illusions. The operational rules followed by both sides, however, precluded the establishment of such a direct channel. The Japanese put out many feelers, but they never sent anybody abroad with official instructions to discuss surrender terms with the United States. Although direct contacts with the United States were necessary to dispel the Japanese illusions about the Moscow channel, these very illusions prevented Tokyo from even considering such contacts. On the American side, on the other hand, confidential conversations with the enemy for the purpose of determining a possible basis for surrender were ruled out on principle. The prolongation of the war until August was the result of these two rigidities. The Japanese attitude being what it was, the United States could have broken the log jam only if it had made a very determined effort to establish contact with the beaten enemy.

But could a victorious power be expected to embark on such a course? Was it not up to the loser to take the initiative? One might argue that elementary considerations of prestige necessarily prevent winners from taking the initiative for confidential surrender talks. But this argument, echoed by Stimson in his dictum that the United States could not do the surrendering for Japan, does not seem to be absolutely valid. The closest analogy to the terminal situation in the war with Japan was not a "boxing match," as Stimson supposed, but the siege of a fortress. And in a siege situation it is natural for the strong besieger to initiate contacts with the besieged party with a view to securing surrender so as to avoid the necessity of storming the fortress. Further, such contacts should properly be confidential. If the besieger wants to avoid having to take the fortress by storm, he is well advised not to limit himself to public appeals for surrender while he waits for the commander of the fortress to run up a white flag.

One may speculate on what the course of events would have been if the American government had handled the situation on the "siege," rather than the "boxing match," analogy. The author believes that the former procedure would have led to Japan's surrender before the Soviets entered the war, resulting in a far more favorable postwar balance of power in the Far East. But this approach was precluded by the prevailing rules of unconditionality.[81]

Another, more fundamental misconception also vi-

tiated the strategic and political handling of the last
stage of the war with Japan: the failure to distinguish
between defeating an enemy and obtaining surrender
from him. The United States acted as if the problem
were that of defeating Japan, when in fact the problem
was to avoid an unnecessary last battle *after* Japan was
defeated. The same misconception prevented the United
States from assessing the real significance of Japanese
last-ditch resistance. Since the American leaders could
not keep the concepts of "defeat" and "surrender" apart,
they saw in Japanese resistance at Iwo and Okinawa proof
that the Japanese did not recognize that they were defeated and needed convincing.

Some uncertainty, of course, is always involved in
estimating at any given time whether strategic victory
has been achieved or whether the enemy acknowledges
his strategic defeat and is ready to act accordingly. The
Allies' terminal policy toward Japan, however, did not
go astray because of faulty intelligence on these points.
Its basic flaw was, rather, a defect of doctrine. All terminal resistance whatsoever was regarded as necessarily
incompatible with the enemy's awareness of his strategic defeat. (As we have seen above, even Italian terminal resistance was interpreted along such lines.)

Not only does this fundamental error prevent the
winner from doing what the terminal situation requires;
it also warps his strategic plans by inducing him to treat
the question of strategic victory as an open one when it
no longer is so. This is what happened during the last
stage of the Pacific war, with disastrous consequences.
Impressed by the strength of Japan's residual capabilities, the United States came to the conclusion that Russian help was needed to "defeat" Japan.

Stalin was able to exploit this American feeling for his own ends. When he told Roosevelt at Teheran that "by our common front we shall defeat Japan," he wanted to put it on record that Japan could not be defeated by the Western Allies' unaided effort. In 1943 there were still legitimate doubts about this. But by the end of 1944, when Japan's fleet and air force were practically nonexistent and all that the Allies faced was terminal resistance, there was no justification for basing strategy on a joint effort to "defeat" Japan. It is true that American belief in the necessity for Russian help grew weaker as Japan's military position weakened, but the agreements entered into earlier could no longer be undone.

The fact that the preferred method for forcing Japan into surrender was that of stepping up destructive warfare reflects the same misconception. That method culminated in the dropping of the atomic bombs, an act that constituted a heavy moral liability for the United States and that, as now seems certain, made no essential contribution to Japan's surrender without a last battle. The American government, of course, could not know at that time what we know now, and those who made the decision were convinced that many lives, American as well as Japanese, would be saved by it. But this conviction would not have prevailed if the nature of the problem of obtaining surrender, as distinct from that of achieving defeat and impressing this fact on the enemy, had been clearly realized.

The final American decision to spare the Emperor's position, which made possible capitulation without the final holocaust, shows that the American government was by no means wholly blind to the nature of the problem of surrender. Although its strategic doctrine was deficient in this respect, it turned out to be impossible not to be "disarmed" by Japan's residual strength. Moreover, there were well-informed and intelligent people in policymaking positions whose knowledge of Japanese conditions enabled them to hit upon the right approach. Thus American surrender policy avoided what would have been the worst of the disasters toward which the cult of "unconditional surrender" was pressing.

CONCLUSIONS

The Japanese surrender illustrates the use of a defeated power's residual strength, combined with an insular position and an extreme will to resist, for the purpose of obtaining political concessions in return for surrender. Although the minimum condition posed by Japan was extremely unpalatable to the most vocal section of American opinion, and although it challenged an essential part of the American doctrine of unconditional surrender, Japan turned out to have a sufficiently strong bargaining position to get the condition accepted. American interest in cutting losses was the chief factor in Japan's bargaining strength.

The reorientation of Japan, i.e., the redistribution of political influence within Japan whereby the military leadership was toppled from its dominant position, failed to produce a notable disarming effect on the Allies, because they had no idea of the power struggle that had taken place within Japan. The political complexion of the group around the Emperor and the Emperor's own attitude were totally unknown to all but a tiny number of Americans. So far as the American public was concerned, Japan, with the Emperor as her ruler, was still unregenerate when she surrendered. In spite of this, the disarming tendency became dominant over tendencies toward hostility.

The Japanese surrender also illustrates the importance of communications during the "interaction" phase preceding surrender. The defectiveness of channels, due to extreme rigidity on both sides, needlessly dragged out the process of liquidating hostilities that no longer had a strategic meaning. The lack of communications was thoroughly exploited by the Soviet leadership, which was able to inject itself as a controlling factor into the surrender process, owing to the radically mistaken political strategy adopted by the Japanese.

PART THREE

UNCONDITIONAL SURRENDER

Seven

THE ALLIES' POLICY
IN WORLD WAR II

THE MEANING AND RULES OF UNCONDITIONAL
SURRENDER

It was axiomatic with the Allies that the war had to be fought to total victory. Since the strategy employed was that of attrition, this meant fighting until the enemy was reduced to surrender. Moreover, the peace terms were to be unilaterally imposed rather than negotiated. All this, however, did not necessarily imply that surrender was to be unconditional. The Allies could decide to announce their political terms while the war was in progress and still insist on the enemies' capitulation. This procedure, however, was ruled out. As Cordell Hull put it,

We . . . concluded that it would be unfortunate were any of these three governments [the United States, Great Britain, and Soviet Russia] to express any willingness to enter into commitments regarding specific terms of the postwar settlement. We would, of course, expect a continuation of discussions among the several governments toward the fullest possible agreement on basic policies and toward later agreements at the proper time and with public knowledge. When Hitler was defeated, the Soviet Government would participate no less than Britain and the United States in an effort to restore peace and order. But no commitments as to individual countries should be entered into at this time lest they jeopardize the aims we all shared in common, looking toward an enduring peace. It would be unfortunate if we approached the peace conference thus hampered.[1]

The belief that specific agreements among the Allies on the peace terms to be imposed would jeopardize lasting peace was one of the elements of the unconditional-surrender policy as it developed during the war. There was, however, more to that policy than the decision to leave the formulation of precise terms until after victory. According to President Roosevelt and his advisers, the ultimate aim of securing a permanently peaceful postwar world was also bound up with the manner in which the enemy's surrender would be handled. They considered this neither a short-range nor a technical problem. The entire political future hinged on it, since the handling of surrender would determine whether or not all the roots of aggression were pulled up. The policy of unconditional surrender was specifically designed to make sure that the winners, in accepting surrender, would not unwittingly permit the survival of potential forces of aggression.

We may distinguish two stages in the development of the policy of unconditional surrender: (1) the pre-terminal stage, concerned with psychological and political warfare on the theme of victory and lasting peace; and (2) the terminal stage, in which the Allies specified rigid rules governing their relations with the surrendering enemy.

When President Roosevelt proclaimed the principle of "unconditional surrender" at the close of the Casablanca Conference on January 24, 1943, it struck those present as a casual improvisation. Roosevelt himself told Hopkins later that the phrase just "popped into his mind;"[2] and Churchill, speaking to the House of Commons on July 21, 1949, said that he first heard the expression when Roosevelt used it at the Casablanca press conference. In a later Commons debate (November 17, 1949), and in his war memoirs, however, Churchill corrected this statement. Examining his papers, he found that the Casablanca communiqué, including the phrase "unconditional surrender," had been discussed with the President beforehand (January 20), and even submitted to the British War Cabinet, which approved it.[3] The U.S. Joint Chiefs of Staff had discussed this formula earlier, on January 7.[4] These facts suggest that the principle was not conceived on the spur of the moment, but was an organic part of Allied thinking about the problems of war, victory, and peace.[5]

This policy of unconditional surrender represented a studied contrast with President Wilson's political conduct of the war in 1918. Wilson had laid down the principles on which the peace settlement was to be based. The Fourteen Points proclaimed, in essence, that all self-aggrandizement was to be forsworn at the peace table. The weakness of the losing powers would not result in their losing territory unless justice and the principle of national self-determination required it.

President Roosevelt and his advisers felt that the Germans had been left with the impression that they had quit in 1918 not because they had been defeated but because they had been offered acceptable terms. Moreover, within a few years the Germans considered their moral and material position strong enough to permit them to reopen the issues of 1919 on the grounds that the settlement imposed upon them at Versailles was at variance with the Fourteen Points. The American leaders were determined to prevent similar developments after World War II. Allied political warfare had to steer clear of all moral commitments toward the enemy; the role of superior force in deciding the war must be made as impressive as possible. That, and that alone, could ensure a lasting peace. In view of these requirements, the policy of unconditional surrender seemed the most suitable basis for the conduct of political and psychological warfare.[6] In addition, by strengthening the Western Allies' determination to pursue the war to total victory, it served to forestall German attempts to split the United Nations coalition.[7]

The "anti-Wilsonian" aspect of the unconditional surrender policy was negative rather than positive: the Allies would refrain from committing themselves to any postwar policy that would entail the slightest concession to the enemy, although the possibility of such concessions, freely granted by the Allies if and when they deemed fit, was by no means excluded.[8]

As to a positive formulation of the aftermath of unconditional surrender, there was broad agreement among the coalition members on a number of the terms to be imposed.[9] Stalin insisted that these be publicly specified, but Churchill and Roosevelt were unwilling to go along with his proposal.[10] They felt that publication of even severe terms would smack of surrender "on terms" and had to be ruled out for that reason.

As the terminal stage of hostilities drew near, however, it appeared imperative not to leave the implications of the unconditional-surrender principle wholly indeterminate, but to define some precise rules for dealing with enemy governments suing for peace.

What were these "rules of unconditionality"? First, there was the "no negotiation" rule, prescribing that there could be no dealings with enemy leaders except to instruct them about details of orderly capitulation.

Second, there was the "no recognition" or "vacuum" rule, prescribing that immediately after capitulation the enemy leaders would cease to exercise any political authority whatever, and that no other indigenous body would be recognized as representing the losing society —i.e., the enemy's acceptance of a political vacuum at the top was made a necessary condition for ending hostilities. The vacuum was to exist during a transitional period, which would fill the gap between the termination of active hostilities and the establishment of normal interstate relations, and during which top governmental functions in the losing countries would be exercised by military governments installed by the winners.[11]

These rules made no allowance for any reorientation of the loser's policy by defeatist elements within the existing war-making regime. To the morally oriented Allies, any abatement from the strict rules of unconditionality meant that some element of the evil past would survive after the loser's surrender and make their victory meaningless and worthless. The Allies' aim was to introduce democratic forms into the countries that had been wrested from totalitarian rule, but this could be done, they believed, only by first creating in each of these countries a political vacuum.

APPLICATION OF THE RULES OF UNCONDITIONALITY

It was not easy to put the rules of unconditionality into effect. Sooner or later the Allies had to face the fact that the creation of a political vacuum could coincide with surrender only if surrender were delayed until the losing nation was occupied. This happened in Germany, which was fully occupied before it formally capitulated. Italy and Japan, however, were summoned

to surrender, and did so, before the Allies were in occupation, with the result that their surrender could not
be handled on the basis of the strict unconditionality
rules.

Neither Italy nor Japan could be occupied unless
the Allies first sacrificed the vacuum policy. In Japan's
case, occupation before the conclusion of a surrender
agreement, though certainly feasible, would have been
too costly. Japan was strategically defeated, but her
insular position and her possession of large, cohesive,
and determined residual forces would have enabled her
to inflict heavy losses on an invading force. The Allies
therefore had a strong interest in obtaining surrender
before occupation, and the Japanese were willing to
offer it, but only on condition that the Allies confirm
the Emperor as Japan's nominal sovereign. Renunciation of the political vacuum in return for avoiding heavy
losses during the terminal stage of the war appeared
too advantageous a trade to reject. The service rendered by the Japanese in capitulating was important
enough to outweigh the Allied reluctance to leave remnants of the war regime in place.

Italy's surrender was demanded and accepted on
the basis of the strict unconditionality rule; the Allies
refused to extend recognition to the surrender regime,
reserving their right to remove it after occupation, even
though that regime promised the Allies not only
to cease resistance but to enter the war on the Allied
side. Even this radical reorientation of policy failed
to move the Allies, who saw the Italian abandonment
of terminal resistance merely as leaving them all the
more free to proceed on the basis of their "vacuum
doctrine." Soon after Italy's unconditional surrender,
however, it became apparent that occupation could not

follow immediately because strong German forces barred the way up the peninsula. This made it imperative for the Allies to salvage and utilize all they could of the remaining elements of Italian military strength, even though these were already weak and were deteriorating rapidly. To do so they had to employ the authority of the royal regime. The Allies could neither remove nor ignore the regime without depriving themselves of active Italian cooperation against the Germans. Thus they were compelled to reverse their original position, and to recognize the Italian surrender regime as a cobelligerent less than two months after its unconditional surrender.

Germany's surrender contrasted sharply with Italy's and Japan's. To begin with, no political reorientation preceded it. Even if the 1944 *coup d'état* against Hitler had succeeded, it is doubtful whether the Allies would have made any allowances for a German reorientation; they indicated no readiness to do so. The question did not arise, however, since the German strategic surrender was carried out by remnants of the German war regime that neither repudiated Hitler nor imposed the surrender in opposition to an extreme prowar group.

The Germans' residual forces could not be used as a bargaining counter—i.e., they could not be invoked to induce the advancing Allies to modify their unconditional surrender policy. In fact, German military behavior during the last weeks of the war amounted to throwing away any opportunities that might have existed on this score. During the winter of 1944–45, the Germans had tried to maintain equal defensive pressure on their eastern and western fronts. Later, however, resistance became selective. By April 18, 1945, the entire Army Group B and other elements in the Ruhr had capitulated, and surrender negotiations were in progress on the southern front. Thereafter, the advance of the Western Allies into Germany was only feebly opposed. But German soil was still being stubbornly defended against Soviet forces in the East.[12]

Political considerations obviously influenced this selective pattern of resistance. Although German military leaders did not dare speak openly about surrender to either East or West, their behavior indicated that their real objective was to surrender to the Western Allies alone, while continuing the fight against Russia. Perhaps they thought that the Western Allies might recognize that they needed Germany as an auxiliary against the "common enemy of the West" and hence abandon the coalition. Selective resistance offered the Allies time to revise their coalition policy. Besides that, of course, it demonstrated that the Western Allies were less feared than the Russians.[13]

The Allies accepted the tactical surrender of such German forces in their path as laid down their arms. But when it came to strategic surrender, they insisted on simultaneous action in East and West. The only tangible result that the Germans achieved through their strategy of selective resistance, apart from cutting losses, was the opportunity to transfer military personnel and civilian populations from Soviet- to Western-controlled territory. Stalling during the last few days, when German-held territory had shrunk to almost nothing, gave the Germans the time needed to carry out a considerable salvage operation of that sort. Although they could not split the coalition, they were at least able to use one enemy as a shield against the other. It would have been impossible for the Germans to obtain such a concession by overt talks. The selective use of their residual force, however, enabled them to obtain the desired end, as it were, surreptitiously.

This sequence of events enabled the Allies to handle the German strategic surrender on the basis of the strict unconditionality rules, without having to pay a heavy price in terms of military losses. Surrender occurred only after occupation, but the prolongation of the terminal stage was not costly for the Allies, since the Germans welcomed, rather than opposed, Western occupation. Therefore the priority of the ideological objective over that of cutting losses and securing quick surrender was not put to a real test in Germany, for the two aims were achieved together. When it was put to the test in Italy and Japan, it did not survive.

The Role of the Unconditional-Surrender Formula in Prolonging the War

The unconditional-surrender policy has been severely criticized on the ground that it needlessly prolonged the war.[14] The demand for unconditional surrender, it is argued, rallied the German people behind the war regime and induced them to fight to the last. Faced with the demand for unconditional surrender, which was tantamount to the annihilation of their national existence, the Germans and the other Axis powers had no choice but to fight as long as was physically possible. If a less severe formula had been used in Allied war propaganda, or even if very severe but specified surrender terms had been offered, resistance would have come to an end sooner.[15]

This criticism clearly refers to the negative, "anti-Wilsonian" phase of the unconditional-surrender policy. It is undeniable that the formula, when it was launched, furnished ammunition to Nazi war propaganda. Göbbels made copious use of it to counteract the disastrous effects on morale of the defeats Germany suffered in Africa and at Stalingrad.[16] But this alone does not prove that the unconditional-surrender policy prolonged German resistance.

That the war would have been shorter if the Allies' basic war aim had not been total victory is, of course, true. Ending the war by a negotiated peace would have resulted in a shorter war and possibly in a better political situation after the war. But few critics maintain that this would have been the correct policy.[17] Most critics, rather, take the objective of total victory for granted and argue that it would have been attained more quickly and more easily if a more positive formula than unconditional surrender had been used.

Fuller, for example, maintains that "the Allied policy of unconditional surrender, by deliberately preventing the surrender of Germany on terms, could mean but one of two things to every German—either victory or annihilation."[18]

Actual German behavior during the latter part of the war, however, cannot be squared with this judgment. For Hitler, annihilation was indeed the only alternative to victory, but not because surrender on terms was ruled out by the Allies. The Nazis' official doctrine of the war did not allow for surrender on terms. On the other hand, there were many Germans who saw that the war was lost but who refused to admit that this necessarily meant total national extinction. They looked to a third alternative, recognizing that the solution lay in ending the hopeless struggle by capitulation if necessary. Although it certainly cannot be said that they acquiesced in unconditional surrender, it would be equally wrong to maintain that "surrender on terms" was the only formula to which such Germans would subscribe. As we have seen in the case study of the German surrender, there was no German last-ditch resistance inspired by the feeling, "If you accept surrender on terms, all right, but if you refuse to do so, nothing remains for us to do but go down fighting to the last." This pattern was present in Japanese, but not in German, behavior.

The major stumbling block in the way of an active surrender policy was the fact that, as long as Hitler was commander in chief, no military leader could initiate surrender without becoming guilty of flagrant insubordination. To the typical officer surrender was well-nigh unthinkable, no matter how senseless and suicidal continued resistance appeared to him. Germans had to choose between military rationality, which implied surrender, and military loyalty, which involved continued resistance. For the military leaders, the latter was a moral imperative. In determining their choice, all purely political questions, including unconditional surrender, played a lesser role. The authors of the July 1944 plot certainly hoped to obtain qualified surrender, despite the Allies' verbal insistence on unconditional surrender. They did not conclude from the unconditional-surrender policy that they had no alternative but to continue a hopeless struggle. Those Germans who at that time chose to fight to the end did so more because they could not bring themselves to break faith with the Führer than because of Allied statements.

As pointed out above, German terminal resistance was selective—stubborn in the East, almost nonexistent in the West. Had the slogan of unconditional surrender made all the difference between last-ditch resistance and surrender, this selective resistance could not have happened, especially since the Western Allies practically had a copyright on the slogan. The Russians used mostly themes other than unconditional surrender in their propaganda in Germany. Stalin used the formula in his order of the day of May 1, 1943, in order to allay Allied uneasiness about his seductive propaganda to the Germans, but later (notably in his speech of November 6, 1943) he again reverted to an appealing language that was in open contrast to the Allied handling of the theme of surrender. If use of the slogan was a propagandistic blunder, the Russians largely avoided it, but their sagacity in this respect was by no means rewarded. It was the Western Allies who obtained the advantage of slackening final resistance by Germany.

This indicates that the generally assumed causal relationship between the *formula* of unconditional surrender and the length of the war is illusory. The length of the war was determined largely by other factors, including the Allies' objective of total victory and Hitler's (and the Japanese war extremists') refusal to admit the possibility of any kind of surrender.[19] The terminal behavior of the Germans also indicates that unconditional surrender to the Western Allies was not unthinkable for them; it was the loss of German territory to the Russians that they viewed as the ultimate catastrophe. Lord Hankey's statement, "Not one of the German leaders was willing to sign such humiliating terms as unconditional surrender,"[20] is directly contradicted by the facts:

both anti-Nazi dissidents and Nazi loyalists were willing to do just that, as our case study of the German surrender shows.

Fuller propounds the thesis that the announced policy of unconditional surrender was the reason that hostilities did not end quickly after strategic decision had been reached in the West:

> In a sane war, Rundstedt's defeat in the Ardennes would have brought hostilities to an immediate end; but because of unconditional surrender the war was far from being sane. Gagged by this idiotic slogan, the Western Allies could offer no terms, however severe. Conversely, their enemy could ask for none, however submissive.[21]

General Westphal, however, who was Rundstedt's chief of staff during the war, reviewed the terminal situation as it appeared from the German side and made the following comment:

> Yet, it is said, at least he [Rundstedt] could have stopped the fighting in the West and capitulated. He would have been only too willing to make an end to the mounting losses of men and the destruction of even more German cities from the air. Should he then make contact of his own accord with Eisenhower? His military upbringing ruled that out. Perhaps nowadays these basic principles are thought to be out of date. But no one can jump over his own shadow.[22]

In the next sentence, Westphal mentions "unconditional surrender" as an additional reason why Rundstedt could not offer capitulation. But this had nothing to do with the harshness of the formula. The western front had to he held, Westphal says, in order to "defend the rear of the army in the east." Capitulation in the West had to be ruled out, otherwise "the front against the Russians would necessarily collapse also." Had it not been for this consequence, capitulation by the field commanders would have been clearly indicated, where it was not rejected out of loyalty to their superiors.

It remains true, however, that the war may have been needlessly lengthened by the unconditional-surrender policy, not because of the effect of the slogan, but because the rules of unconditionality prevented the Allies from handling surrender situations in the most efficient and expeditious manner.

The Rules of Unconditionality and the Duration of the Terminal Stage

As seen above, the two rules of unconditionality could not be imposed simultaneously in the cases of Italy and Japan. The "vacuum" requirement was abandoned prior to Japan's surrender and shortly after Italy's, when events made it clear that further insistence upon the rule would be ruinous for the Allies themselves. The no-negotiation rule, however, was strictly adhered to in both cases. Prior to surrender, the Allies limited their dealings with these countries to the transmission of unilateral appeals to surrender and to instructions about how capitulation was to take place.

The combination of adherence to the no-negotiation rule and abandonment of the vacuum rule did result in a certain prolongation of the terminal stage of hostilities. How much more quickly hostilities could have been liquidated if the Allies had proceeded on entirely different rules is difficult to tell. In Italy, the delay caused by adherence to the rules was only a matter of a few weeks, whereas, in Japan, conversations on qualified surrender might perhaps have been successfully initiated immediately after Germany's capitulation, if not before.

But the main damage done to the Allied cause by

insistence on the rules was not the delay as such; it was that the delay enabled third parties to make gains at the expense of vital Allied interests. In the Italian case, it was Germany who profited by the unconditional-surrender policy; in the Japanese case, it was Soviet Russia. The Allies overlooked the fact that, in both cases, speedy qualified surrender would have been better from their point of view than either strictly unconditional surrender or delayed qualified surrender. Both situations, therefore, called for negotiated surrender without a political vacuum, but that was precluded by the no-negotiation and no-recognition rules.

In Japan the greatest damage was done by the no-negotiation rule. The no-recognition (vacuum) rule was not rigidly binding on American policymakers, and many of them had opposed it all along. Thus, when a formal surrender offer was made by Japan on a qualified basis, the vacuum rule was not insisted on and no further delay occurred on that score. Earlier agreement forestalling Soviet intervention could have been reached, however, had the Allies departed from the no-negotiation rule.

In Italy's case, on the other hand, it was the vacuum rule that had the most disastrous effects. Several weeks were lost after Mussolini's ouster because the new Italian regime could not establish contact with the Allies for technical reasons. Even so, things might have gone more quickly if the Allies had not acted on the principle, implied in the no-negotiation rule, that all they could do was to wait until the enemy indicated his readiness to surrender unconditionally.

But the real damage, as noted above, was done after the Italian offer of qualified surrender had been received. The offer was rejected in the name of strict unconditionality . The vacuum rule was later abandoned, and relations between winner and loser were put on the basis of qualified surrender, as the Italians had proposed to begin with. But by that time the Allies were no longer in a position to derive much advantage from Italian cobelligerency. Thus, while the unconditional-surrender policy did not result in a significant prolongation of the war with Italy, it certainly facilitated the German deployment in that country, and this may well have contributed to a prolongation of the war as a whole.

No needless delay in winding up hostilities can be attributed to the application of the rules of unconditionality in Germany. Some last-minute stalling permitted a surreptitious salvaging operation in the East, but the surrender behavior of the Germans in the West was almost perfectly adjusted to the rules of unconditionality. Their leaders recognized fully that, once surrender became unavoidable, it could only be unqualified, and they neither threatened nor actually engaged in last-ditch resistance in order to obtain something better.

Their last-ditch resistance on the eastern front cannot be blamed on the unconditional-surrender policy. On the contrary, had the Western Allies departed from that policy during the terminal stage, German resistance in the East might have been greatly facilitated because Western conversations with a German surrender regime or the search for an alternative to a political vacuum would have brought the latent tension within the wartime coalition to the fore. The Russians were so suspicious that even the military surrender negotiations with the Germans on the Italian front in the spring of 1945 drew a sharp protest from them.[23] Later, when the Allies left Admiral Dönitz in office temporarily in order to ensure the quick disarmament of German forces, Soviet commentators vehemently declared that "reactionary circles in the Allied countries" were trying to preserve "fascist governments" in order to prevent the "victory of the democratic forces of freedom-loving peoples."[24] It is easy to imagine what the Russians would have said if the Allies had initiated talks prior to surrender with a view to recognizing an interim regime.

Such considerations precluded Western dealings with the political and military opposition that tried to overthrow Hitler in July 1944. The problem of relations with this dissident group was handled in accordance with the rules of unconditionality, which embodied ideological and political, rather than military, considerations. The Allied leaders remembered that the sole purpose of the German generals between the two wars had been to rebuild Germany's military strength in order to subvert the peace settlement by force or by the threat of force. The generals had thrown their influence behind Hitler and thus made the Nazi regime possible. Was it not folly, then, to allow the German military caste to dissociate itself from Hitler's doomed enterprise, maintain its influence behind a peaceful façade, and start the same game over again?

Critics of Allied policy in World War II argue that this negative attitude was unwarranted. They maintain that the postwar situation would have developed much more favorably from the Allies' point of view if Germany's military leaders had been encouraged to eliminate Hitler and to make peace. In the light of hindsight, a considerable case can be made for this position. But no matter how desirable it might have been to encourage Germany's political transformation and conclude peace with a regenerate regime, the Allied governments could not endorse such a policy, even if they had wished to, except in concert with Soviet Russia. There was little chance of such a concerted procedure, however, for basic goals and interests were too far apart. The Russians were interested mainly in promoting radical social changes in Germany, so as to set the stage for a fundamentally anti-Western reorientation of German society after the war. Therefore, any Allied attempt to work out a common platform would have risked splitting the coalition no less than independent action by the West. The only sure way of avoiding a split was by conceding the German prize to Russia, but that, of course, would have been suicidal for the West.

Substitution of a policy of negotiation or qualified surrender for that of unconditional surrender during the war with Germany would have threatened to split the coalition. As the end was drawing near, however, no mitigation of the formula was needed to cut short last-ditch resistance by the Germans in the West; no such mitigation could affect their determination to hold out in the East as long as was necessary to save their people from the Russians. In the West, the Germans, for reasons of their own, chose to let military resistance subside; in the East, no blandishments on the part of the Soviet Union could induce them to abandon their last-ditch resistance.

THE FALLACIES OF UNCONDITIONAL SURRENDER

What the record indicates is that the mere verbal expression of Allied policy exercised no major influence upon the stubbornness of enemy resistance and the duration of the war. The belief that the Allies could have shortened the war appreciably if they had mitigated the excesses of their verbal behavior is a myth. This myth is readily believed because it is consonant with one of the pervasive beliefs of our age, the belief in manipulation as the main factor determining human conduct. Addicted to a naïve stimulus-response philosophy, we tend to take it for granted that people's actions depend on nothing but the momentary stimuli they receive, stimuli that we, the manipulators, can control at will. Where this philosophy holds sway, the possibility that conduct might also have other sources is not even taken into consideration. There is no room for the "autonomous" sources of conduct in the simplistic philosophy that colors so much of our present political thinking. Accordingly, during the war, the enemy's own permanent and deep-rooted loyalties, his own spontaneous assessment of his interests, and similar autonomous factors were not taken into account when we tried to foresee and influence his conduct in the terminal situation. Nothing seemed to matter except what we did to him and what we told him then and there. Even in retrospect, we indulge in fantasies to the effect that everything would have happened differently if our verbal manipulation of the enemy's actions had been more skillful. This line of criticism is worthless because it is based upon the manipulative fallacy, a misconception that the critics share with the policymakers whose decisions they scrutinize.

There is, however, an even more fundamental flaw in this kind of criticism of the unconditional-surrender policy. The main question to which it is addressed, namely, whether the policy of unconditional surrender has "prolonged the war," is irrelevant. This sort of question was centrally relevant to the assessment of the merits of basic strategic decisions in World War I, where it turned out in retrospect that victory, though fully achieved, had no real, lasting value for the principal winners, France and England, because they had bled themselves white in pursuing it. The drain on their resources involved in coming out of the war in possession of a complete monopoly of armed strength turned out to be more important in the long run than that monopoly itself. For France and Britain, victory was Pyrrhic because the war "lasted too long"; i.e., it was too costly in lives and material goods. The victory the West achieved in World War II also turned out to be hollow, but not owing to the length or costliness of the war as such. The war, of course, had been tremendously destructive, and it may well be argued that the political aftermath would have been better if the Allies had been less adamant in ruling out political concessions to new, regenerate regimes on the enemy side. But it was not the undue prolongation of the war that was primarily responsible for the hollowness of the victory, nor was the excessive length and destructiveness of the war caused by the lack of a sensible strategic concept on the eventual winners' side.

In World War I, the West's holding out for complete victory was ill-advised because it entailed exhaustion. For this reason alone, a policy of compromise would have been preferable. (It is not inconceivable, though it is by no means certain, that a compromise settlement could have been worked out with Germany.) In World War II, however, the western conduct of operations at least did not involve the insane strategic concept of symmetrical, mutual attrition, i.e., months and years of almost uninterrupted slaughter, "justified" by the hope of still having some divisions left when the enemy had none. The West's attrition strategy in World War II was more destructive than it need have been, but at least it was, by and large, asymmetrical, as a genuine winning strategy must be. For the United States, politically the leading power of the West, the war had not been total at all, and if the postwar period found the West in a politically disadvantageous position, it was not because the human and economic substance of its leading component had been drained away. Nor was the West's political intransigence the chief reason why fighting continued far beyond the point where strategic victory was assured: blindness and fanaticism on the eventual losers' side would probably have led to this result even if the eventual winners had been less intransigent.

It seems, then, that fastening upon the "unnecessary prolongation" of the war as the main criterion of weakness in the Allied war leadership is just one more instance of the well-known tendency of strategic thinking to lag one war behind. As we have seen above, the unconditional-surrender policy itself was conceived largely in an effort to avoid a supposed mistake made in the previous war; its critics, however, are apparently not above falling into similar errors.

To find fault with many critics of the Allied policy of unconditional surrender, however, is not to say that this policy was free from basic fallacies. We have seen that in two cases, those of Italy and Japan, the policy could not even be put into practice, while in a third, that of Germany, it worked because it fitted in with German preferences and calculations of which its authors were not aware. If leaders enjoying overwhelming military superiority nevertheless managed to set themselves objectives that cannot be attained, there must be something wrong with their basic thinking and doctrine. It will be useful at this point to identify the main fallacies of the unconditional-surrender policy.

The first fallacy was the Allied policymakers' failure to distinguish between the problem of inflicting strategic defeat on the enemy and that of inducing him to surrender. Whereas the former problem involves only violent interaction, the latter concerns the transition from violence to nonviolence. At this stage, there must be some give-and-take. A surrender agreement is essentially a political bargain. To aim at obtaining surrender while ruling out all bargaining on principle is a contradiction in terms. It is quite true that belligerents strong enough to impose surrender, and thus to obtain a monopoly of fighting strength, need not conclude a compromise peace; they can dictate terms. Dictation, however, does not mean that the winner, in fixing the terms, must act as if the loser had no bargaining assets at all. The fallacy inherent in the unconditional-surrender doctrine that we have described consists in supposing that before the beaten enemy has renounced the use of his last significant capabilities his bargaining strength is exactly nil.

We should be clear about the penalties for acting on this fallacy. These penalties do not include exhaustion of the winner's resources, undue prolongation of the war, or other major calamities of this kind. The winner will find, rather, that his objectives, framed in the light of a fallacious doctrine, are unrealistic. As he enters the terminal stage of the conflict he will discover too late that he cannot avoid making payments proportionate to the loser's residual bargaining strength. He must either revise his original policy or make involuntary payments to the loser, to third parties, or to "nature" (as the game theorists would put it).[25]

It is poor policy in general to treat an enemy nation as if it were a *quantité négligeable*. Victorious leaders who impose a political vacuum on the defeated enemy act on this questionable premise. Political nature no less than physical nature, however, abhors a vacuum; imposing one is bound to lead to ultimate disappointment. The consequences of the Allies' vacuum policy in World War II were largely negative, where they were not positively harmful. Where, as in West Germany, the political vacuum eventually gave way to the development of a democratic regime, the same thing could also have happened had there been no vacuum. In this case only time was lost, but in East Germany, communism rushed into the vacuum. Japan might have fallen under communist domination had the Allies succeeded in imposing integral unconditional surrender there. In Austria, where no vacuum was imposed, the communists did not seize power even in that part of the country that was under Soviet occupation.

Whereas the vacuum policy actually jeopardized prospects for a democratic development in the defeated countries, it recommended itself to the instigators of unconditional surrender precisely because they saw in it an indispensable preliminary condition for the healthy development of political democracy and thus for a peaceful future. This brings us to the second major fallacy, or cluster of fallacies, involved in the doctrine of unconditional surrender. The main inspiration behind the policy was the passionate belief that the more completely the enemy was stripped of power at the end of hostilities, the more securely peace would be established. The smallest shred of power and influence surviving on the losing side was to be feared as a possible focus of infection from which the disease of war might spread again. This summed up the problem of war or peace.

This belief, preposterous as it is, was not pulled out of a hat; there was seemingly solid historical evidence behind it. World War II did grow out of Germany's desire to turn the tables on the powers that defeated her in 1918; had she been more thoroughly stripped of power, this could not have happened. It could also be argued that lasting peace might have been secured after World War I by treating Germany not more sternly but more leniently. But it is impossible to settle this question one way or another, and we must admit in any case that revenge by the defeated was one of the possible threats to peace after World War I. The mistake was only to believe that this threat would necessarily persist, and be the dominant factor in international relations, after World War II as well. The Western leaders and peoples overlooked the fact that a vast transformation was taking place in the political universe, completely overshadowing the German-Western and Japanese-American differences inherited from the era of the Baghdad railway, the Tirpitz fleet, and the Open Door in China. Instead of planning to settle the problems germane to World War II, they resolved to end it by doing everything that would have been needed to prevent it from breaking out.

Even on this premise, however, the approach embodied in the unconditional-surrender policy was fallacious. Even if weakening the former enemies in order to prevent them from ever again becoming threats to peace had been a valid objective (which, given the very favorable outlook for their spontaneous "reorientation," was not the case), unconditional surrender was not the key to it. If the Western leaders had read history correctly, they would have realized how fleeting a thing is a wartime monopoly of military strength. Dangers such as revenge by a defeated power cannot be indefinitely warded off by unilateral disarmament or even by occupation and the imposition of a political vacuum. There are only two ways in which such dangers can be nullified. A defeated power, even if it does not reorient its policy, can cease to be dangerous either if it goes into decline by losing vitality or if an international grouping is set up facing it with overwhelming odds. The main reason Germany remained dangerous after World War I was not that she had not been given a stern enough lesson, but that the coalition that might have been strong enough to discourage her plans for revenge fell apart.

Two problems were germane to securing lasting peace after World War II: Was German and Japanese revenge the main danger to avert? And if so, was a firm and stable countercoalition available? The Allied leaders unfortunately answered the first question with "yes," although the correct answer was "no." As to the second question, they did not even raise it, because they did not recognize that peace was a matter of the international balance. They put their faith instead in unconditional surrender, in going to the farthest conceivable limit in dismantling the German and Japanese power structure. They reduced the problem of forestalling further wars to that of administering to the disturbers of the peace a lesson they would never forget.

This pedagogic fallacy was perhaps the most salient feature of the Western approach to the problem of war and peace. Western leaders and their nations did not know, alas, how quickly people forget even the most painful lessons, how differently the same lesson can be interpreted by those who administer it and by those who receive it, and how soon it can become irrelevant because of changed circumstances. Permanent peace rests on a weak foundation indeed if it depends on the undying memory of a just chastisement. This, however, was the foundation we prepared for it by adopting the unconditional-surrender policy.

It is idle to debate whether the mistake was an avoidable one. In all probability it was not: as we suggested in Chapter Two, the tendency to expect lasting peace from the destruction of all germs of aggression located in the enemy society has deep roots in the American tradition. It would have been extremely difficult, if not impossible, for Americans to sustain the war if they had not been inspired by this expectation. From this point of view, the pedagogic fallacy inherent in the policy of unconditional surrender was a pragmatically valuable illusion during the war. And this leads to a question of conscience: if an illusion is pragmatically valuable, if it works, is one justified in corroding it by rational criticism?

The answer is that illusions of this sort do not collapse merely because rational analysis corrodes them; our experience of "losing the peace after winning the war"—an experience repeated twice in the last fifty years—has done more in this respect than any amount of abstract analysis. We have never been slow to see the flaws in our specific war ideologies after the event, but this has not, so far, induced us to give up the habits of thought that produce such fallacies.

There are some signs that as a people we are moving away from the kind of fallacious thinking about the prob-

lem of peace and war that expressed itself in the unconditional-surrender policy. An indication of this is the
recent growth of a considerable body of literature, critically analyzing the traditional moralistic, all-or-nothing
American approach to the problem of war and peace.
Some recent political experiences, such as the Korean war
and the ups and downs of the cold war, also may have
contributed to the development of less rigid, more elastic
ways of thinking about the international conflict and international harmony. But deeply ingrained emotional
patterns die hard, and old fallacies, no matter how thoroughly hindsight demolishes them, have a way of crop-
ping up again when a new challenge is to be met. Hence,
scrutinizing them is no wasted effort.

PART FOUR

SURRENDER IN
FUTURE STRATEGY

Eight

AWAY FROM
THE SIEGE STRATEGY

THE CHANGED OUTLOOK FOR STRATEGY

It is safe to assume that future armed conflicts will not be dominated by the strategy of attrition that determined the character of World Wars I and II. The destructiveness of present (and, *a fortiori*, future) weapons is such that strategic decisions can no longer center upon the gradual wearing down of the enemy's mobilizable potential.[1] Hence, we no longer can visualize terminal situations of the "classic" World War I and II type, essentially representing the last stage of a siege. The main feature of that pattern was the unimpaired cohesive structure of the loser's residual forces (and, in World War II, even of his political and social fabric), together with the drying up of sources of supplies and reinforcements. What present weapons portend, however, is an extreme *disruptive* effect, which goes far beyond the disruption achieved by earlier "battle" strategies.[2] Full-scale nuclear warfare threatens its target with a level of destruction so high that coordinated activities must largely come to a stop. In such a situation, the loser cannot offer "surrender" in the shape of handing to the winner control over cohesive residual capabilities and over a society that is still a going concern.

The strategic picture is also bound to change in an

even more fundamental sense. The immediate payoffs of "victory" and "defeat," possession of unimpaired armed strength on one side and lack of all defensive capabilities on the other, will no longer circumscribe the major strategic alternatives facing the belligerents. The worst strategic outcome will no longer be defenselessness but utter destruction of the entire society, and in full-scale nuclear war this fate may overtake both sides. It is questionable whether an asymmetrical winning strategy can be developed at all for unlimited nuclear war between the two great world powers:[3] such a war conceivably can have only losers, although this is by no means certain.

With such changes in basic strategic factors, the political aspect of international conflict is bound to change too. Under the new conditions, maximally total war can no longer serve such political aims as the dictation of terms, temporary "pedagogic" occupation, or even outright conquest. All this presupposes that something worth dictating to, reeducating, or annexing survives on the losing side. The only political objective appropriate to all-out nuclear war is the elimination of the adversary, something that probably cannot be achieved except at the risk of self-elimination.

Adopting such an objective, coupled with such risks, is, of course, not strategy but lunacy. People, however, sometimes act in an insane fashion. In the course of the above analysis, we touched on "insane" strategies—those which aim at complete victory without having the characteristics of asymmetry that alone can make a strategy a winning one. Insane or not, such strategies have been applied in the past. Where is the guarantee that even more insane ones will not be applied in the future?

There can be no such guarantee, but the probability

that any power will deliberately embark on such a suicidal course must be considered extremely small. In World War I, the belligerents stumbled into the strategy of mutual attrition because past doctrine provided them with no other possibility, and also because they did not know what the consequences would be. What mutual nuclear attrition would mean, however, is only too clear to everyone. But if this course is extremely unlikely to be chosen deliberately, it may nevertheless grow out of miscalculation, for example underestimation of the enemy's ability to hit back. If this happens, the political outcome will not be strategic surrender of the World War I and II type but mutual devastation, with whatever political adjustment may subsequently be possible.

We must also mention the possibility that a power might develop a perfect winning strategy for all-out nuclear war, i.e., the strategy of a first strike that eliminates all significant retaliatory capabilities on the adversary's side. Needless to say, a power whose enemy develops strategic capabilities of this sort is in mortal danger: the enemy can, if he chooses, eliminate that power with relative impunity. Once this happens, strategic surrender (at least strategic surrender of the classic type discussed above) will be irrelevant. But this kind of situation points to the possibility of surrender of a different sort: surrender without fighting. If one power has a monopoly of such a winning strategy, and its adversary knows it, a mere threat of attack might induce the latter to surrender politically.

SURRENDER IN NUCLEAR WAR

Strategic surrender may become germane to the terminal stage of other possible variants of total nuclear warfare. For example, even without possessing a perfect winning strategy, one side may achieve a victorious, asymmetrical outcome, if it comes out of unlimited nuclear war with much larger operational capabilities, and particularly in a much less disrupted state, than the other. If the latter then still possesses even a small, residual nuclear capability that is well protected, the surrender of this capability will be important to the former. While the victory itself will be predicated on differential disruption rather than on divergent attrition, the characteristic element of strategic surrender, dispensing with the use of a residual capability, will still be present.

Similar terminal problems might arise in another conceivable type of nuclear war, a war that is waged entirely in the form of counter-force operations (the pure air-counter-air war). This stratgy is, if course, one of pure disruption. But if one side wins the battle, surviving small units on the other side will be potentially dangerous (as small units surviving after decisive non-nuclear battles were not), so that it will be important to secure their surrender.

Although the nuclear variants of surrender just discussed necessarily differ in many respects from the older, non-nuclear ones surveyed in this study, the permanent characteristics of surrender specified in our analysis will be present if strategic surrender becomes a factor in the context of nuclear war. Thus, surrender will still be essentially a bargain, calling for counterpayments; it will still not be synonymous with omnipotence for one side and zero bargaining power for the other. Those who may have to deal politically with surrender will have to keep this in mind.

Nine

NUCLEAR STRATEGY AND LIMITED WAR

The emergence of nuclear weapons not only changed the possible significance of strategic surrender, but also rendered questionable the compatibility of victory in any meaningful sense with the waging of total war. The new weapons are so destructive that, if they are used to the full limit of their destructiveness, the losses they cause must far outweigh any political advantage that might be derived from victory. If we disregard the asymmetrical case in which one side can prevent any critically telling use of the opponent's capabilities, we have to recognize that the concept of strategic victory will be meaningful in the future only in wars that are nontotal, i.e., wars that end when a significant part of destructive potential of both sides has not been put to use.

The concept of nontotal war has been discussed in Chapter Two of this study. The essential condition for a conflict's remaining nontotal, we suggested there, is that the belligerent who is frustrated by the outcome of early engagements nevertheless accepts their verdict as final. Such behavior, we said further, presupposes the initial loser's (or at least nonwinner's) belief that he cannot secure for himself a better total payoff by prolonging the war, either because the later engagements would end as poorly for him as the early ones had, or because securing a larger slice of what is politically at stake, though feasible, would not be worth the additional cost. This analysis was carried out with the known historical past in mind. We shall now consider what the novel facts of the nuclear age imply concerning the problem of the limitation of war.

The first thing we have to recognize is that the pattern of gradually mounting costs and losses, a pattern that is central to classic nontotal war no less than to classic attrition strategy, is alien to the nature of nuclear war. One cannot keep such a war nontotal simply by cutting it short; if waged in all-out fashion, it can become very highly total in the first exchange of blows. This means that any limitation of nuclear war, any holding back of destructive capabilities for its entire duration, must be in a sense artificial. It can only result from a decision to do much less than one could from the very beginning, rather than from a decision to quit after the first results of *un-limited* efforts are in. One may say, in fact, that in the classic pattern single efforts are unlimited, in the sense that (given substantial equality among the contenders) decisions about what forces to commit are based solely on what the enemy has readily available: the only upper limit is what is thought necessary to overmatch him. In a nuclear war, however, the first exchange would lead to total destruction if its vehemence were determined by this criterion. Therefore, an "artificial" limiting criterion is needed.

The necessity for an artificial limitation poses exceedingly difficult theoretical and practical problems. How can one determine the nature and extent of necessary and sufficient artificial limitations? And supposing that this is done, how can prospective enemies reach an agreement on this basis? No attempt can be made here to answer these questions; we must limit ourselves to a few general remarks.

Strategies involving artificial limitations are not altogether inconceivable: the classic principle of unlimited single efforts in the above sense does not have the force of a law of nature. To be sure, the drafting of explicit agreements about artificial limitations of single efforts is an exceedingly difficult, if not impossible, task. But artificial limitations might come to be observed without an explicit agreement; each belligerent might, for example, spontaneously decide to pull his punches in cautious fashion, hoping that his adversary will also do so. Such a pattern can be quite stable as long as neither side sees an opportunity for achieving a quick knockout by a single unlimited blow that leaves the enemy no chance for a telling riposte. Belief in the existence of such a winning strategy, of course, would automatically wipe out all limitations, regardless of whether or not they are explicitly codified in international agreements.

The artificial limitation of single blows, however, does not in itself ensure that the whole war will be nontotal. The essential question in this respect is not whether single blows are limited, but whether a peace settlement is made on the basis of a military outcome achieved while very considerable capabilities remain unused on both sides. Whether this happens or not depends primarily on the attitude of any belligerent who is dissatisfied with the outcome of the partial use of capabilities. We have here, indeed, an invariable principle valid for *all* nontotal war, no matter how strategic patterns change. Novel nuclear capabilities, however, pose problems in connection with keeping a war nontotal that do not exist in non-nuclear war.

Even in nuclear war, acknowledging defeat (or any other unsatisfactory outcome, such as stalemate) on the strength of the result of a partial effort is not unduly difficult when the political stake is low. Low-stake wars tend to remain nontotal in any case. The crucial problem that arises in connection with limiting nuclear war is how to conclude a high-stake war with considerable capabilities held in abeyance on both sides.

There is a ready solution of this problem in the classic context. It is based on strategic foresight. Whatever the stake, additional efforts are warranted only if they may be expected to change the trend. Where this is ruled out, i.e., where an adverse trend pointing toward defeat or stalemate is clearly seen to be irreversible, the result of partial operations mirrors that of more total ones. The partial operations, in other words, constitute a representative sample of any more complete cycle of operations. Such judgments, however, can be made with cogency only where the classic principle of unlimited single blows holds. When the single blows are unlimited, there may be a basis for concluding that the outcome will not change when their number is increased. But when the partial result is based on artificial limitations, such extrapolations are necessarily problematic. The partial outcome may still cogently imply that one side is relatively stronger, but it *cannot* prove that the stronger side would be in a position to achieve a *monopoly* of military strength if the war were to become more total. Hence, even if the partial outcome strongly favors one side, it cannot serve as a firm basis for setting peace terms predicated upon unimpaired strength on one side, defense-lessness on the other. If the winner of partial operations were to demand the surrender of the loser's significant unused capabilities, yielding would mean that the loser would be exposed in the future to the constant danger of extinction, and to the certainty of continuous un-bearable exactions. This he can prevent as long as he still has considerable unused capabilities; by employing them in a last, suicidal outbreak of despair, he can at least prevent the winner from enjoying the fruits of his victory.

Under classic conditions, such possible despair re-actions do not present a significant problem, because any reasonable extrapolation from an irreversible losing trend implies that the longer desperate, hopeless resis-tance goes on, the less telling will be the blows that the loser might still inflict on the winner. Any small addi-tional loss that the winner will be made to suffer will have as its counterpart a large additional loss for the loser. The gradualness characteristic of the classic stra-tegic picture excludes any sudden and startling jump in loss levels. Totally suicidal and murderous despair reactions at the terminal stage can enter into the strategic picture only when capabilities are nuclear.

In dealing with the political problem of securing a settlement on the basis of partial nuclear operations, the winner must take into account the loser's ability to unleash a last orgy of destruction, together with the reasons he might have for doing so. When it comes to setting terms, the possibility of a last explosion of des-pair must be counted as part of the loser's bargaining strength. But this implies that in nontotal nuclear war, the final political payoffs must be moderate: in general, such wars can leave no room for extreme settlements. The logic of the situation cannot entail political terms based on a monopoly of armed strength on one side, with the other side reduced to defenselessness. Since the loser has a desperate last recourse, he cannot be treated as if he were defenseless. To be sure, it is not an absolute certainty that the loser in nontotal nuclear war will prefer a suicidal last battle to surrender; it is only a possibility. But this is enough to make insistence on total surrender prohibitively risky for the winner.

Now we can formulate the solution to the problem under consideration: that of limiting nuclear war when the political stakes are very high. The solution is that in high-stake nuclear wars that are nontotal the political payoffs must be small, in spite of the high stakes, if the belligerents are rational. It is as if the belligerents were playing poker for unlimited stakes, each having a loaded revolver and ready to shoot his opponent if he should try to collect very high winnings. In other words, such wars cannot reasonably be expected to result in complete victory in the political sense. What the winner can reasonably expect is only a relatively modest gain, not departing significantly from the status quo. Since nuclear war costs and losses are necessarily very high even if limitations are observed, this means that just keeping what one has is likely to be a very costly proposition if there is any war at all. Just leaving the status quo unchanged is infinitely cheaper and cannot be much worse politically for either side. This is, I think, instinctively recognized by political leaders everywhere. Hence, no major challenge to the existing status quo is likely, unless and until someone develops a winning strategy that can, in his opinion, overcome the dilemma. Crises of critical magnitude may arise, unfortunately, even if no great power deliberately challenges the status quo: we must not forget the totally unsettling effects that conflicts between minor powers may have upon the international equilibrium. But we cannot pursue this topic further here.

Belief in the possession of an asymmetrical winning strategy predicated on unlimited strikes that also prevent critically effective counterstrikes can, as we have seen, prompt a power to start a war in the expectation of eliminating its opponent. But it is conceivable that there might be winning strategies that ensured great political gains and also limited the destructiveness of single blows. The pure air-counter-air strategy, mentioned above, is a case in point. This strategy involves a considerable limitation of single blows, since it implies that only air capabilities in being are attacked. Since many such capabilities are located near population centers, even such a "limited" strategy is bound to result in extremely heavy civilian losses. It is only relatively less destructive than, say, a counter-industry or counter-population strategy; but the limitation seems sufficient to permit the survival of the society under attack.

If one side achieves complete victory in such an air-counter-air battle, it will reduce the other to practical defenselessness.[1] At this point the winner can dictate political terms, subject only to the necessity of making political payments for the surrender of the loser's residual capabilities. Such a victorious war, in fact, would be limited *only* as regards single efforts; it would not be a nontotal war by our definition, since no significant capabilities would remain unused on the

losing side. It is one of the novelties of nuclear strategy that it makes a type of war possible in which single
efforts are artificially limited while the war itself is total. But it appears that the pure air-counter-air war
represents the only kind of artificial limitation that does
not necessarily result in nontotal war, and hence permits large political payoffs even under nuclear conditions. Other possible types of artificial limitations (such
as limiting nuclear weapons to tactical uses) do not have
this property. Wars in which such limitations are re-
liably observed but in which neither side has a totally
successful counterforce strategy are necessarily nontotal,
and hence permit only compromise settlements.

A war ending on moderate terms may nevertheless
have very far-reaching political consequences. For example, it may result in considerable, or even revolutionary, political changes in either of the war-making
societies. If one side is very pleased to see such changes
occur in the other, the former may reckon them as a
high net political payoff accruing to it. But we must
distinguish such payoffs from those that winners impose on losers on the strength of the strategic outcome.
In a nontotal nuclear war, the imposed terms cannot
reasonably be expected to be other than lenient. One
has to approach the peace table in such a war in a spirit
of moderation to avoid the risk of total war.

A few words remain to be said about low-stake
wars in the nuclear age. Such wars obviously can end in
complete victory in a political sense: if the stake is low,
the military loser will give it up entirely without much
difficulty. If the stake is low, however, the means employed to achieve victory or to avert defeat must be
limited; and if the belligerents possess nuclear weapons,

this means that single efforts will be subject to stringent artificial limitations, possibly to the extent of excluding the use of nuclear weapons altogether.

Are low-stake conflicts possible in the nuclear age? The creation of a small, insignificant *fait accompli* by a big power may well give rise to such a conflict. Such incidents are unimportant by definition, but a great power whose interests are hurt by them may prefer taking active countermeasures, amounting to a low-stake war, to acquiescence.

Meaningful counteraction, however, is possible in such cases only if forces that can operate on a level of low destructiveness are available. "Massive retaliation" cannot undo a small *fait accompli;* it can only create a very large new one, changing the status quo to a considerable extent. A power that has only large indivisible packages of destructive potential at its disposal will find that it is not in a position to counter minor breaches of the status quo; nor will it be able to create small *faits accomplis* offsetting those created by its opponent.

Even though the stake involved in any single minor incident of this kind is small, it is unwise to treat it as if it were nonexistent. Major challenges to the status quo, as we have seen, are unlikely in any case; even nuclear wars waged for high stakes cannot result in big shifts in the status quo unless they become total (in which case the shifts may well be ruinous to both sides). Hence the principle that complete acquiescence and nonviolence is the rule to be observed in all cases that are not grave enough to call for all-out counteraction cannot be valid. In the nuclear age the powers must accustom themselves to thinking in terms of relatively small political payoffs.

CONCLUSION: SURVIVAL IN THE NUCLEAR AGE

The major political implications of the new strategic situation brought about by the emergence of nuclear weapons may be formulated as follows: powers may seek to survive in the nuclear age, either by going to extremes of inhumanity and malevolence never imagined before, or by drastically limiting their expectations of gain from the application of armed power. Adjusting to the new conditions is bound to be particularly difficult for the United States, because both of the available alternatives are diametrically opposed to traditional American political attitudes. Systematic malevolence is as alien to the American makeup as overblown emotional expectations of unlimited gains are congenial to it.

We must, of course, cherish our traditions of humanity and benevolence. If the inhuman alternative for survival opened up by the nuclear age is excluded for us because of our nature, so much the better. Let us hope that this alternative will not be open to others either, for practical reasons if not for reasons of character. If we rule out the inhuman solution, then we must act on the other alternative for survival. We shall have to revise some of our deeply rooted traditional attitudes, such as our rejection of compromise and our faith in extreme, ideal solutions when the chips are down. In the past, these propensities served us well in some respects and played us nasty tricks in others. In the future, they can only render us impotent to deal with political reality, and thus jeopardize our very survival.

NOTES

*See Bibliography for full titles
and publication data.*

I

Chapter One: SURRENDER AS A STRATEGIC CONCEPT

1. Clausewitz comments on annihilation of the enemy force in the following terms: "The [enemy's] fighting force must be annihilated, that is, reduced to such a state that it can no longer continue the struggle. We declare herewith that in what follows we shall mean only this by the expression 'annihilation of the enemy's fighting force.'" *Vom Kriege,* p. 22.

2. Hans Delbrück, *Geschichte der Kriegskunst im Rahmen der politischen Geschichte,* IV, 334. See also Gert Buchheit, *Vernichtungs- oder Ermattungsstrategie?,* pp. 11 ff.

Chapter Two: SURRENDER AS A POLITICAL CONCEPT

1. Cf. Gunnar Landtman, *The Origin of the Inequality of Social Classes,* esp. pp. 248 ff.

2. Xenophon, *Anabasis,* IV, 7 (translation by the author).

3. On the rigidities of premodern military establishments that prevented progressive mobilization, see Hans Speier, "Militarism in the Eighteenth Century" and "Class Structure and Total War," Chapters 19 and 20, in *Social Order and the Risks of War.*

4. Cf. Clausewitz's dictum: "The only effective form of activity in war is the battle" (*Vom Kriege,* p. 31); and his definition of strategy: "Strategy . . . is the use of battle for the purpose of war" (*ibid.,* p. 129).

5. Cf. *ibid.,* pp. 149, 151 ff.

II

Chapter Three: THE FRENCH SURRENDER (JUNE 1940)

1. Paul Reynaud, *La France a sauvé l'Europe*, II, 180.
2. Albert Kammerer, *La Vérité sur l'armistice*, 2d ed.,
pp. 14 f.
3. Reynaud, II, 181 f.
4. *Ibid.*, p. 303.
5. *Ibid.*, p. 176.
6. *Ibid.*, p. 303.
7. *Ibid.*, p. 340.
8. *Ibid.*, p. 441.
9. Maxine Weygand, *Recalled to Service* (London,
1952), p. 226. (The French edition appeared in 1950.)
10. At the beginning, the Marshal did not give British
resistance much of a chance. But after the Germans lost the air
battle over London, he understood that the war would last a
long time. This strengthened his interest in not concluding
peace. "The armistice," he often said, "the armistice with
whatever sauce you like, bland or sharp, but no final settlement,
no treaty. I shall never accept another treaty of Frankfurt."
(Du Moulin de Labarthète, *Le Temps des illusions*, pp. 195 f.)
11. Reynaud, pp. 297 f.
12. Sir Edward Spears, *The Fall of France, June 1940*,
p. 193.
13. Kammerer, pp. 107 f.
14. See *The Private Diaries of Paul Baudouin.*
15. Spears, pp. 219 f.
16. Reynaud, p. 315.
17. *Ibid.*, p. 324. This outburst is characteristic in that it
reveals the stubborn survival of the French revolutionary habit
of basing political conduct upon classic models. Weygand, by
the way, later disavowed the stand he had taken; he conceded
that there would have been no point in the French cabinet's
letting itself be captured by the Germans. Another Weygand
outburst is reported by Kammerer: "Vous voulez aller jusqu'au
bout . . . mais vous y êtes, au bout!" [You want to go to the
bitter end . . . but you are *at* the bitter end!], Kammerer,
p. 110.
18. Reynaud, p. 325.
19. Cf. A. Rossi, *Les Communistes français pendant la
drôle de guerre*, pp. 322 ff.

20. Reynaud, pp. 340 f.; Kammerer, pp. 180 ff.
21. Robert Aron, *Histoire de Vichy 1940–1944*, p. 48.
22. *Ibid.*
23. Kammerer, p. 196.
24. Reynaud, pp. 363 ff.
25. William L. Langer, *Our Vichy Gamble*, p. 45.
26. Kammerer, p. 125.
27. According to Robert Aron, the cabinet was unanimously in favor of breaking off armistice talks if the Germans demanded any part of the fleet or of the colonial empire. The military members of the cabinet took a number of measures in preparation for last-ditch resistance in that case; two battleships were sent to Africa, as well as nine hundred airplanes. (See Aron, p. 62.)
28. Kammerer, p. 444.
29. Galeazzo Ciano, *L'Europa verso la catastrofe*, p. 562. See also Aron, p. 74.
30. Ciano, p. 563.
31. B. H. Liddell Hart, *The German Generals Talk*, pp. 144 ff.
32. Ciano, p. 562.
33. Kurt von Tippelskirch, *Geschichte des zweiten Weltkrieges*, p. 111.
34. Ciano, p. 567.
35. *Diaries of Paul Baudouin*, p. 172; Aron, pp. 240 ff.
36. *Diaries of Paul Baudouin*, p. 173.
37. *Ibid.*, pp. 190 f.
38. Ciano, pp. 591–94.
39. J. Paul-Boncour, *Entre deux guerres*, III, 222–38.
40. Du Moulin, p. 24.
41. *Diaries of Paul Baudouin*, p. 110.
42. Ciano, pp. 591–94.
43. Apparently some Germans thought so too; Guderian said later that he had tried in vain to convince Hitler that it was necessary to occupy Northwest Africa after the fall of France. (Langer, p. 60.)
44. Elie J. Bois, *Truth on the Tragedy of France*, pp. 111 f. (Italics in original.)
45. See Rossi, *passim*.
46. Tippelskirch, pp. 33 f.
47. Aron, pp. 249 f.
48. On this diplomatic offensive, cf. Aron, pp. 428 ff.

49. *Ibid.*, p. 433.
50. See William D. Leahy, *I Was There*, pp. 21, 24, 54–61.
51. Aron, pp. 246 ff.
52. *Ibid.*, p. 247.
53. Cf. the Dakar episode of September 1940.

Chapter Four: THE ITALIAN SURRENDER (SEPTEMBER 1943)

1. See Mark W. Clark, *Calculated Risk*, p. 3.
2. Enno von Rintelen, *Mussolini als Bundesgenosse*, pp. 197 ff.
3. *Ibid.*, pp. 209 f.
4. *Ibid.*, pp. 213–15.
5. *Ibid.*, pp. 216 ff.
6. *Ibid.*, pp. 236 ff.
7. Winston S. Churchill, *The Second World War*, Vol. V: *Closing the Ring*, p. 684.
8. *Ibid.*, p. 686.
9. Admiral Franco Maugeri, *From the Ashes of Disgrace*, p. 165.
10. Harry C. Butcher, *My Three Years with Eisenhower*, p. 371.
11. *Ibid.*, p. 372.
12. *Ibid.*
13. Hans Speier, "Psychological Warfare Reconsidered," Chapter 32 in *Social Order and the Risks of War*.
14. Pietro Badoglio, *Italy in the Second World War*; Dwight D. Eisenhower, *Crusade in Europe*, p. 184.
15. Maugeri, p. 157. A similar feeling is expressed in Oscar di Giamberardino, *La Politica bellica nella tragedia nazionale*, p. 226.
16. Maurice Vaussard, *Histoire de l'Italie contemporaine*, pp. 282 f.
17. Butcher, p. 375.
18. *Ibid.*, p. 382; see also Wallace Carroll, *Persuade or Perish*, pp. 171 ff.
19. Churchill to Eden, August 7, 1943, in Churchill, *Closing the Ring*, p. 102.
20. *Ibid.*, pp. 99 ff.
21. Butcher, pp. 391, 398, 405. (These figures seem to have been exaggerated.)

22. Cf. Tippelskirch, p. 371.

23. On this concept, see our discussion of the policy of unconditional surrender in Chapter Seven, pp. 218 f.

24. Butcher, p. 375.

25. *Ibid.*, p. 386.

26. *Ibid.*, p. 394.

27. Churchill, *Closing the Ring*, p. 103.

28. On the instructions to Eisenhower, see *ibid.*, pp. 105 f.

29. Robert E. Sherwood, *Roosevelt and Hopkins*, p. 744.

30. *Ibid.*, pp.. 742 f.

31. Maugeri, pp. 178 f.

32. Badoglio, p. 72.

33. Butcher, p. 410.

34. Vaussard, pp. 293 f.

35. Badoglio, p. 73. Tippelskirch, p. 368, also gives this explanation.

36. Butcher, p. 400.

37. On September 3, day of the signature of the armistice, General Clark warned of the possibility that the Italians might "welsh" on their agreement. (*Ibid.*, p. 407.)

38. *Ibid.*, p. 405.

39. Churchill, *Closing the Ring*, pp. 101 f.

40. Churchill to Roosevelt, September 21, 1943, *ibid.*, p. 189.

41. Badoglio, p. 103. (Author's italics.)

42. Churchill, *Closing the Ring*, p. 201.

43. Sherwood, p. 752.

44. Cf. Admiral of the Fleet Viscount Cunningham of Hyndhope, *A Sailor's Odyssey*, p. 572. (In the book, de Courten's name is consistently misspelled "de Courton.")

45. Badoglio, p. 103. Cf. also Churchill, *Closing the Ring*, p. 201.

46. Carroll, p. 174. The Italian fleet's surrender is flatly attributed to the Algiers broadcasts in Edward W. Barrett, *Truth Is Our Weapon*, p. 47. Actually, the ships steaming into Malta did not come from La Spezia but from Taranto. On the fate of the main naval force that set out from La Spezia, see below.

47. S. E. Morison, *History of U.S. Naval Operations in World War II*, IX, 242 f. The source quoted for Admiral Bergamini's speech is Admiral Fioravanzo, *The Italian Navy's*

Struggle for the Country's Liberation, 1946 (not available to the author).

48. Alberto da Zara, *Pelle d'Ammiraglio*, p. 418.

49. *Ibid.*, p. 419.

50. *Ibid.*, p. 421.

51. *Ibid.*, p. 425. The order to "treat the Italian navy well" was given by Churchill (*Closing the Ring*, p. 115).

52. Badoglio, p. 111.

53. Morison, pp. 243 ff.

54. Clark, p. 2.

55. Cf. Sherwood, p. 65.

56. For Cordell Hull, he was a near-enemy (cf. *The Memoirs of Cordell Hull*, II, 1159 ff.).

Chapter Five: THE GERMAN SURRENDER (MAY 1945)

1. Von Grünau telegram to German Foreign Office, October 1, 1918, in Ralph Haswell Lutz (ed.), *Fall of the German Empire*, II, 459.

2. *Ibid.*, pp. 462 ff.

3. Cf. Hans Rothfels, *The German Opposition to Hitler*, p. 84.

4. On these contacts, cf. Allen W. Dulles, *Germany's Underground*; *The Von Hassell Diaries, 1938–1944*; J. Lonsdale Bryans, *Blind Victory*, pp. 60 ff.

5. The text in Gerhard Ritter, *Carl Gördeler und die deutsche Widerstandsbewegung*, p. 569.

6. According to a statement by Carl Burckhardt, reported by Hassell, this was recognized in London; cf. Ritter, p. 317.

7. The text in Ritter, pp. 570–76.

8. *Ibid.*, p. 572.

9. *Ibid.*, pp. 577 f., 585 f.

10. *Ibid.*, p. 589.

11. *Ibid.*, pp. 589, 599.

12. On military attitudes, cf. Rothfels, p. 70.

13. Ritter, pp. 357 ff.

14. Hans Speidel, *Invasion 1944*.

15. *Ibid.*, pp. 72 ff.

16. *Ibid.*, p. 74.

17. Ritter, pp. 391 ff.

18. *Ibid.*, p. 394. For a different version of Kluge's refusal, see Dulles, pp. 187 f.

19. Cf. Hans Bernd Gisevius, *Bis zum bittern Ende*, II, 299, 322.
20. *Ibid.*, p. 304.
21. Ritter, pp. 386 f.
22. *Ibid.*, p. 387.
23. Dulles, pp. 131 ff.
24. Gisevius, pp. 308 f.; cf. also Dulles, pp. 170 f.
25. Rothfels, pp. 154 ff.
26. Dr. Peter Kleist, *Zwischen Hitler und Stalin*, pp. 230 ff.
27. Ritter, p. 379 f.
28. *Ibid.*, p. 381.
29. Dulles, p. 167.
30. Conversation between Gördeler and Wallenberg, November 1942, in Ritter, p. 314.
31. General Siegfried Westphal, *The German Army in the West*, p. 191.
32. Cf. Adolf Heusinger, *Befehl im Widerstreit*; Erich von Manstein, *Verlorene Siege*.
33. Forrest C. Pogue, *The European Theater of Operations: The Supreme Command*, p. 448.
34. Tippelskirch, pp. 658 f.
35. Albert Kesselring, *Soldat bis zum letzen Tag*, p. 410.
36. Pogue, p. 440; italics in original.
37. Kesselring, pp. 409, 423.
38. Pogue, pp. 477 f.; Kesselring, pp. 411, 418 ff.
39. Pogue, p. 482; Kesselring, p. 421.
40. *Ibid.*
41. Ritter, p. 390; the source of the story is Stuttgart's Mayor Strölin.
42. Quoted in H. R. Trevor-Roper, *The Last Days of Hitler*, p. 82.
43. Pogue, pp. 476 f.; Trevor-Roper, pp. 131, 165; Walter Schellenberg, *The Labyrinth*, pp. 392 ff.
44. Trevor-Roper, pp. 130 f.
45. *Ibid.*, p. 208.
46. Milton Shulman, *Defeat in the West*, p. 304.
47. The book as it appeared in Germany was Walter Lüdde-Neurath, *Regierung Dönitz* (1951). For the present study, the French edition was used (*Les Derniers Jours du Troisième Reich*, Paris, 1950).
48. *Ibid.*, p. 85.

49. *Ibid.*, p. 86.
50. Pogue, p. 479.
51. *Ibid.*, pp. 480 f.
52. Lüdde-Neurath, p. 108.
53. *Ibid.*, p. 110.
54. *Ibid.*, p. 115.
55. Pogue, p. 505.
56. *Ibid.*, pp. 481 ff.
57. Lüdde-Neurath, p. 121.
58. Pogue, p. 505.
59. *Ibid.*, p. 506.

Chapter Six: THE JAPANESE SURRENDER (AUGUST 1945)

1. Cf. Robert J. C. Butow, *Japan's Decision to Surrender,* pp. 13 f.
2. *Ibid.*, p. 14.
3. *Ibid.*, pp. 20 ff.; U.S. Strategic Bombing Survey (USSBS), *Japan's Struggle to End the War,* p. 3.
4. *United States Relations with China, Based on the Files of the Department of State,* p. 519.
5. Ray S. Cline, *Washington Command Post: The Operations Division,* p. 339.
6. *Memoirs of Cordell Hull,* II, 1309.
7. Sherwood, p. 779.
8. Agreement of February 11, 1945, cited in "The Conferences at Malta and Yalta, 1945," in *Foreign Relations of the United States: Diplomatic Papers,* p. 984.
9. Cf. Memorandum by the United States Chiefs of Staff, January 22, 1945, *ibid.*, p. 395; Cline, p. 338.
10. Joint Chiefs of Staff 1176/6, January 18, 1945, in *Diplomatic Papers,* pp. 389 f.
11. Cf. James F. Byrnes, *Speaking Frankly,* p. 208; Leahy, pp. 369, 422.
12. Cf. Cline, p. 344.
13. Cf. Admiral Ernest J. King and Walter Muir Whitehill, *Fleet Admiral King,* p. 598.
14. Cf. Cline, p. 342.
15. Cf. Leahy, pp. 384 f.
16. John J. McCloy, *The Challenge to American Foreign Policy,* p. 42. (The only member of the Joint Chiefs of Staff not identified with a particular service was Admiral Leahy.)

17. See below, pp. 260 f.

18. On the "no negotiation" principle, see Chapter Seven, p. 218.

19. Joseph C. Grew, *Turbulent Era*, II, 1406, 1411.

20. See below, pp. 312 ff.

21. *Congressional Record*, Vol. 90, No. 139, August 30, 1944, pp. A4113–15.

22. *Ibid.*, Vol. 91, No. 163, September 18, 1945, p. 8816.

23. *Ibid.*

24. *Ibid.*

25. *Ibid.*, p. 8815.

26. *Ibid.*, p. 8819.

27. See below, pp. 305 ff.

28. Henry L. Stimson and McGeorge Bundy, *On Active Service in Peace and War*, p. 627.

29. For a detailed treatment of this point see the section entitled "Japanese Peace Policies," beginning on p. 169 of this study.

30. Butow, p. 14.

31. *Ibid.*, pp. 17 f.

32. *Ibid.*, pp. 24 f. The above account is based on Marquis Kido's testimony before the International Military Tribunal for the Far East. Later in his testimony, Kido added that Shigemitsu told him "on several occasions" during the war that unconditional surrender would be inescapable.

33. Toshikazu Kase, *Journey to the Missouri*, p. 91.

34. USSBS, OPNAV-P-03-100, Vol. II, p. 319.

35. Kase, p. 86.

36. Butow, p. 40.

37. USSBS, *Japan's Struggle*, p. 5. According to Butow, Koiso's position was unduly weakened by a fatal oversight: he failed to secure appointment as Minister of War, in which position he would have had a better chance to control the officers' corps. (Butow, p. 37.)

38. Butow, pp. 40 f.

39. *Ibid.*, p. 55.

40. *Ibid.*, p. 69.

41. *Ibid.*, p. 77.

42. *Ibid.*

43. The political complexion of the Council was mixed: the War Minister and the two Chiefs of Staff were antipeace die-hards; the Foreign Minister and the Navy Minister (Yonai)

were antiwar; the Premier, Suzuki, was vacillating between the
two groups, but tended to defer to the prowar group.
    44. *Ibid.*, p. 91; Kase, p. 170.
    45. Butow, p. 93.
    46. Kase, p. 184.
    47. Butow, pp. 121 f.
    48. *Ibid.*
    49. Testimony of Admiral Toyoda, USSBS, OPNAV-P-
03-100, Vol. II, pp. 318 f.
    50. Kase, pp. 193 f.; Walter Millis (ed.), *The Forrestal
Diaries*, p. 74.
    51. Kase, p. 205.
    52. *Ibid.*, p. 222.
    53. *Ibid.*
    54. Butow, p. 129, with references to Byrnes, *Speaking
Frankly*, p. 205; Churchill, *The Second World War*, Vol. 6:
Triumph and Tragedy, pp. 641–42; David H. James, *The
Rise and Fall of the Japanese Empire*, pp. 329–30.
    55. *The Forrestal Diaries*, pp. 74–76.
    56. The text in *Documents on American Foreign Relations*,
1945–46, pp. 105–6.
    57. Butow, pp. 103 ff., 134.
    58. Harry S. Truman, *Memoirs*, I, 396.
    59. Butow, pp. 142 f.
    60. *Ibid.*, p. 143.
    61. *Ibid.*, p. 145.
    62. On "mokusatsu," see Kazu-Kawaii, "Mokusatsu," *Pa-
cific Historical Review*, November 1950, pp. 409–14, and William J. Coughlin, "The Great Mokusatsu," *Harper's Magazine*,
March 1953, pp. 31–40. For these references, the author is
indebted to Louis Morton's article, "The Decision to Use the
Atomic Bomb," *Foreign Affairs*, January 1957, p. 350.
    63. Cf. Stimson and Bundy, p. 625. On the background of
this decision, see Morton's excellent account in *Foreign Affairs*,
January 1957, pp. 334–39.
    64. Quoted in P. M. S. Blackett, *Fear, War and the Bomb*,
p. 128. Professor Blackett also quotes an article by Dr. Karl
T. Compton in the December 1946 *Atlantic Monthly*, in which
the writer states: "I believe with complete conviction that the
use of the atomic bomb saved hundreds of thousands—perhaps
several millions—of lives, both American and Japanese; that

without its use the war would have continued for many months."
In a letter to Dr. Compton dated December 16, 1946, President Truman endorsed his conclusions and added: "I imagine the bomb caused them to accept the terms." (Blackett, pp. 128 f.)

65. Byrnes, pp. 211 f.
66. Reproduced in Stimson and Bundy, pp. 617 ff.
67. Stimson and Bundy, p. 625.
68. USSBS, *Japan's Struggle*, p. 13.
69. Stimson and Bundy, p. 628.
70. *Ibid.*, p. 627.
71. *Ibid.*, p. 629.
72. Cf. Butow, pp. 168 ff.
73. *Ibid.*, p. 172.
74. *Ibid.*, p. 175.
75. *Ibid.*, pp. 152 f.
76. *Ibid.*
77. *Ibid.*, p. 180.
78. *Ibid.*, pp. 193 ff.
79. Cf. *Documents on American Foreign Relations, 1945–1946*, pp. 107–8; William Hardy McNeill, *Survey of International Affairs, 1939–1946* (America, Britain, and Russia), pp. 637 f.
80. Butow, pp. 207 f.
81. On these rules, see below, pp. 218 ff.

III

Chapter Seven: THE ALLIES' POLICY IN WORLD WAR II

1. *Memoirs of Cordell Hull*, II, 1166.
2. Sherwood, p. 696.
3. Churchill, *The Second World War*, Vol. IV: *The Hinge of Fate*, pp. 686 ff.
4. Eisenhower, *Crusade in Europe*, p. 489, fn. 7. See also Chester Wilmot, *The Struggle for Europe*, p. 122.
5. On the genesis of the unconditional-surrender policy, see Günter Moltmann, "Die Genesis der Unconditional Surrender-Forderung," *Wehrwissenschaftliche Rundschau*, Vol. VI, Nos. 3–4, March and April, 1956.

6. Cf. Sherwood, p. 697; Churchill, *The Hinge of Fate*, pp. 690 f. (quoting his speech in the House of Commons, February 22, 1944).

7. Cf. Roosevelt on February 12, 1943, in Samuel I. Rosenman (ed.), *The Public Papers and Addresses of Franklin D. Roosevelt*, 1943 volume: *The Tide Turns*, pp. 71 ff.

8. Cf. Churchill's explanation in the speech referred to in note 6 above: "Unconditional surrender means that the victors have a free hand. It does not mean that they are entitled to behave in a barbarous manner, nor that they wish to blot out Germany from among the nations of Europe. If we are bound, we are bound by our own consciences to civilization. We are not bound to the Germans as the result of a bargain struck. That is the meaning of unconditional surrender."

9. Churchill, pp. 689 f.

10. On Roosevelt's negative reaction to a Soviet proposal on defining unconditional surrender, see *Memoirs of Cordell Hull*, II, 1573 f. Later, American military leaders repeatedly pressed for a specification of surrender terms in order to hasten surrender: Carroll, pp. 306 f., 313 f., 319 f.; Butcher, p. 518. These proposals also remained without effect.

11. Such a "vacuum rule" is appropriate when surrender ends a war of secession: the very object of the war is to extinguish the sovereignty of the secessionist state once and for all. In World War II, however, the rule was applied to international conflict, where the vacuum, as it happened, was not intended to achieve this end.

12. On this selective pattern, see Chapter Five, pp. 132 ff.

13. Rothfels, p. 154.

14. *Memoirs of Cordell Hull*, II, 1581 f.; Wilmot, p. 122; J. F. C. Fuller, *The Second World War*, pp. 258 ff.; Lord Hankey, *Politics, Trials and Errors*.

15. As we have seen, this critique of the unconditional-surrender policy was put forward not only in retrospect; the policy of "severe but specific" terms was vigorously supported in high Allied quarters during the war.

16. Louis P. Lochner (ed.), *The Goebbels Diaries 1942–1943*, p. 325.

17. This line is adopted by Russell Grenfell (*Unconditional Hatred*, pp. 166 ff.) and F. O. Miksche (*Unconditional Surrender*).

18. Fuller, p. 275.

19. Cf. Hans Speier's analysis in "War Aims in Political Warfare," Chapter 29 in *Social Order and the Risks of War*.

20. Hankey, p. 45.

21. Fuller, p. 355.

22. Westphal, p. 192.

23. Cf. Stalin's cable to Roosevelt on April 3, alleging that Marshal Kesselring "has agreed to open the front and permit the Anglo-American troops to advance to the east . . . At the present moment the Germans on the western front in fact have ceased to wage war against England and the United States. At the same time, the Germans continue the war with Russia, the ally of England and the United States." On this incident, see Leahy, pp. 386 ff.

24. On Soviet comments in this vein, see Boris Meissner, *Russland, die Westmächte und Deutschland*, pp. 57 f.

25. In the theory of games, first developed systematically by John von Neumann and Oskar Morgenstern, there is a convenient rule to the effect that losses accruing to one "player" must be counted simultaneously as gains accruing to another. The war losses of a belligerent, however, cannot be reckoned as gains accruing to his opponent; to satisfy the rule, then, such losses are treated as gains made by a fictitious third party, called "nature."

IV

Chapter Eight: AWAY FROM THE SIEGE STRATEGY

1. For a similar argument, see Colonel Robert C. Richardson III, "Atomic Weapons and Theater Warfare," *Air University Quarterly Review*, Vol. VII, No. 3, Winter 1954–55, pp. 11, 14. The writer says: ". . . the limiting factor will be that an atomic war of the future will not be a war of attrition. D-Day will find both contestants armed with adequate stocks of destructive power to permit hope of an early decision if the power is properly employed. The situation points to a short conflict in which the primary target system would consist of 'quick pay-off' objectives."

2. On the disruptive effect of massive nuclear attack, see Harrison Brown, "How Vulnerable Are We?," *Bulletin of the Atomic Scientists*, Vol. XIII, No. 9, November 1957.

3. See Richardson, *op. cit.*, pp. 9 f.

Chapter Nine: NUCLEAR STRATEGY AND LIMITED WAR

1. Complete defenselessness, of course, presupposes the destruction of *all* forces in being, including land and naval forces. A pure counter-force strategy such as the one envisaged by Richardson (see note 1 to Chapter Eight) aims not only at the enemy's air capabilities but at his other capabilities as well. But victory in the air battle, eliminating the loser's missile as well as manned aircraft capabilities, would mean that his other forces could not survive for long.

BIBLIOGRAPHY

Aron, Robert. Histoire de Vichy, 1940–1944. Paris, 1954.

Badoglio, Pietro. Italy in the Second World War. New York, 1948.

Barrett, Edward W. Truth Is Our Weapon. New York, 1953.

Baudouin, Paul. The Private Diaries of Paul Baudouin. London, 1948.

Blackett, P. M. S. Fear, War and the Bomb. New York and Toronto, 1948.

Bois, Elie J. Truth on the Tragedy of France. London, 1940.

Bryans, J. Lansdale. Blind Victory. London, 1951.

Buchheit, Gert. Vernichtungs- oder Ermattungsstrategie? Berlin, 1942.

Butcher, Harry C. My Three Years with Eisenhower. New York, 1946.

Butow, Robert J. C. Japan's Decision to Surrender. Stanford, 1954.

Byrnes, James F. Speaking Frankly. New York, 1947.

Carroll, Wallace. Persuade or Perish. Boston, 1948.

Churchill, Winston S. The Second World War. Vol. IV, The Hinge of Fate (Boston, 1950); Vol. V, Closing the Ring (Boston, 1951); Vol. VI, Triumph and Tragedy (Boston, 1953).

Ciano, Galeazzo. L'Europa verso la catastrofe. Milan and Rome, 1948.

Clark, Mark W. Calculated Risk. New York, 1950.

Clausewitz, Karl von. Vom Kriege. Edited by Karl Linnebach. Berlin, 1937.

Cline, Ray S. Washington Command Post: The Operations Division. Department of the Army, Washington, D.C., 1951.

Congressional Record, Vols. 90 and 91.

Cunningham of Hyndhope, Viscount. A Sailor's Odyssey. London, 1951.

Delbrück, Hans. Geschichte der Kriegskunst im Rahmen der politischen Geschichte. Berlin, 1920. Vol. IV.

Documents on American Foreign Relations, 1945–46. Published for the World Peace Foundation. New York, 1948. Vol. VIII in a series.

Dulles, Allen W. Germany's Underground. New York, 1947.

Du Moulin de Labarthète, Henry. Le Temps des illusions. Brussels and Paris, 1946.

Eisenhower, Dwight D., Crusade in Europe. Garden City, N.Y., 1948.

Foreign Relations of the United States: Diplomatic Papers. Washington, D.C., 1955.

Forrestal, James V. The Forrestal Diaries. Edited by Walter Millis. New York, 1951.

Fuller, J. F. C. The Second World War. New York, 1949.

Giamberardino, Oscar di. La Politica bellica nella tragedia nazionale. Rome, 1945.

Gisevius, Hans Bernd. Bis zum bittern Ende. Zurich, 1946. Vol. II.

Goebbels, Joseph Paul. The Goebbels Diaries, 1942–1943. Edited by Louis P. Lochner. Garden City, N.Y., 1948.

Grenfell, Russell. Unconditional Hatred. New York, 1953.

Grew, Joseph C. Turbulent Era. Boston, 1952. Vol. II.

Hankey, Lord. Politics, Trials and Errors. Chicago, 1950.

Hassell, Ulrich von. The Von Hassell Diaries, 1938–1944. Garden City, N.Y., 1947.

Heusinger, Adolf. Befehl im Widerstreit. Tübingen and Stuttgart, 1953.

Hull, Cordell. The Memoirs of Cordell Hull. New York, 1948. Vol. II.

James, David H. The Rise and Fall of the Japanese Empire. New York, 1948.

Kammerer, Albert. La Verité sur l'armistice. 2d ed. Paris, 1945.

Kase, Toshikazu. Journey to the Missouri. New Haven, 1950.

Kesselring, Albert. Soldat bis zum letzten Tag. Bonn, 1953.

King, Ernest J., and Walter Muir Whitehill. Fleet Admiral King. New York, 1952.

Kleist, Peter. Zwischen Hitler und Stalin. Bonn, 1950.

Landtman, Gunnar. The Origin of the Inequality of Social Classes. London, 1938.

Langer, William L. Our Vichy Gamble. New York, 1947.

Leahy, William D. I Was There. New York, 1950.

Liddell Hart, B. H. The German Generals Talk. New York, 1948.

Lüdde-Neurath, Walter. Regierung Dönitz. 1951. Translated as Les Derniers Jours du Troisième Reich. Paris, 1950.

Lutz, Ralph Haswell, ed. Fall of the German Empire. Stanford, 1932. Vol. I.

Manstein, Erich von. Verlorene Siege. Bonn, 1955.

McCloy, John J. The Challenge to American Foreign Policy. Cambridge, Mass., 1953.

McNeill, William Hardy. Survey of International Affairs, 1939–1946 (America, Britain, and Russia). London, New York, and Toronto, 1953.

Maugeri, Franco. From the Ashes of Disgrace. New York, 1948.

Meissner, Boris. Russland, die Westmächte und Deutschland. Hamburg, 1953.

Miksche, F. O. Unconditional Surrender. London, 1952.

Morison, Samuel Eliot. History of U.S. Naval Operations in World War II. Vol. IX. Boston, 1954.

Paul-Boncour, Joseph. Entre deux guerres. New York, 1946. Vol. III.

Pogue, Forrest C. The European Theater of Operations: The Supreme Command. Department of the Army, Washington, D.C., 1954.

Reynaud, Paul. La France a sauvé l'Europe. Paris, 1947. Vol. II.

Rintelen, Enno von. Mussolini als Bundesgenosse. Tübingen and Stuttgart, 1951.

Ritter, Gerhard. Carl Gördeler und die deutsche Widerstandsbewegung. Stuttgart, 1955.

Roosevelt, Franklin D. The Public Papers and Addresses of Franklin D. Roosevelt. 1943 volume: The Tide Turns. New York, 1950.

Rossi, A. Les Communistes français pendant la drôle de guerre. Paris, 1951.

Rothfels, Hans. The German Opposition to Hitler. Chicago, 1948.

Schellenberg, Walter. The Labyrinth: Memoirs of Walter Schellenberg. New York, 1956.

Sherwood, Robert E. Roosevelt and Hopkins. New York, 1948.

Shulman, Milton. Defeat in the West. New York, 1948.

Spears, Sir Edward. The Fall of France, June 1940. Vol. II of Assignment to Catastrophe. London, 1940.

Speidel, Hans. Invasion 1944. Chicago, 1950.

Speier, Hans. Social Order and the Risks of War. New York, 1952. Chaps. 19, 20, 29, 32.

Stimson, Henry L., and McGeorge Bundy. On Active Service in Peace and War. New York, 1948.

Tippelskirch, Kurt von. Geschichte des zweiten Weltkrieges. Bonn, 1951.

Trevor-Roper, H. R. The Last Days of Hitler. New York, 1947.

Truman, Harry S. Memoirs by Harry S. Truman. Vol. I, Year of Decision. Garden City, N.Y., 1955.

United States Relations with China, Based on the Files of the Department of State. Department of State Publication 3573, Far Eastern Series 30. Released August 1949.

U.S. Strategic Bombing Survey (USSBS). Japan's Struggle to End the War. July 1, 1946.

Vaussard, Maurice. Histoire de l'Italie contemporaine. Paris, 1950.

Westphal, Siegfried. The German Army in the West. London, 1950.

Weygand, Maxime. Recalled to Service. London, 1952.

Wilmot, Chester. The Struggle for Europe. London, 1952.

Zara, Alberto da. Pelle d'Ammiraglio. Rome, 1949.

INDEX

Abetz, Otto, German Ambassador to France, 66

Abruzzi, Italian cruiser, 112

Aegean Sea, 105, 126

Air-counter-air strategy, 248; and limitation of war, 255 f.

Alexandria, 105

Algeria, 47, 50

Algiers, 67, 85, 99, 104

Allies, Western: landings in North Africa, 68; surrender policies toward Italy, 74–104, 113–17; misjudge requirements of Italian situation, 84 f., 99 f.; failure to prepare for military cooperation by Italy, 86, 104; distrust of Badoglio and King of Italy, 89, 98, 110; plan to send airborne troops to Rome, 90; policy on Italian cobelligerency, 100 f.; moral crisis over Italian cobelligerency, 114; agreement with Darlan, 114 f.; Italian surrender policy evaluated, 113–17; and German opposition, 132 f., 135, 231; Germans' image of, 141, 222; purely military conception of surrender, 153 f.; policy toward Japan, 157 f.; estimate of Japanese military strength, 158; Japanese efforts to enlist Soviet mediation, 185–89; unconditional-surrender policy, 215–41; war aim defined as total victory, 215 f., 224, 226

Allies, tension between Eastern and Western, 127; minimized by West, 133, 148, 153, 154, 222; Soviet suspicion of West, 230 f.; potential split of coalition over Germany, 232

Alsace-Lorraine, 126

Altmayer, French general, 38

Ambrosio, Vittorio, Italian Chief of Staff, 73

American attitude toward power and aggression, 25 f.

American Civil War, 1, 17

Anami, Korechika, General, Japanese Minister of War, 176, 190, 194

Annihilation policy of Hitler, 144 f.

Aosta, Italian cruiser, 112

Appeasement, 60 f.

Armistice, French, 44 f., 50 f.

Armistice, Italian, 90, 92

Army Group B, German, 142

Army Group G, German, 144

Aron, Robert, on Vichy regime, 68, 261 n., 262 n.

Artificial limitation of war, *see* Limitation of war

Asymmetry, strategic, 18 f., 22, 235, 246, 249, 255

Atomic bomb, 165 f., 184; and Japan's surrender, 191–206, 209

Attilio Regolo, Italian cruiser, 112

Attlee, Clement, British Prime Minister, 185, 188

Attrition, in strategy, 7–9, 13; divergent, 9; and surrender, 21; in World Wars I and II, 7, 71, 119, 234 f.; in nuclear war, 247

Australia, 165

Austria, 17; *Anschluss* to Germany, 60; German antiwar group's position, 125 f.; no political vacuum imposed after World War II, 237

Austro-Prussian War, 17

Autonomous sources of conduct, 233

Avranches, breakthrough in World War II, 120, 137

Axis powers, 89, 156, 223

Badoglio, Pietro, Italian marshal and Prime Minister, 112, 115, 191; assumes government, 74; seeks to conclude armistice with Allies and to hoodwink Germans, 74, 77–81; basic policy of not announcing surrender until Allies can give military protection, 78, 89; consultations on forming cabinet, 79; conference with Hitler at Tarvis, 79; difficulty in starting negotiations with Allies, 81; Allies' suspicions of double game, 82 f., 84, 89, 110, 116; record of cooperation with Fascist regime, 87 f., 100 f.; passivity, 90; plan of airdrop of Allied troops near Rome, 90 f.; requests postponement of armistice, 92; flight from Rome, 92, 96; cryptic instructions on fighting Germans, 93 f., 106 f.; could not go back to German side, 98; complains about Allies' treatment of Italy, 99; Hopkins memorandum opposing recognition, 101; on air and naval cooperation with Allies, 103, 106; protest about fleet, 109

Baggë, Widar, Swedish diplomat, 174–76

Baghdad railway, 238

Balkan peninsula, 99

Baltic Sea, 140

Banfi, Alberto, Italian naval officer, 108

Bargaining strength of losers, 16, 69, 115 f., 127, 152, 158, 210, 236 f., 248, 253

Barrett, Edward W., 263 n.

Battle, in strategy, 5, 22, 245

Battle of France, 31 f., 63 f.

Baudouin, Paul, French foreign minister, 45, 50; at Supreme War Council meeting, 38 f.; on chances of preventing German invasion of North Africa, 52; on decision to send Admiral Darlan to North Africa, 67

Beck, Ludwig, German general, member of anti-Hitler group, 125, 129, 132, 135, 136

Belgium: capitulation, 31; remains outside western security system, 60; strategic importance, 63

Benoist-Méchin, Jacques, French cabinet member, 66

Bergamini, C., Italian admiral, 105, 113

Berio, Italian diplomat, mission to Tangiers, 81

Berlin, 44, 129, 134, 146, 184

Bernadotte, Count Folke, Swedish diplomat, 145

Berne, 187

Biddle, Alexander J., U.S. diplomat, 45

Blackett, P. S. M., 268 n.

Blitzkrieg, 31, 56

Blum, Léon, French Socialist leader, 58

Blumentritt, Günther, German general, 48

Bône, North African port, 105

Bonifacio, Strait of, 113

Bonomi, Ivanoe, Italian Socialist leader, 79

Bordeaux, temporary seat of French cabinet, 42; cabinet meetings, 43 f.

Borotra, Jean, French cabinet member, 36

Brandenberger, Erich, German general, 144

Briare, Supreme War Council meetings, 38

British War Cabinet, 75; on Italy's unconditional surrender, 75; on unconditional-surrender policy, 217

Brittany redoubt, 38

Burckhardt, Carl, Swiss diplomat, 264 n.

Butcher, Harry C., on Eisenhower's attitude toward Italian surrender, 76 f.; on press opposition to leniency toward House of Savoy, 80; on fading hopes for Italian surrender, 83; on Italian "flip-flop," 85; on Eisenhower's refusal to postpone announcement of Italian surrender, 94

Butow, Robert J. C.: on Japan's surrender, 169 f., 173, 185, 199; on role of atomic bomb, 203

Byrnes, James F., U.S. Secretary of State, 185; on Soviet intervention against Japan, 160; on atomic bomb, 192

Cadiz, 52

"Cadorna," Italian naval division, 106

Caio Duilio, Italian battleship, 106

Cairo Declaration, 157, 170–74, 178

Calvi, in Corsica, 112

Campbell, Sir Ronald, British diplomat, 43 f.

Canada, diplomatic relations with Vichy regime, 67

Carboni, Giacomo, Italian general, 91

Carroll, Wallace, on propaganda myth concerning surrender of Italian fleet, 104 f.

Casablanca conference, 74 f., 216 f.

Cassibile in Sicily, armistice signed, 90, 105

Castellano, Giuseppe, Italian general, head of armistice mission, 81, 86, 105

Catholic party, German, 124

Chamberlain, Neville, British Prime Minister, 126

Chautemps, Camille, French Vice-Premier, 43 f.

Chile, 81

China, 157, 165, 170 f., 238

Chungking, 171

sonable, 58; foreign policies, 65 ff.;
rejects cobelligerency, 66; yields to
German pressure, 67; collapse of political strength, 68
Victor Emmanuel III, King of Italy,
94, 98, 109 f., 115; dismisses Mussolini, 73 f.; record of cooperation
with fascism, 87 f., 100 f.; flight
from Rome, 92; recognition criticized, 101
Victory: in strategy, 1 f., 19; relativity of, 20, 23; Allied doubts, 208 f.;
total, as war aim, 216, 224, 226; in
World Wars I and II, 234; in future war, 246, 249
Vietinghoff, Heinrich von, German
general, 143
Vistula, 131
Vittorio Veneto, Italian battleship, 112
Volkssturm, 139

Wallenberg, Jakob, Swedish banker,
136
War, total and nontotal, 17–21; political stake, 19, 22, 254–57; as
crusade, 26; of revenge, how to
avoid, 239
War aims, Allies', 215 f., 224, 226
Washington, 76, 195, 200
Westphal, Siegfried, German general,
227
Weygand, Maxime, French general, 35,
260 n.; on Britain's defeat, 36 f.;
comment on armistice policy, 37;
against Brittany redoubt, 38; criti-
cizes cabinet, 40; on communist danger, 40 f.; against purely military
capitulation, 42 f.; against accepting

German demands going beyond armistice, 50; motives for favoring
armistice, 57, 64
Wherry, Kenneth S., U.S. Senator, 167
Wilson, Woodrow, 217
Wolff, Karl Friedrich, SS general, 143
Woodruff, Roy O., U.S. Representative, 164
World War I, 17, 22, 31, 125, 238 f.;
attrition strategy, 7; strategic surrender, 121 f.; comment by Goerde-
ler, 128; reference in Cairo Declaration, 157; Allied promises to Russia, 171; Roosevelt on political conduct, 217; long-range effect of victory, 234
World War II, 17, 22, 125 f.; attrition, 7; ends without revolution, 24;
"crusade" character, 26 f.; early period, 62 ff.; turning point, 119; terminal stage, Germany, 120, Japan,
197; becomes total, 136; Allied
handling of political aspect, 215–41;
origin, 238

Xenophon, 13 f.

Yalta conference, 154, 159 f., 178, 185
Ybarnégaray, J e a n, French cabinet
member, 44
Yonai, Mitsumasa, Japanese admiral,
cabinet member, 173, 179, 267 n.
Yoshida, Shigeru, Japanese politician,
155, 169
Yugoslavia, 60

Zara, Alberto da, Italian admiral, on
surrender of fleet, 106–9.

Introduction to the Theory of Games
J. C. C. McKinsey, 1952
Weight-Strength Analysis of Aircraft Structures
F. R. Shanley, 1952
The Compleat Strategyst: Being a Primer on the Theory of Games of Strategy
J. D. Williams, 1954
Linear Programming and Economic Analysis, Robert Dorfman, Paul A. Samuelson, and Robert M. Solow, 1958

PRINCETON UNIVERSITY PRESS, PRINCETON, NEW JERSEY:

Approximations for Digital Computers
Cecil Hastings, Jr., 1955
International Communication and Political Opinion: A Guide to the Literature
Bruce Lannes Smith and Chitra M. Smith, 1956
Dynamic Programming, Richard Bellman, 1957

PUBLIC AFFAIRS PRESS, WASHINGTON, D.C.

The Rise of Khrushchev, Myron Rush, 1958
Behind the Sputniks: A Survey of Soviet Space Science
F. J. Krieger, 1958

ROW, PETERSON & COMPANY, EVANSTON, ILLINOIS:

German Rearmament and Atomic War: The Views of German Military and Political Leaders, Hans Speier, 1957
West German Leadership and Foreign Policy
Hans Speier and W. Phillips Davison (eds.), 1957

TL DUE